Inflation accounting

An introduction to the debate

Management and Industrial Relations Series

Edited for the Social Science Research Council by
DOROTHY WEDDERBURN
Principal of Bedford College, London
MICHAEL BROMWICH
Professor of Finance and Accounting, University of Reading
and
DOUGLAS BROOKS
Director, Walker Brooks and Partners

Social science research has much to contribute to the better understanding and solution of problems in the field of management and industrial relations. The difficulty, however, is that there is frequently a gap between the researcher and the practitioner who wants to use the research results. This new series is designed to make available to practitioners in the relevant fields the results of the best research which the Social Science Research Council (SSRC) has supported in the fields of management and industrial relations. The subjects covered and the style adopted will appeal to managers, trade unionists and administrators because there will be an emphasis upon the practical implications of research findings. But the volumes will also serve as a useful introduction to particular areas for students and teachers of management and industrial relations.

The series is jointly produced by the Cambridge University Press and the Social Science Research Council.

Other books in the series
1 *Lost managers: supervisors in industry and society* by JOHN CHILD and BRUCE PARTRIDGE
2 *Tackling discrimination in the workplace: an analysis of sex discrimination in Britain* by BRIAN CHIPLIN and PETER SLOANE

Inflation accounting
An introduction to the debate

GEOFFREY WHITTINGTON

CAMBRIDGE UNIVERSITY PRESS

Cambridge
London   New York   New Rochelle
Melbourne   Sydney

Published by the Press Syndicate of the University of Cambridge
The Pitt Building, Trumpington Street, Cambridge CB2 1RP
32 East 57th Street, New York, NY 10022, USA
296 Beaconsfield Parade, Middle Park, Melbourne 3206, Australia

First published 1983

Printed in Great Britain at
the University Press, Cambridge

Library of Congress catalogue card number: 82–9657

British Library Cataloguing in Publication Data
Whittington, Geoffrey
Inflation accounting.——(Management and industrial
relations series)
1. Inflation (Finance) and accounting
I. Title   II. Series
657'.48   HF5657

ISBN 0 521 24903 1 hard covers
ISBN 0 521 27055 3 paperback

Contents

To Alan and Richard

Preface

In 1979 I was awarded a Social Science Research Council Professorial Research Fellowship in Inflation Accounting, to enable me to spend two years, commencing in October 1979, studying the theory and practice of inflation accounting. My intention was to write, in collaboration with David Tweedie, a book entitled *The Debate on Inflation Accounting*. This would survey the theory of the subject and the history of its international development, including the important debates in professional and government circles during the 1970s. It would conclude with an attempt to summarise the present state of affairs, and to identify future developments which are implicit in it, broader lessons to be learned for the development of and interaction between accounting ideas and accounting practices, and areas requiring further research.

As is the way with these things, once I set foot on the mountain, it appeared to be much larger than it had seemed from a distance, and, in order to help the reader whose interest and stamina do not justify his attempting to follow the whole journey, it was decided to split the project into two stages. The first resulted in the present book, which attempts to provide a concise and clear summary of the present state of the theory of inflation accounting. It is intended as an introduction to the theoretical issues in the debate, and knowledge of its contents will be assumed in the second book, *The Debate on Inflation Accounting*, which is currently being written in co-authorship with David Tweedie, and which covers the remaining topics on my original agenda. However, it is hoped that this introductory book will stand on its own as an introduction to the theory of the subject, for those who do not wish to study the historical and institutional aspects of the debate, or feel that they already know enough (or possibly too much) about this. Equally, it is hoped that the second volume, on the debate, will stand on its own for those who feel that they already have an adequate knowledge of the theory but need to know more about the evolution of the subject in both theory and practice.

Needless to say, both David Tweedie and I hope that many readers will stay the whole course and read both books. The division between the two is convenient, but both parts are inter-dependent: it is impossible to evaluate the debate without a theoretical framework and it is impossible to understand the present state of theory without knowledge of the history of both ideas and practice out of which it has evolved. It is also possible that those who think that they know enough about either the theory or the debate should consider reading the relevant book as a revision course. If they do this, they are quite likely to discover that their state of knowledge is not as complete as they thought: certainly my own experience of working on this project has resulted in my being less confident of my knowledge of the subject when I finished than when I started. It is perhaps in the nature of research that the process of answering questions leads to yet further questions, so that our knowledge may expand, but, in the process, our awareness of what we do not know also increases.

Even if, as in this book, we confine ourselves to financial accounting, rather than to management accounting, the literature of inflation accounting is vast, and still developing, as can be seen from the length of the Bibliography to this book. There are therefore many 'loose ends' and areas requiring further research, which I have tried to point out. The difficulties are compounded by the fact that the inflation accounting problem goes to the heart of what accounting is about. For example, Current Cost Accounting is an alternative model to the traditional Historical Cost system even in the absence of inflation, although it was presented by the Sandilands Committee (1975) as a system of 'inflation accounting'. If there were more agreement about the fundamental model of accounting in the absence of inflation, then inflation accounting would be a simpler matter. However, agreement on these issues is far away, despite the efforts of the Financial Accounting Standards Board in the USA and the Accounting Standards Committee in the UK to define a 'conceptual framework' for accounting, and it is possible that the search for a precise model for accounting is fundamentally ill-conceived, because different types of accounting information may be needed for different purposes. In these circumstances, I have concentrated on analysing the arguments for and against alternative models, and have deliberately refrained from attempting to adjudicate a contest to establish 'the winner', a system which is a universal panacea for all ills. This is because my own view is that most of the theoretical arguments advanced are logically valid: it is merely the assumptions which vary, and different assumptions might be appropriate in different circumstances or for different uses of the accounting data. Thus, if I have a strong prejudice, it is against those who conduct single-minded campaigns for their own preferred solution, without recognising the merits of alternatives, which are not necessarily inconsistent. Accounting has more than its fair share of such monologuists, possibly because it is in an early stage of development as an area of scientific endeavour. Perhaps the search for an ideal accounting system should be likened to the search for the philosopher's stone or the elixir of life, which marked the earlier days of some other sciences which have since achieved more secure status.

It is a great pleasure to acknowledge the support of those who enabled me to write this book. The Social Science Research Council were responsible not only for funding the project but also for initiating it by creating a Fellowship specifically in Inflation Accounting. Price, Waterhouse and Co. gave further financial support and intellectual stimulus by enabling me to visit the USA, where I was attached to their National Office in New York, as a Faculty Fellow, during the Summer of 1980. My colleagues at Bristol took on extra responsibilities in my absence, particular thanks being due to Don Egginton who took over responsibility for organising Accounting teaching, and Esra Bennathan and Angus Deaton each of who did an out-of-turn stint as Head of the Economics Department. The Master and Fellows of Fitzwilliam College, Cambridge, gave me a Visiting Fellowship and the Department of Applied Economics (whose Director, Wynne Godley, was an important contributor to the inflation accounting debate) provided office facilities, for the Lent and Easter terms of 1980, during which the first draft was written. The University of Bristol Library provided excellent facilities for the extensive literature search which I undertook in the Autumn of 1979 and at Easter 1980 (including a computer search using the Lockheed Dialog system). I am particularly grateful to the following academic colleagues who unselfishly gave up time from

Preface

their own work to read and comment on my manuscript: Michael Bromwich, Don Eggington, John Forker, John Kay, Geoff Meeks, Brian Reddaway, Maurice Scott and David Tweedie, and John Beath and Angus Deaton who commented on Chapter 4. The inevitable disclaimer must be made, that they are not responsible for any remaining imperfections (although David Tweedie will not retain this exemption in the companion volume), but they have all contributed significant improvements. My wife, Joyce, read the entire manuscript in the rôle of the elusive 'general reader' and was surprisingly encouraging, although that may be the result of having had low initial expectations. Finally, all stages of the manuscript were typed with efficiency and good humour by Val Harvey.

GEOFFREY WHITTINGTON
Bristol
June 1981

List of abbreviations

Institutions

APB	The Accounting Principles Board. (The predecessor of the FASB in the USA).
ASC	The Accounting Standards Committee. (Previously, until 1975, the ASSC. The professional standard-setting body in the UK).
ASSC	The Accounting Standards Steering Committee. (Became the ASC in 1975).
CCAB	Consultative Committee on Accountancy Bodies. (A committee of professional institutes, which supervises the ASC in the UK).
ED	Exposure Draft. (A draft accounting standard, issued for discussion).
FAS	Financial Accounting Standard. (Issued by the FASB).
FASB	Financial Accounting Standards Board. (The private-sector standard-setting body in the USA).
ICAEW	Institute of Chartered Accountants in England and Wales.
PSSAP	Provisional Statement of Standard Accounting Practice. (Issued by the ASSC).
SEC	Securities and Exchange Commission. (The US government agency responsible for supervising securities markets and financial information disclosure).
SSAP	Statement of Standard Accounting Practice. (Issued by the ASC).

Technical

CCA	Current Cost Accounting.		
CoCoA	Continuously Contemporaneous Accounting.		
CPP	Constant (or Current) Purchasing Power Accounting.		
HC	Historical Cost.	PV	Present Value.
NRV	Net Realisable Value.	RC	Replacement Cost.

1
An introduction to inflation accounting

1 Introduction

The scope and context of this book were described in the Preface. The object of this chapter is to give a broad survey of the problems which will be analysed in more detail in subsequent chapters.[1] Firstly, we shall briefly discuss accounts and their uses, and then we shall consider the nature of inflation and its impact on accounts. The variety of methods of 'inflation accounting' which have been proposed will then be illustrated by means of a simple numerical example and the quantitative importance of various adjustments will be illustrated using recent British data. Finally, the course of the argument of the rest of the book will be outlined.

2 Accounting

Accounting can be defined broadly as the provision of information relating to economic transactions. For present purposes, we shall narrow this to exlude the special problems of national income accounting and of non-business organisations. We shall be concerned primarily with the accounts of business enterprises, and the field will be further narrowed by being concerned only with the financial accounts and not with the management accounts of these organisations. Financial accounts are the financial statements which have traditionally been drawn up on a periodic basis, usually for a year or six months, mainly for the benefit of the providers of finance of the firm, i.e. the shareholders and the creditors in the typical case of a company. As we shall see, the range of users and uses has widened in recent years. Management accounts are prepared for the internal use of the managers of the firm, to help them with their decision-making and control activities. The range of management

1

accounting information is very broad and its form is not specified by statute, so that management accounting practice is more heterogeneous than that of financial accounting. The correct treatment of inflation accounting in management accounts is obviously important, because misleading information could lead to bad management. The reason for avoiding special analysis of management accounting problems here is merely one of simplicity: financial accounting has quite enough problems to suffice for present purposes.[2]

A number of important decisions are based on financial accounts. Traditionally, these include the decision by the directors of a company to declare dividends, the decision by a potential creditor to lend to a firm, the decision by an investor to buy (or to sell) shares in a company, and the decision by a shareholder to support the present management by re-electing directors. During the twentieth century, an increasingly important use of financial accounts has been as a means of establishing the basis for company taxation. Although the tax base usually involves the adjustment of amounts reported in the financial accounts, such as depreciation charges, to comply with special rules laid down in the tax statutes, taxation has nevertheless played an important part in the debate on inflation accounting, because it is always possible that a convention adopted for accounting purposes will be acepted for tax purposes. A recent example of this has been the Stock Relief, granted in Britain in 1974 as a temporary relief against Corporation Tax, pending the introduction of a system of inflation accounting. Ironically, when a system of inflation accounting was finally implemented by the Accounting Standards Committee in 1980, it was not used as the basis of the new stock relief scheme (introduced in the 1981 budget).

In recent years, increasing stress has been laid on the use of financial reports for users of accounts other than the providers of finance. Evidence of this will be found in the reports of two professional committees, The Trueblood Report (1973) in the USA and *The Corporate Report* (Accounting Standards Steering Committee, 1975) in the UK, and in two official government publications in the UK, the Sandilands Report (1975) and the Green Paper, *The Future of Company Reports* (Secretary of State for Trade, 1977). Prominent amongst these users are employees, who may wish to use reported profits as evidence that their employers can afford wage increases, and who may also wish to use financial reports to assess their future employment prospects. Government also has a substantial interest in financial accounts as providing information for economic policy decisions. For example, during periods of price restraint, profits reported in the accounts have been used as evidence[3] relating to pricing policy, price increases being allowed only if they are necessary for the achievement of an adequate profit. The monopolies and restrictive practices legislation also allows the use of reported profits as one criterion to be considered in assessing whether the consumer is being over-charged.

These examples of the range of uses of financial accounts should serve to demonstrate that financial accounting is an important activity, because important economic decisions may rest partly on the use of the information which it provides. Thus, the adjustment of financial accounts for the effects of inflation is also potentially important, since it can influence such important matters as the levels of taxation, dividends, wages and prices. It is therefore not surprising that the debate on different methods of inflation accounting has been a very spirited one, despite the superficial appearance of the subject as being somewhat dry and technical. The choice of inflation accounting technique can affect the allocation of resources, and the various affected parties have a strong incentive to support the particular technique which seems to favour them most.

Before discussing inflation and its effects on accounts it is important to consider another implication of the widening range of uses of accounting information. It is unlikely that one piece of information, such as a single profit figure, will meet all of the wide variety of needs which financial accounting is meant to satisfy. For example, it is not necessary that the measure of profit used for tax purposes should be the same as that used for setting an upper limit to the dividends which can be distributed to shareholders: the fact that taxable profit and distributable profit differ under current British legislation is evidence of this. Despite this, the debate on inflation accounting is bedevilled by the implicit belief on the part of many participants that a single number can be found which will provide 'all the answers'. This problem is compounded by the fact that most of the individual questions potentially have a number of answers: for example, it is by no means clear that corporation tax should be based on profits rather than net payments to shareholders,[4] and it seems that the dividend decision should be constrained by consideration of measures of liquidity as well as of profitability.[5]

An introduction to inflation accounting

3 Inflation

Inflation may be loosely defined as a decline in the purchasing power of money, due to an increase in the general level of prices. It has been experienced throughout history, e.g. as a result of currency debasement, or, as in the sixteenth century, when gold from America was imported into Europe. Inflation has been a particularly acute problem in the twentieth century, when the reliance on fiat money has combined with increasing demands on government expenditure, often financed by borrowing rather than taxation, to make inflation the typical condition in many economies. In some countries, such as Germany after the First World War and certain Latin American countries in more recent years, inflation has reached extremely high levels which amounted to a collapse in the value of the currency and has followed or been followed by serious political problems. More often, inflation has been at more moderate rates which nevertheless have important economic consequences (e.g. at average annual percentage rates of 20 per cent or less). During the 1970s, particularly following the oil crisis of 1973, inflation increased on a world-wide scale and many countries, including the United Kingdom, experienced sustained inflation at levels (typically greater than 10 per cent per annum) previously unknown in times of peace.[6] Evidence of recent inflation rates in market economies (as opposed to centrally planned economies) is given in Table 1.1. In the United

Table 1.1. *World market economies: rates of change in consumer prices 1971–79*

Country groups (averages)	Annual average 1971–78	Annual rates		
		1977	1978	1979
Developed market economies	8.1	8.4	7.5	9.9
Major industrial countries	7.7	7.7	6.8	9.4
Other industrial countries	7.9	7.3	5.5	5.3
Primary producing countries	13.5	18.1	17.3	20.3
Developing market economies	15.0	21.5	20.7	32.6
Oil-exporting countries	12.1	15.8	11.0	14.3
Non-oil-exporting countries	15.9	23.3	23.4	36.5

Source: United Nations, *World Economic Survey 1979–1980*, Table III-1. The numbers are annual percentage point increases.

Kingdom the price level approximately quadrupled between 1969 and 1981.

We have implicitly made the common assumption that inflation is approximately measured by changes in a broadly-based consumer price index, which reflects the general level of prices. However, such an index represents the cost of living (and its inverse, the purchasing power of money) strictly only for an individual who buys commodities in proportion to their weighting in the index. For others, the index is an approximation whose accuracy will be reduced to the extent to which their expenditure pattern diverges from that assumed by the index and the prices of the divergent expenditures change out of proportion with the index. For example, a non-smoking, teetotal vegetarian might consider inappropriate to his needs a consumer price index which includes tobacco, alcohol and meat, in periods when this group of commodities varies in price relative to the other commodities which are in the index, and which he does consume in the same relative proportions as they are represented in the index.[7]

This type of objection assumes less importance at higher rates of inflation, at which most prices tend to move upwards and, for all but the most perverse of consumers, fiat money tends to be a less satisfactory measure of purchasing power than a 'real' unit calculated by reference to a broadly-based index. Thus, it is not a coincidence that it has been in countries with persistently high rates of inflation, such as Brazil, that the use of general indices to alleviate the distortionary measurement effects of inflation has been most popular. In countries with lower inflation rates, there has been more controversy about the usefulness of measuring inflation by the use of general indices. In Britain, for example, the Report of the Sandilands Committee (1975), an official government committee of enquiry into inflation accounting, came to the conclusion that 'inflation is not a phenomenon capable of objective measurement affecting all individuals and entities equally' (para. 48) and used this as an argument to justify the complete rejection of the use of general indices in the system which they proposed, their system being based solely on specific price changes.

If we can, for the present, ignore the difficulties of measuring the general price level, we can make important conceptual distinctions between the general price level, specific prices and relative prices. The general price level is a measure of the purchasing power of

5

money, as represented by some general index. Specific prices are the observable prices of specific goods and services. These specific prices may change relative to one another and to the general price level. If a specific price changes over a period, we may divide the change into two components, that which is due to changes in the purchasing power of money in general (provided we can measure it), and that due to the change in the price of the specific commodities relative to that of other commodities, the 'real' increase in the price of the specific commodity. Thus, if the price of a specific commodity rose from £10 to £15 in a period in which the general price level rose by 20 per cent (the rate of inflation), we might attribute £2 of the increase to inflation and £3 to a relative price change.[8] These distinctions are important components of some systems of inflation accounting.

4 Inflation and accounts

Since accounts are concerned with the measurement of economic activity and inflation affects the value of the conventional unit of measurement, the currency unit, inflation can clearly have an important effect on accounts. This is especially so in the case of accounts prepared on the traditional historical cost (HC) principle, in which assets and liabilities are recorded at their nominal values at the time of acquisition rather than their current values. In times of inflation, current monetary values are likely to exceed historical values by considerable amounts. Equally, when measuring income, the monetary value of the capital which must be maintained by a business before recognizing a profit (i.e. the amount of capital which will maintain the business, or its proprietors, as 'well off' at the end of a period as it was at the beginning) will also need to reflect inflation and does not do so on the traditional historical cost convention.

It is these problems which are at the root of the fierce debates which have taken place in recent years over such issues as whether the increase in the nominal (i.e. monetary rather than real) value of stocks held by companies ('stock appreciation') should be regarded as profit, and whether firms which are financed by borrowing have made a 'gain on borrowing' as a result of inflation, because they are able to repay their loans in currency units whose purchasing power has depreciated. These issues will be taken up in more detail in later chapters.[9] The next section of this chapter gives an introduction to (but not a complete survey of) the techniques of inflation accounting, by means of a simple numerical illustration, and the following section offers some quantitative evidence as to the practical importance of the choice between alternative methods. Both the numerical illustration and the quantitative evidence will show that our assessment of the profitability of an individual business, and of business in general, can be changed radically by our choice of accounting method.

5 A numerical illustration

This numerical example was inspired by a leading member of the accounting profession who, in an address to a group of industrial accountants, attempted to justify the system of current cost accounting (CCA), recently enforced by the Accounting Standards Committee,[10] in the following terms:

'It's all quite simple really. Imagine old Fred, who's a street trader. One morning he goes to the wholesale market and buys a hundred pineapples for £1.00 each. He sells them for £1.50 each so he works out his profit for the day by the traditional historical cost method, as:

	£
Sales	150
Less Historical cost of goods sold	100
Profit	£ 50

He feels that he has had a successful day and goes to the pub and spends his £50 profit. The next day, he arrives at the wholesale market and finds that, when he was selling his pineapples the previous day, the wholesale price had risen to £1.25. He looks into his pocket and realises that he has only £100 to spend, so that he can't replace his stock of 100 pineapples: he can only afford 80 pineapples. On the other hand, if he had done current cost accounting, he would have calculated his profit after charging the current replacement cost of his pineapples:

	£
Sales	150
Less Current cost of goods sold	125
Profit	£ 25

He would then have spent only £25 in the pub, and he would have preserved enough cash to maintain his capital stock of 100 pineapples.'

This simple tale was no doubt adequate for its purpose of communicating the spirit of current cost accounting, and our object is not to offer carping criticism of it, but to demonstrate a few implicit assumptions which lie behind even this simple and apparently innocuous problem. Before doing this, it should be noted that financial accounting is normally concerned with periods greater than one day, but those who are dissatisfied with this can pretend that the period is a year rather than a day. Equally, those who find Old Fred and his pineapples a rather unimportant corner of the economy can pretend that Old Fred is their favourite oil company and that the figures are expressed in millions of pounds. A more serious objection to the example is that Old Fred holds only cash at the end of the day, whereas most companies hold fixed assets and stocks of goods: we shall return to this problem later, when it will be shown to add to the variety of answers which are available to the problems of inflation accounting, Now, let us turn to an analysis of Old Fred's problem, beginning with some objections which might be raised against the case which was made out for Current Cost Accounting (CCA), over the traditional Historical Cost (HC) method.

Firstly, Fred might well object that he started the day with £100 in cash and ended with £150. Surely, then, he has gained an income of £50 which he is entitled to spend, leaving himself as well off at the end of the day as at the beginning, with £100. After all, he did not actually spend the £125 charged as cost of goods sold under the current cost accounting system.

The reply to this, by the advocates of CCA, is that the difference between the £100 actually paid and the £125 is a holding gain, the rise in the cost of his stock of pineapples between when he bought them and when he sold them. This is Fred's reward for buying early when prices were lower, rather than later, when they were higher. It should not be regarded as part of his profit, bur rather as a 'capital gain'; something which must be preserved (rather than being spent in the pub) if he is to maintain the substance of his business (100 pineapples).

Fred's reply to this might well be that he does not care about maintaining a stock of pineapples: he is in business to make money, not to accumulate a heap of perishable stock. Furthermore, if pineapples have become relatively expensive in the wholesale market and the retail price has not risen proportionately, he might prefer to switch to oranges, or some other potentially more profitable line, and his £100 might buy even more oranges today than it did yesterday.

It thus transpires that our CCA advocate supports the 'entity' view of the business: its specific physical substance, either in terms of assets or that seductive but elusive concept 'productive capacity', must be maintained before we recognize an increase in the value of the assets of the business as giving rise to a profit which is regarded as a suitable object for distribution (as dividends in the case of an oil company, at the pub in the case of Fred) or taxation. This point of view has been associated, in the recent debate on inflation accounting, with Messrs Merrett and Sykes, who have a number of eloquent and influential[11] pleas for a concept of physical capital maintenance, based upon the need to protect the operating capacity of British industry against the ravages of taxation and excessive dividends which might result from the 'paper profits' reported by traditional accounts in a period of inflation. This concept has a natural appeal for managers and other employees whose jobs may depend upon the preservation of the operating capacity of the business.

Fred, on the other hand, is an advocate of the 'proprietary' view of the business, which is not surprising, since he is the proprietor. This views the business as a financial fund administered by the management for the benefit of the proprietors, who provide the finance. On this view, the objective of the business is not to maintain its productive capacity, but to maximise the wealth of the proprietors, and a profit is an increase in the wealth of the proprietors. The dispute between these two points of view explains a great deal of the controversy on inflation accounting and will be discussed further in Chapter 6, but we must, having raised the issue, pass on to yet further complications.

It will be observed that the example so far has not taken any account of inflation in the sense described in the previous section of this chapter. If we assume that inflation was zero, or negligible, during the period (which is plausible if we assume it to be a day), then no adjustment is necessary. Thus, CCA cannot be simply a system of inflation accounting, since it produces different figures from those of traditional HC even when there is no general inflation. This is because CCA deals with *specific* price changes, which, as we found earlier, can be due to *general* price level changes (inflation or deflation) or to *relative* price changes, or both. If we assume no inflation, our example is one solely of relative price changes (pineapples relative to other goods).

At the other extreme, we might assume that the rise in the price of Fred's pineapples was attributable entirely to general inflation: this is more plausible if we assume that the period is a year rather than a day, although high daily rates of inflation have occurred, e.g. in the German hyper-inflation of 1923. In such a case, we might say that Fred was wrong, even on his own 'proprietary' assumptions, because he failed to take account of the declining value of the monetary unit. His wealth in this case can be measured in pineapples, since they represent constant command over other goods and services. After maintaining this wealth intact, he has £25 left over to spend, and, incidentally, these current pounds will buy him only four fifths of the number of pints of beer which they would have bought before the inflation price rise.

However, it is more plausible to assume that inflation exists but at a rate different from that of the change in the price of a specific commodity, such as pineapples. In such a case, Fred should aim to maintain his 'real' wealth, i.e. his command over goods and services in general (not pineapples specifically) before recognizing a profit, if he takes the proprietary view. Thus, if we assume that inflation took place at 10 per cent,[12] we would regard Fred's closing capital requirement as £110 and his profit as £40. His profit calculation could be re-cast as follows:

	£
Sales	150
Less Historical cost of goods sold, in current £s	110
Profit	£ 40

The purchases have been re-stated to allow for the fact that, since purchase, the £ has effectively been devalued in terms of its general purchasing power, so that the cost of the original purchases expressed in current £s must be increased to be equivalent (£100 × 110/100). This is an example of Constant Purchasing Power (CPP) accounting, as advocated by the accounting profession in 1973.[13]

An alternative way of presenting this would be:

	£
Sales	150
Less Current cost of goods sold	125
Operating profit	25
Add Real holding gain on stock	15
Profit	£ 40

This yields the same profit figure as CPP in this instance,[14] but it tells the story of how the profit was made in a different, and possibly more revealing manner, which might help Fred towards a better understanding of the sources of his gains. First, we are told Fred's current cost operating profit (£25): this is the cash profit which he would have made had he bought his stock at current prices. However, he bought early and cheap, saving money by doing so. This holding gain was £25 in money terms, but we deduct from this the £10 allowance for inflation, the general devaluation of money which has taken place since the purchase. If we wanted to be yet more informative, we would distinguish in our profit statement between the nominal holding gain (£25) and the adjustment for inflation (£10).

This alternative presentation is the profit and loss account associated with a 'real terms' accounting system, which combines the useful features of both CCA and CPP. It has a respectable intellectual history, having been advocated by the great pioneer of inflation accounting, H. W. Sweeney (1936), and by some of the most important theoretical writers since then, such as E. O. Edwards and P. W. Bell (1961). It was also advocated in practice by the Consultative Committee of Accountancy Bodies in their initial response to the Sandilands Report (CCAB, 1975), and certain features of it are incorporated in the current United States standard on accounting for changing prices (FAS33: FASB, 1979). However, it must ultimately stand or fall by its own merits, rather than its respectable ancestry, and one important merit stands out: it is capable of telling Old Fred rather more than either of the simpler but narrower answers stated earlier. Of course, if he is content with a simple and narrow answer, there is no point in providing him with a more complicated one, but, if it is accepted that there is something to be said for both the CPP and CCA solutions, a system which combines the two seems to avoid an invidious choice.

However, our choice of capital maintenance concepts does not end here. In the United Kingdom at present, the 'real terms' method of allowing for inflation with a CCA system has been rejected in favour of a 'gearing adjustment', which is an alternative method of assessing the gain on borrowing when prices change. This would not affect Fred in our example as it has been stated to date, because he has no 'gearing', i.e. his business is not financed by borrowing. However, let us now suppose that half of his £100 has been lent to Fred by his Aunt Mabel, or, if we prefer to think in grandiose terms, suppose that our oil company is financed by £50 million equity shares and £50 million loan stock, i.e. its 'gearing ratio' is 50 per cent. To keep matters simple, we shall assume that no interest is payable on the loan. The HC statements of profit and loss will be unaffected by the existence of the loan, if no interest is paid: profit remains at £50. Under the CCA systems, equally, there will be no change, if no gearing adjustment is made. Under the CPP and real terms system, if we assume inflation at 10 per cent, Fred's profit will now be £45. This is because he now has to put aside only £5 to maintain the real value of his initial capital (£50): the remainder of the capital was provided by Aunt Mabel, who will require payment only of 50 depreciated pounds, not of the real purchasing power she invested (which she would have preserved by investing in Granny Bonds, i.e. 55 depreciated pounds). Thus, Fred has made a 'gain on borrowing' of £5.[15] The precise calculation is as follows:

CPP		£
Sales		150
Less Historical cost of goods sold, in current £s		110
Operating profit		40
Add Gain on borrowing		5
Total profit		£ 45

Real terms		£
Sales		150
Less Current cost of goods sold		125
Operating profit		25
Add Real holding gain on stock	£15	
Gain on borrowing	£ 5	
Total holding gains		20
Total profit		£ 45

The real holding gain and operating profit figures are calculated as in the previous example. The 'gain on borrowing' represents the loss of general purchasing power of the nominal pounds which Fred owes to

An introduction to inflation accounting

Aunt Mabel: her loss is his gain. The greater the rate of inflation, the more important will this item become.

There is, however, another way of looking at the problem of the gain on borrowing, namely the 'gearing adjustment', which is incorporated in the current United Kingdom accounting standard, SSAP16. This takes the view that the gain or loss on borrowing should be related not to changes in the general purchasing power of money (a concept which extreme advocates of CCA, such as the Sandilands Committee, reject) but to changes in the prices of the specific goods and services bought by the firm. Thus, in Fred's case, the gain on borrowing would be related to the change in the price of pineapples, a 25 per cent increase, which, on a loan of £50, amounts to a gain of £12.50p. The way this is introduced is through the gearing adjustment:

General Income	£
Sales	150
Less Current Cost of Purchases	125
Operating profit	25
Add Gearing Adjustment	12.50
Geared income	£ 37.50

The gearing adjustment is calculated by multiplying the 'realised holding gain', i.e. the difference between what Fred paid for his pineapples and what they would have cost him at the time of their sale (£125 − £100 = £25), by the geared proportion,[16] i.e. the proportion of loans to Fred's total finance (£50/£100 = 0.5). This is convoluted, but it is also an ingenious way of introducing a gain on borrowing into the CCA system without making use of a general price index.

Of course, the gearing adjustment does not produce the *same* gain on borrowing as the 'real terms' system. The reason is that the gearing adjustment does not recognise the effect of general inflation in eroding Fred's own equity capital but rather assumes that he must maintain his share of the physical capital. Thus, on his share of the capital he cannot recognise any holding gain on his pineapples as profit. The real holding gain on the pineapples financed by his capital (half of the total real holding gain) is £7.50: this is the difference between real terms profit and geared profit, the latter failing to recognise the gain as profit.

The gearing adjustment is controversial, because it seems to some commentators to be an uneasy mixture of the proprietary and entity concepts of capital maintenance. Particularly contentious is the split-

13

ting of real holding gains into those which can be recognized as income because they are loan financed and those which must be capitalised because they are equity financed. There are also a number of technical difficulties in its implementation (how does it apply to unrealised holding gains, do we calculate gearing on the basis of the opening balance sheet, or as an average for the year, do we regard preference shares as equity or loans? etc.). The same could be said of a corresponding adjustment, the monetary working capital adjustment, which is incorporated in the present UK standard. However, a theoretical justification of the gearing adjustment is possible: perhaps its most persuasive advocate is Professor Charles Kennedy (1978a and 1978b). These issues will be discussed further in Chapter 6. The main purpose of the present discussion is not to denigrate the gearing adjustment but to show that it represents yet another alternative view as to how Fred might calculate the capital which must be maintained intact before recognising a profit.

A final alternative, which would find strong support in economic theory, is that Fred need not require any particular configuration of assets to be maintained intact. Rather, he should look to the future and regard his income as 'the maximum amount the individual can spend this week, and still expect to be able to spend the same amount in each ensuing week' (Hicks, 1946): if inflation is anticipated he would wish to define his spending in real terms, i.e. in terms of constant command over goods and services. In this case, Fred's assessment of his income would depend upon the future course of prices in general, the cost of pineapples and the selling price of pineapples. For example, he might regard the £50 which he spent at the pub as profit if he expected the next day to buy 80 pineapples for £1.25 and sell them for £1.94 each to give receipts of £155 (approximately) and a surplus of £55, i.e. £50 with compensation for an anticipated 10 per cent inflation, with similar adjustments in future selling prices to compensate for rising costs and inflation.

This might seem to be relevant to a small businessman like Fred, but not to a large public company, but this is not so. The shareholder's return on his shares is the dividend (unless the firm goes into liquidation) and he will value the shares as a claim to a future dividend stream. If we translate 'able to spend' into 'able to distribute as a dividend', the concept becomes relevant to the company, and the sustainable constant 'standard stream' dividend is a useful device for valuing shares. An annuity of this type can be valued simply by dividing by an appropriate discount rate. Thus, if the sustainable dividend on a particular share is £1 per annum and the appropriate discount rate (allowing for risk and also for inflation when the return is defined in nominal rather than real £s) is 10 per cent, then the value of the share is £1/0.1 = £10. The most persuasive advocate of the 'standard stream' approach to financial reporting is the economist, M. FG. Scott (1976), who has argued for its relevance to share valuation as one of its particular merits.

We have now found that poor Old Fred's financial affairs are more complicated than he originally might have thought. Despite starting the day with cash and finishing with cash, thus avoiding the problem of valuing stocks and fixed assets which commonly afflict trading and manufacturing businesses, he still faces a choice of five approaches to defining the capital to be maintained before he recognises a gain in his resources as profit. These are:

1. Money capital (as in traditional HC)
2. Physical capital (as in CCA operating profit)
3. Real capital (as in CPP or 'real terms')
4. Geared capital (as in current UK version of CCA)
5. That capital which will maintain future consumption or dividends.

We could add to this complicated picture by discussing asset valuation, if we chose to endow Fred with assets other than cash at the end of the day, e.g. supposing that he had some unsold pineapples. Apart from the traditional historical cost method (HC is what Fred actually paid for his pineapples), we have two other types of current market values, 'entry' values which would represent the cost to the business of acquiring the assets (in Fred's case, the price of pineapples in the wholesale market) and 'exit values' which would represent the amount realisable by their being sold by the business (in Fred's case, the price which his retail customers are prepared to pay for pineapples). Also in the case of fixed assets (those held for use in the business over a number of accounting periods) the economist's method of valuation may be appropriate: the asset is valued at 'net present value', i.e. the present value, after charging interest, of the future benefits which the firm will derive by using the asset. The valuation of shares by reference to a standard stream of expected dividends, described earlier, was an example of such a calculation. Finally, there are eclectic methods of valuation which use one or other of these methods depending on the circumstances. The current British and US standards, for example, make use of the 'value to the firm' concept: assets are valued at replacement cost (an entry value) or 'recoverable amount' (the higher of exit value or present value in use), whichever is the lower.

The complications do not end here. Each of the broad methods of valuation described above contains a variety of alternatives. For example, if we choose entry value, do we estimate the replacement cost of the specific asset, or the replacement cost of the service provided by the asset, which may, as a result of technical change or relative price changes, be most economically provided by a different asset? If we choose exit value, do we choose selling price in the ordinary course of business (which must take time), or do we choose the immediately realisable price in enforced liquidation (which may involve offering a substantial discount to induce customers to come forward immediately)? If we choose discounted present value, what future use do we envisage for the asset (its present use or a more profitable alternative which may offer itself in the future) and how do we assess the appropriate discount rate? Added to these conceptual problems are the practical ones of subjectivity: current values are often described as 'soft', lending themselves to manipulation by unscrupulous preparers. However, historical cost involves some difficulties and is not as 'hard' as its advocates might wish, e.g. the assessment of depreciation of partly-used fixed assets is subjective, and advocates of CPP would have us re-state historical cost in units of constant purchasing power, using a general index.

Further difficulties are raised by the fascinating problems of allocation and aggregation, which have been rigorously exposed by the work of Arthur L. Thomas (1969 and 1974). In valuing used assets, where secondhand values are not readily ascertainable, we may have to resort to 'writing off' as depreciation a proportion of the price of a new equivalent asset just as, in the traditional historical cost system, a proportion of original cost is written off. This raises the time allocation problem, that any allocation of the cost of the asset to specific periods (in order to determine how much of the asset has been used up) is arbitrary in cases in which the purchase of the asset is essentially the purchase of the asset's services over its whole lifetime, not for separable sub-periods. Equally, we may be faced with a different type of allocation problem, occurring between assets rather than between time periods, when we calculate net present values. When a number of assets are engaged in a joint productive process, we may face the problem of allocating the joint return between individual assets. The allocation problem is concerned with dividing or allocating a joint product amongst the factors which were responsible for producing it, or allocating a shared factor amongst its various products. The aggregation problem involves the reverse process of assembling the whole from the sum of its parts. Thus, if we aggregate a set of individual asset values, we face the problem of interpreting the total: is the total equal to the total value of the firm, and if not what is its significance? This question is obviously important in relation to profit measures which start by comparing the total of closing assets with the total of opening assets. Here, we encounter the problem of goodwill, the excess of the value of the whole firm over the sum of the values of the individual assets: what is its nature and how can it be measured? Asset valuation is discussed further in Chapter 5.

Subsequent chapters will elaborate upon these problems and the relative merits of alternative accounting methods. For the moment, this simple illustration should have persuaded the reader that financial accounting in general and inflation accounting in particular face difficulties which are more complex than is popularly supposed. These problems do not lend themselves to simplistic solutions of a general purpose type, although this does not mean that they are not amenable to logical investigation or that their importance cannot be assessed by empirical research.

6 Some quantitative evidence

There is a great deal of evidence both for the USA and the United Kingdom as to the quantitative differences between the various methods of accounting described in the previous section. Brief reviews of such studies will be given in the appendices to subsequent chapters, which review empirical research results. For the present, a single illustration will be given, to demonstrate that the amounts involved in the various adjustments are far from trivial.

This illustration is taken from the work of Basil Moore (1980), and is based upon the recent experience (1961–77) of the United Kingdom quoted company sector. It is an aggregate study and it should be borne in mind that aggregate figures will tend to mask the variability of the experience of individual companies, an above-average adjustment in one company being offset by the below-average adjustment of others, in the aggregation process. The study is also confined to those companies engaged primarily in manufacturing and distribution, and it therefore omits the financial sector and oil companies, each of which groups would be expected to have results widely divergent from the average, but for very different reasons.[17] It is also, of necessity, based upon the use of indices rather than the specific revaluation of individual assets, so that the adjustments for stock appreciation, current cost depreciation and real holding gains can be regarded only as broad estimates of the order of magnitude of these adjustments. Finally, the figures are all in current £s of the individual years: no attempt has been made to translate them into a unit of constant purchasing power, which would make them comparable in real terms between different years, as in a fully developed system of CPP accounting (described in Chapter 4).

Despite these reservations, Table 1.2 provides vivid evidence of the quantitative importance of the various alternative adjustments. Rows 1 to 5 contain a summary of the conventional published profit and loss account data, based broadly on the historical cost principle. Thus, Row 5 is an estimate of 'HC' profit (less tax) as described in the numerical example earlier in this chapter. It will be observed that the broad trend of profit, indicated by Row 5, is broadly upwards. This increase is, of course, illusory due to the recording of profits in £s of the particular year: the retail price index (based on 1970 = 100) rose from 89 in 1968 to 249 in 1977 (a 180 per cent increase), so that a rise from £million 1,580 in 1968 to £million 4,308 in 1977 (a 173 per cent increase) does not represent an increase in real terms. However, even setting aside the problem of inter-year comparability of the measurement unit, the pattern of profitability is profoundly affected by the choice of accounting technique.

Rows 6 and 7 contain the adjustments necessary to charge the cost of goods sold (Row 6) and depreciation of fixed assets (Row 7) at current cost. Deducting these from conventional (HC) profit gives us (in Row 8) an estimate of Current Cost profit (CCA) as in our earlier numerical example. This is an approximation to the Current Cost Operating Profit (less tax) proposed by the Sandilands Committee. The effect of these adjustments is to wipe out entirely the apparent increase in nominal profits which took place in the period of high inflation, 1973–77, showing losses for the period 1974–76. This is primarily because this concept of profit excludes stock appreciation, which was particularly high during this period, as a consequence of inflation.

However, charging current cost depreciation and eliminating stock appreciation adjusts only for the deleterious effects of inflation on profitability and ignores some of the possible gains. Rows 9 and

Table 1.2. *Reported and adjusted profits of UK quoted companies 1968–77*

	1968	1969	1970	1971	1972	1973	1974	1975	1976	1977
1. Reported net trading profits	2,843	2,880	2,814	3,234	4,252	5,486	5,916	6,171	8,334	7,615
2. *Less* net interest payments	123	165	394	405	480	655	1,033	1,212	1,178	955
3. Reported equity profits	2,720	2,715	2,420	2,830	3,772	4,831	4,883	4,958	7,156	6,660
4. *Less* corporation tax (excluding tax on dividends)	1,140	1,180	1,042	1,149	1,350	1,926	2,076	2,118	2,948	2,352
5. Reported net after-tax equity profits	1,580	1,535	1,378	1,681	2,422	2,905	2,807	2,840	4,208	4,308
6. *Less* stock appreciation	322	405	570	550	695	1,940	3,292	2,972	3,362	2,035
7. *Less* current cost depreciation adjustment	144	175	259	389	475	634	995	1,499	2,058	1,957
8. Current cost profit, after tax	1,114	955	549	742	1,252	331	−1,480	−1,631	−1,212	316
9. Monetary working capital adjustment	−92	−72	−81	−43	−120	−113	−54	183	185	172
10. Gearing adjustment	169	230	300	306	422	826	1,261	1,085	1,142	774
11. SSAP16 after tax net profits	1,191	1,113	768	1,005	1,554	1,044	−273	−363	115	1,262
12. Gain on net borrowing	242	254	503	548	667	933	2,183	3,379	2,169	1,597
13. Real holding gains on assets	−469	−58	−102	530	−163	1,179	2,144	−2,462	3,526	584
14. 'Real terms' profit	887	1,151	950	1,820	1,756	2,443	2,847	−714	4,483	2,497

Source: Moore (1980), as corrected by Wiles (1981).

Notes: All figures are expressed in £million. The companies are the larger UK quoted companies engaged in manufacturing and distribution, the basic source being the aggregate data published in *Business Monitor* (M3). Arithmetic consistency between rows is as follows:

Row 5 = Rows 1 − 2 − 4, Row 8 = Rows 5 − 6 − 7, Row 11 = Rows 8 + 9 + 10, Row 14 = Rows 8 + 12 + 13.

10 introduce two further adjustments which are incorporated in the current United Kingdom standard (SSAP16). The monetary working capital adjustment is an attempt to reflect the effect of inflation on eroding the net monetary working capital of the business. Monetary working capital consists primarily of short-term amounts owed to the business (trade debtors) less amounts owed by the business (trade creditors). This can be positive or negative (i.e. creditors can exceed debtors), and when it is negative inflation will lead to a gain (a form of gain on borrowing). The net effect of this adjustment is usually small in any year, but it varies considerably (from positive to negative) across the years. The gearing adjustment was described briefly in the preceding section. The form used here is that currently used in practice: it is an abatement of the stock appreciation and current cost depreciation charges to reflect the proportion of assets financed by borrowing. Its effect is therefore always to increase measured profit, when prices are rising, and the effect is substantial in the years of high stock appreciation. The effect would be even greater if the adjustment were applied to the unrealised gain in the value of fixed assets (i.e. that portion which has not been realised through the asset being used and depreciated) as was advocated by the original authors of the gearing adjustment (Godley and Cripps, 1975). The net result is an 'SSAP16' profit figure which lies between the original HC figures and the pessimistic CCA figure.

Finally, Rows 12 and 13 estimate the amounts of the alternative adjustments to CCA profit (Row 8) which would be made in order to calculate 'real terms' profit (Row 14). The gain on borrowing (Row 12) represents the decline in the real burden of net debt due to inflation (Aunt Mabel's £5 loss, in the numerical example of the previous section). This is always positive when inflation is positive, and the amounts involved are very large in the period of high inflation (1973–77). The real holding gains on assets represent the change in value (on a current cost basis) of assets held by the business, relative to changes in a general index. These depend upon relative price movements and can therefore be either positive or negative. The methods used to estimate the figures in Row 13 are necessarily crude, and great reliance should not be placed upon them, but they serve to demonstrate the huge potential impact of real gains and losses on assets held by the business, and the potentially misleading nature of accounts which ignore such gains. Because of the volatility of the holding gains, the 'real terms' profit figure does not bear a consistent relationship to the other measures, being lower then CCA (Row 7) in one year, and higher than historical cost in three others, but more often between the two.

One measure of profit which does not appear separately in Table 1.2 is Constant Purchasing Power (CPP) profit. It will be recalled that, in the simplified example presented in the preceding section, CPP profit equalled 'real terms' profit because no non-monetary assets were held at the end of the period. In the real world, as represented in Table 1.2, non-monetary assets are very important and, in order to convert 'real terms' profit into CPP profit, it would be necessary to eliminate the unrealised proportion of the holding gains (or losses) on these assets (a significant fraction of the adjustment in Row 13) and to add back any unrealised real holding gains of previous years which were realised in the current year (which would be included in the current year's profits by HC and CPP, but in previous years' profits by the 'real terms' holding gain adjustment of Row 13). However, the gain on borrowing (Row 12) is common to both CPP and real terms,[18] and this adjustment is large enough to demonstrate the quantitative importance of the CPP adjustments relative to the traditional historical cost and alternative current cost measures. As was pointed out earlier, the full application of the CPP philosophy would also require that, the profits having been calculated on a CPP basis within each period in £s of that period, they should be converted into £'s of a single period for comparative purposes.[19]

7 Plan of the book

The object of this chapter was to introduce the main problems of inflation accounting and some of the more commonly advanced solutions, on a relatively superficial level. The remaining chapters will cover the same ground in much greater detail and discuss the issues involved much more thoroughly.

Chapter 2 will elaborate upon the framework of financial accounting, which was discussed briefly in section 2 of this chapter. Chapter 3 will develop this discussion further by examining the properties of historical cost accounting. This is important because the traditional historical cost methods have severe limitations even in the absence of inflation, but the debate on this subject has become associated with the debate on inflation accounting. Chapter 4 then elaborates upon the measurement problems created by inflation and the use of

An introduction to inflation accounting

CPP techniques to deal with these problems. Chapters 5 and 6 then survey the various methods of current value accounting which have been proposed, Chapter 5 concentrating on the valuation of assets and liabilities and Chapter 6 dealing with the various capital maintenance concepts which could be used for income measurement purposes. Finally, Chapter 7 provides a review of the alternative systems and suggests some possible future developments both in research and in practice.

2
Fundamentals

1 Introduction

It was explained in Chapter 1 that this book is concerned with the effects of inflation on the financial accounts of companies, i.e. the accounts which are published, under statutory obligation, for the shareholders and other interested parties external to the company organisation. The two principal statements with which we shall be concerned are the balance sheet and the profit and loss account.

Our task is to establish the nature of the problem which inflation poses for financial accounts, and to explain and evaluate the various remedies which have been proposed to deal with it. The first stage of this analysis must be to establish the nature and purpose of financial accounts: without an understanding of this and the attendant problems, it is unlikely that we will understand the additional problems imposed by inflation. This first step will be attempted in this chapter.

2 Financial accounts and their uses

The traditional function of financial accounts is that of stewardship.[1] In the case of a company, this implies that the board of directors, who are responsible for the management of the company's assets, give a periodic account to the proprietors (the shareholders) of how they have carried out this function. In its narrowest traditional sense, this implies a statement of past transactions, in historical cost terms,[2] which provides a check on the honesty of the steward, but not necessarily on his efficiency, which might be assessed in terms of how the current value of the company's assets has grown. Apart from their use by shareholders, accounts have traditionally been used by creditors, to assess the security for their loans, and creditor protection has been an important factor in accountants' application of conservative valuation principles. The general public also has been given the right of access to company accounts (except in the case of 'exempt private companies', a category which was abolished for limited liability companies by the 1967 Companies' Act).

In recent years, the range of uses which company accounts are expected to meet has broadened considerably.[3] Some of these uses were outlined in Chapter 1. This development may partly be due to the growth of very large companies with diffused shareholdings and a consequent increase in the separation of ownership (shareholders) from control (directors), which has placed more responsibility on the financial accounts for communication between the two groups, whereas shareholders who exercise direct control will have access to management information. Another important factor has undoubtedly been the increased concern of government with the affairs of companies. This is most obvious in the field of taxation: income tax and corporation tax now give the government a claim on UK company profits which is of a similar order of magnitude to that paid out to shareholders.[4] The government has also created a financial interest in companies by various investment incentive and regional development schemes, and accounting information has been used in the implementation of price and dividend controls, and competition policy. Finally, other groups within the community such as employees and consumers are also showing an increased interest in the financial affairs of companies, which expresses the changing economic, political and social environment in which companies operate.

The result of these developments has been a recognition that accounts serve a wide variety of users and uses. This has long been recognised by some academic writers (notably H. C. Daines (1929), who can claim to be a pioneer of the user-oriented approach to the design of accounting information), but it has penetrated professional circles relatively recently. *The Corporate Report* (ASSC, 1975) epitomises this development and provides a good summary of the user-oriented approach and its implications. Although *The Corporate Report* was a discussion document, and has not been adopted as a statement of policy, it nevertheless emanated from a professional committee of high standing and provides a sharp contrast with the conservative, narrow stewardship approach of the earlier *Recommendation on Accounting Principles* (*N15*) issued by the Institute of

Chartered Accountants in England and Wales in 1952. Many of the proposals put forward in *The Corporate Report* were subsequently adopted in the government's Green Paper on *The Future of Company Reports*,[5] and the progressive widening of the disclosure requirements in the Companies' Acts of 1967 and 1979 suggests that future legislation is likely to support the broad user-oriented approach to financial reporting. There have been similar changes in the orientation of professional and governmental attitudes to financial reporting in the USA.[6]

The movement towards user-orientation has had two consequences. Firstly, it has led to the idea that accounting information should be related to the decisions which users will make, and, since decisions are made in the present and relate to the present or future, rather than to the past, this has created dissatisfaction with historical cost as a valuation base (except where it can be shown to provide data which have predictive value) and a preference for current market values or values based upon an assessment of future prospects. This in turn has led to a conflict between objectivity and relevance. Historical cost data are more easily verified (e.g. by examining documents relating to purchase or sale) and are relatively objective,[7] in the sense that two independent accountants applying the same rules should arrive at a similar figure,[8] but it is often argued that objectivity is of no value when the data themselves are irrelevant.[9] Current value data, or 'economic' present values obtained by discounting prospective receipts, are clearly less easy to verify and less objective (since they depend upon what might happen rather than what did happen), but they are obviously relevant to decisions which are made in the present and will have consequences in the future. The unresolved debate as to whether past, present, or future values (or a combination of them) should be recorded in accounts could have occurred in the absence of inflation, but in fact it has occurred at a time when inflation is perceived as being a serious problem. This is not an accident: one of the consequences of inflation is that, if a nominal currency unit (such as the £ sterling) is used as the unit of measurement, the apparent difference between historical cost and current value, measured in currency units, is likely to be greater. This led the Sandilands Committee on Inflation Accounting (1975) to conclude that their current cost accounting system based on current values, but making no direct adjustment for changes in the general purchasing power of money, was an adequate system of inflation accounting. Thus, the debate on inflation accounting is inter-twined with the debate on the valuation basis of accounts.

A second consequence of user-orientation is the recognition that there is a variety of users and uses, each of which might have different information requirements. This raises the possibility that there may be a conflict of interest between different users, whose information needs differ, if financial accounts are to be of the 'general purpose' type. A greater degree of disclosure will help to overcome such problems, by providing more detail or even reporting alternative valuation bases, but this will entail additional costs on both the producers of accounts (the cost of producing the additional information) and on the users (the cost of interpreting more complex information).[10] The various proposals that forms of inflation-adjusted statements should be provided as a supplement to the accounts,[11] rather than as an integral part of them, provide an illustration of practical attempts to resolve the latter problem.

It might, of course, be argued that there is a substantial area of overlap between the information requirements of various users, and that it is more fruitful to concentrate on these areas of common interest than on the differences. It is certainly the case that such matters as the value of the economic resources commanded by a business, the means by which this is financed, and the capacity of the business to add to those resources from both internal (retained profit) and external (borrowing and new issues) sources are of interest to a wide variety of users. However, the traditional 'general purpose' financial statements, the balance sheet and the profit and loss account, calculated broadly on historical cost principles, have failed to provide such information. This is partly because historical cost accounts are not well designed to meet decision needs, since decisions are made in the present and have consequences in the future, and any possible relationship between historical costs and present values is likely to be weakened by rising prices. Another contributory factor, which would apply to any attempt to devise a multi-purpose system, is the wide variety of uses, which implies a wide range of information requirements which may have little in common with one another. This problem is compounded by the wide variety of information which is potentially relevant in a world which is characterised by uncertainty. Uncertainty implies that *ex post* measures of income and value do not necessarily equal *ex ante* measures,[12] and that the present economic value of an asset or a firm (i.e. discounted present value of future receipts) cannot be established objectively in the absence of perfect and complete markets.[13] Thus, uncertainty adds to both the variety and the subjectivity of the available valuation methods. This may be reinforced by the existence of disequilibrium or imperfect markets,[14] which will add to the subjectivity of current market values and will imply that replacement cost (buying price) can diverge from net realisable value (selling price).

Thus, an attempt to report the 'true' value of the firm's assets or its profit for the period will encounter the problem of uncertainty, and a single choice from among the variety of measures available is unlikely to meet the needs of all potential users. In the face of this difficulty, some writers[15] have concluded that accountants should not attempt to be valuers, but should concentrate on supplying relevant information to the user, who will estimate his own subjective value. An alternative approach would be for the accountant to attempt to calculate such variables as income but to provide different measures for different potential uses: this approach is exemplified in the 'different incomes for different purposes' literature.[16] The narrowest approach of all is to report a single measure of income (or similar summary measure of economic performance) and to justify this on the ground that it is the best proxy or 'surrogate' for the 'true' measure, which would satisfy all users in the absence of uncertainty or market imperfections. There has been a considerable debate on the validity of the surrogate approach to measuring economic income.[17] So far, the surrogate relationship has been shown to hold only under circumstances which are so restrictive that the relationship is unlikely to be a suitable basis for accounting practice.[18]

However, although it may not be possible to measure precisely such concepts as income and capital, they are crucial components of the traditional form of accounts (although the substance of the actual measurement has traditionally left much to be desired) and it seems likely that their measurement will be an important step in many uses of accounts. It is therefore important to clarify these concepts and their traditional rôle in accounting before considering the effects of inflation on accounts. This is the purpose of the next section of this chapter.

3 Income, value and capital

The traditional financial accounts of a business enterprise consist of a balance sheet and a profit and loss account. These two accounts are 'articulated', i.e. they arise from a common double entry system, and the profit for a period recorded in the profit and loss account matches the change in net worth in the balance sheet during the same period, in the absence of capital introductions and withdrawals by the proprietors or transfers to and from capital reserves such as are often associated with methods of inflation accounting.[19] Thus, the balance sheet is a statement of assets and claims at a point in time:

Balance Sheet of firm A at time t

Claims	£	Assets	£
Proprietors' interest	P	Non-monetary (i.e. fluctuating	
Liabilities	L	money value)	N
		Monetary (i.e. fixed money	
		value)	M
	$\overline{P+L}$		$\overline{N+M}$

Since the proprietor's interest is a residual claim on the assets of the business, we have the definition:

$$P_t \equiv N_t + M_t - L_t \tag{2.1}$$

where t indicates the common point in time, and the balance sheet identity:

$$P_t + L_t \equiv N_t + M_t \tag{2.2}$$

which ensures that the balance sheet always balances.[20] There are two features of this identity which are extremely important in considering inflation accounting.

Firstly, money is conventionally used as the unit of measurement. If, therefore, money fluctuates in value and different components of the balance sheet are measured in units of different value, it might be argued that the residual claim (Proprietors' interest, P) is not measured in homogeneous units, i.e. it is not legitimate to aggregate the components of the balance sheet. Current Purchasing Power Accounting (CPP) (which is discussed further in Chapter 4) is a system which has been advocated to overcome this difficulty.

Secondly, the valuation of assets and liabilities is crucial in determining the amount of the residual claim, P. Valuation is the process of translating assets into monetary units. We have therefore distinguished between those assets, such as cash or deposits, which have a clearly defined fixed money value, M, and those assets whose values in monetary terms will fluctuate, N. This distinction is useful in theoretical discussions about inflation accounting, although in practice there may be difficulties in assigning certain assets to either category. For the moment, we shall assume that liabilities, L, are also fixed in monetary value, although there are certain cases in which this does not occur: most obviously that of long-term fixed-interest loans, whose market value fluctuates inversely with the rate of interest.

The balance sheet identity holds at any point in time. We may therefore difference any pair of balance sheets, relating to the same accounting entity at different points in time, to produce a self-balancing statement of how the balance sheet structure has changed over the period intervening between the two balance sheet dates:

$$N_{t+1} + M_{t+1} \equiv L_{t+1} + P_{t+1} \tag{2.3}$$

and deducting (2.2) above gives:

$$(N_{t+1} - N_t) + (M_{t+1} - M_t) \equiv (L_{t+1} - L_t) + (P_{t+1} - P_t) \tag{2.4}$$

This relationship is the basis of the flow of funds statement, which has become an important financial statement in recent years,[21] but it is also the basis of a statement which has, historically, been of even more importance, the profit and loss account. As stated earlier, in a firm with no other transactions on or adjustments to the proprietors' capital account, the change in proprietors' interest is solely attributable to the profit of the period. Rearranging (2.4), profit may then be defined[22] as:

$$(P_{t+1} - P_t) \equiv (N_{t+1} - N_t) + (M_{t+1} - M_t) - (L_{t+1} - L_t) \tag{2.5}$$

The appendix to this chapter provides a simple numerical illustration of these algebraic relationships.

We should note certain features of this definition of profit, which will be of great importance in the subsequent discussion of inflation accounting. Profit measurement is dependent upon the measurement conventions incorporated in the balance sheets. Thus, the assumption that the unit of measurement should be homogeneous will be violated if all figures in both balance sheets are not measured in the same units. Equally, the valuation conventions used in measuring the assets and liabilities in both balance sheets will affect the income measure, over-valuation of assets in the closing balance sheet and under-valuation in the opening balance sheet both leading to the over-statement of profit. It should particularly be stressed that income measurement requires consistent measurement between two balance sheets as well as within each balance sheet. Since the two balance sheets refer to different points in time, there is a possibility (in practice, a probability) that the purchasing power of the monetary unit (as measured by a general consumer price index) will have changed between the two dates, and that the relative prices of specific assets will also have changed. The problems of recording and isolating the effects of general and specific price changes have been the central concern of the debate on inflation accounting. Adherents of various forms of Current Purchasing Power (CPP) accounting have sought to deal primarily with the general purchasing power problem, and adherents of various forms of Current Cost Accounting (CCA) have sought to deal mainly with the problem of specific price changes, whilst adherents of Real Terms Accounting have attempted to deal simultaneously with both problems.

The accountant's method of calculating income is, superficially, consistent with that of the economist, described in the next paragraph: income is the surplus net worth accruing during the period after maintaining opening capital (net worth) intact.[23] However, the valuation conventions used by the accountant in measuring opening and closing net worth have traditionally differed from those of the economist, the former preferring historical cost, modified by conservatism, as being a relatively objective basis for practical implementation, and the latter preferring current market values or net present values based on discounting prospective returns, as being more relevant to decision making.[24]

The most widely quoted economist's definition of income is that of Hicks (1946), who offers three definitions:

(1) 'Income No. 1 is . . . the maximum amount which can be spent during a period if there is to be an expectation of maintaining intact the capital value of prospective receipts (in money terms).'

(2) 'Income No. 2 . . . (is) . . . the maximum amount the individual can spend this week, and still expect to be able to spend the same amount in each ensuing week.'

(3) 'Income No. 3 must be defined as the maximum amount of money which the individual can spend this week, and still expect to be able to spend the same amount *in real terms* in each ensuing week.'

Each of these definitions is an *ex ante* concept, adopting the forward-looking approach which is ideally relevant to decision-making, but there is a parallel set of three *ex post* concepts, defining the income of the past week, which are clearly of more relevance to the financial accountant, who is typically concerned to report past events in accordance with his traditional 'stewardship' function. However, as Kaldor (1955) points out, even the *ex post* measures involve the estimation of future events, in order to assess 'the capital value of prospective receipts' (No. 1 definition) or the expectation of the amount available for expenditure in subsequent weeks (definitions Nos. 2 and 3). Thus, although the No. 1 definition might superficially appear to be similar to the accountant's traditional method of calculating income for a firm,[25] the underlying valuation methods are very different. Not only is the economist's definition of income more subjective than the accountant's, which leads to greater uncertainty about the valuation of assets at any point in time, but also, under conditions of uncertainty, *ex post* valuations will not necessarily equal *ex ante* valuations. Thus the estimate of the income for a period will depend upon the state of knowledge at the time when the estimate is made. In the case of an *ex post* measure made at the end of a period, at, say, time $t + 1$, this means that the estimate of opening net worth at time t may be different when viewed from time $t + 1$ than it was when viewed from the state of knowledge at time t. Thus, the capital to be maintained intact (net worth at time t) is not unambiguously determined and we have to make a decision as to how to treat the windfall gain or loss,[26] which is the source of the discrepancy between the two evaluations of opening net worth.

It might seem that the treatment of windfalls is a trivial issue, but in fact it is central to the economist's model of income, because, apart from windfalls and assuming a constant rate of discount, the income of a period is simply the opening net present value, multiplied by the discount rate:

$$V_0 = \sum_{t=1}^{n} \frac{Q_t}{(1 + r)^t} \qquad (2.6)$$

Fundamentals

where V_0 = present value at time zero
Q_t = Cash receipts (positive)
or payments (negative) t periods hence
r = Discount rate per period

If we assume certainty or correct expectations, one period hence, if the cash receipt Q_1 is not consumed, we will have:

$$V_1 = \sum_{t=2}^{n} \frac{Q_t}{(1 + r)^{t-1}} + Q_1 = V_0(1+r) \qquad (2.7)$$

and income,

$$Y = V_1 - V_0 = V_0 r \qquad (2.8)$$

Thus, from knowledge of the net present value and the discount rate, we can infer the income for the period (and, with an additional assumption about the reinvestment rate, for all future periods) in the case in which initial expectations are fulfilled. When expectations are not fulfilled, windfalls will play a crucial rôle in *ex post* evaluation, since they comprise deviations from previously planned returns. The construction of an *ex post* accounting income measure suitable for the evaluation of deviations from previous plans is one of the objectives of financial accounts assumed by Edwards and Bell (1961) in their classic work on business income measurement.

Another important feature of the economist's definition of income is now apparent. If we know present value, it seems likely that, for many purposes, we shall not require an income measure, since present value summarises in present terms all the future flows which are expected to occur.[27] The investment decision rule derived from capital budgeting theory is to accept investments whose present value exceeds initial cost: no estimate of income is required. Attempts to make investment decisions on the basis of expected profits or rates of return are cumbersome and less satisfactory from a theoretical standpoint.[28] Even the internal rate of return method of investment appraisal, which is derived from the basic discounting relationship,[29] is generally less satisfactory than the net present value method.[30] An important example of a case in which knowledge of net present value would render income measurement redundant is share valuation, if we assume that the shareholder's valuation is the present value of the future dividends which he expects to receive from ownership of his share.

However, the fact that knowledge of net present value under conditions of certainty might make income measurement redundant for some purposes does not make it redundant under conditions of uncertainty or for all purposes. We have already seen that, in conditions in which expectations are not fulfilled, windfall gains and losses measure the effect of these changes in expectations, so that they (and therefore their separation from anticipated income) provide information relevant to *ex post* evaluation and control. More importantly, we do not usually know net present value and an income measure may be an important input into the estimation of present value. This takes us away from the realm of the 'Hicks No. 1' capital maintenance approach, and towards that of the 'Hicks Nos. 2 and 3' consumption maintenance approach stated above and described briefly, in the context of accounting, in Chapter 1. If we can estimate a 'standard stream' of constant periodic consumption, in the case of individuals, or distributions to shareholders, in the case of companies, which is expected to be maintainable[31] over the definite future, we have a very simple means of assessing present value. It is well known that, in the case of a perpetual constant stream of expected receipts, at the rate of $\bar{Q}$ per period, expression (2.6) reduces to:

$$V_0 = \frac{\bar{Q}}{r} \tag{2.9}$$

Thus the present value of the equity interest in the firm is the standard stream income per period, attributable to equity, divided by the appropriate discount rate, r. The estimation of the appropriate discount rate is, of course, a difficult problem, especially when we introduce risk into the analysis, but, since this is a matter involving the subjective preferences of the shareholder, it is possible to argue that the accountant's rôle should stop with the estimation of $\bar{Q}$, leaving the valuation problem to the shareholder. Furthermore, it is possible that the accountant should concentrate on providing information relevant to the estimation of $\bar{Q}$, rather than attempting his own evaluation.[32].

The design of the accounting system explicitly to report a measure of Hicks No. 2 or 3 standard stream income is a formidable undertaking because of the subjectivity involved in estimating future returns. Scott (1976) has made some suggestions as to how this might be done, although it is extremely doubtful whether his suggestions could be made acceptable to the accounting and auditing professions, since they inevitably involve a large dependence on assumptions about the future.[33] The difficulties inherent in this approach have led others, such as Kay (1976), to advocate some form of cash flow reporting,[34] although this still encounters the problem of forecasting future events. Some of the recent contributors to the debate on inflation accounting in Britain, particularly as regards the gearing and monetary working capital adjustments (such as Gibbs (1976)), have seemed to be concerned with liquidity rather than profitability and come close to advocating forms of cash flow accounting,[35] although they have continued to use the language of income measurement (e.g. referring to the variable of central interest as a profit measure). However, if they *are* really concerned with income measurement it seems to be with a 'standard stream' measure of the Hicks No. 2 or 3 variety, rather than with the Hicks No. 1 capital maintenance type which emerges more naturally from the methods used traditionally by accountants. The Sandilands Report's emphasis on the predictive value of current cost operating profit might be interpreted in this light, as an example of standard stream income measurement.[36]

We may summarise the main points of the above discussion of business income measurement as follows:

(1) There are two basic models of income, one based upon capital maintenance and one based upon consumption maintenance, or, in the case of a company, dividend maintenance.

(2) The former model, capital maintenance, is, formally at least, consistent with the manner in which accountants have traditionally measured income, but the valuation basis used by accountants has traditionally been historical cost, whereas economists based their model on current values. In a world characterised by uncertainty and imperfect markets, the economist's ideal method of calculation is ambiguous and we face a choice between various current entry values (purchase prices, or replacement costs), current exit values (selling, less costs of disposal) and present values (discounted present values of returns expected from use in the ordinary course of the business). All of these measures involve a degree of subjectivity, which is particularly acute in the case of present values. The choice between measures might be expected to differ as between different individual users and different uses.

(3) The latter model, consumption maintenance, is burdened with a strong expectational element. Clearly, the maximum amount which can be consumed (or distributed) per period over an indefinite future depends crucially upon expectations about purchase prices, selling prices and productivity. The capital maintenance approach can at least hope to use current market prices, which are observable, but the consumption maintenance approach is entirely dependent upon future expectations, unless it is to resort to arbitrary assumptions.[37] On the other hand, the consumption maintenance approach does avoid the problem of assessing current values. An alternative route out of this dilemma might be to abandon income measurement entirely and resort to an accounting system based on cash flows, with both *ex ante* projections and *ex post* statements of actual cash flows, such as is advocated by Lee (1972 and 1979).

(4) The reservations about income measurement expressed above indicate that we are unlikely to be able to measure a single general-purpose income number under the conditions which prevail in the real world in which practising accountants operate. Thus, in considering inflation accounting, we do not have a simple standard by which to judge alternative techniques. It is quite possible that different techniques will be satisfactory in different circumstances or for different purposes, so that the choice of accounting technique can be viewed as a problem of social choice, involving judgement between the competing claims of different users of accounts. However, we can at least hope to ascertain whether particular techniques live up to the claims made for them and to identify the precise assumptions which are necessary for this to be the case.

4 Conclusion

In this chapter, we have considered some of the central problems of financial accounting. It is clear that, even in the absence of inflation, accounting faces serious difficulties in a world characterised by uncertainty and imperfect markets and by the competing claims of different users of accounting information. Thus, it is not surprising that the debate on inflation accounting has become inextricably linked with the debate on the other problems of accounting. Such questions as how to value fixed assets are related both to our fundamental model of how to measure capital and income and to our view on how to allow for the effects of inflation on those measurements.

It is also clear that there is not a single model of accounting, or a single summary measure, such as an income number, which will meet the needs of all users and uses of accounts in all circumstances. Thus, our subsequent review of the techniques of what can broadly be described as 'inflation accounting', and of the debate on the subject, is not likely to lead to the emergence of an ideal solution. Indeed, one possible criticism of the conduct of the debate on inflation accounting is that the participants have tended to cling rigidly to their own narrowly based 'solutions', without recognizing the merits of alternative methods in alternative situations. What we can hope to do is to identify the assumptions upon which alternative techniques are based, to consider the soundness of the reasoning which derives them from those assumptions, and to consider the uses and the circumstances in which they are appropriate.

Appendix: a numerical example

This numerical example is an extension of that given in Chapter 1. We take the 'geared' case and add the complication that Fred has a stock of 20 pineapples at the end of the period. These stocks are assumed to be worth £20 at historical cost (both selling value and wholesale value being higher).

The relevant facts are now:

(1) Fred has started the period with £100 in cash, of which £50 was lent by Aunt Mabel and £50 was his own (proprietor's) capital.
(2) He then bought 100 pineapples for £1 each.
(3) The wholesale price of pineapples then rose to £1.25p each.
(4) He then sold 80 pineapples for £1.50p each, yielding £120 in cash.

The algebraic accounting relations stated in equations (2.1) to (2.5) in the text are neutral as to the valuation system used. We shall illustrate them using the historical cost method since this is still the most widely practised system, and is also simple in application, avoiding such problems as the restatement of proprietor's interest to allow for changing prices.

Historical Cost Accounts

Balance Sheet at *t* (start of period)

Claims		£	Assets		£
Proprietor's Capital	*P*	50	Cash	*M*	100
Loan (Aunt Mabel)	*L*	50			
		100			100

Balance Sheet at *t* + 1 (end of period)

Claims		£	Assets		£
Proprietor's Capital	*P*	90	Stock	*N*	20
Loan (Aunt Mabel)	*L*	50	Cash	*M*	120
		140			140

It can easily be seen that the balance sheet identities (2.1), (2.2) and (2.3) hold for both balance sheets.

Flow of Funds Computation (period *t* to *t* + 1)

	£		£
$(P_{t+1} - P_t)$	40	$(N_{t+1} - N_t)$	20
$(L_{t+1} - L_t)$	0	$(M_{t+1} - M_t)$	20
	40		40

This demonstrates that identity (2.4) holds. A simple rearrangement would be:

Flow of Funds Statement (period *t* to *t* + 1)

Source of Funds	£
Net funds from trading operations	40

Uses of Funds	£
Increase in stocks	20
Increase in cash balance	20
	40

There are no transactions on the proprietor's capital account, so the increase in its balance (£40) must be the trading profit (identity (2.5)).

Profit and Loss Account for the period t to $t + 1$

	£
Sales	120
Less Cost of goods sold*	80
Profit	40

* Purchases £100, less closing stock £20.

3

Historical Cost accounting

Historical Cost (HC) is the basis of traditional accounting, or what are sometimes called Generally Accepted Accounting Principles (GAAP), although it is not usually applied in its pure form. Common modifications are *ad hoc* revaluations of fixed assets and the doctrine of conservatism, which encourages a downward bias in valuation practices by valuing certain assets, such as stocks, at historical cost or market value whichever is the lower. In this chapter, we shall consider some of the properties of HC accounting. This is a necessary prelude to the study of inflation accounting, for two reasons. Firstly, it is important to establish why there is dissatisfaction with HC in periods of inflation: if such dissatisfaction is ill-founded, then there is no reason to tamper with traditional methods which have stood the test of practical application. Secondly, it is important to discover the properties of HC in the absence of inflation. If these are desirable properties of a financial accounting system, then it might be thought that the object of inflation accounting should be to adapt HC in periods of inflation so that it retains the properties which it possesses in the absence of inflation. This has indeed often seemed to be the reasoning used by advocates of Constant Purchasing Power Accounting (CPP), who seek to eliminate the distortionary effect introduced into HC measurements by changes in the purchasing power of money. On the other hand, if, as some have suggested,[1] HC accounts have little meaning even in the absence of inflation, it would seem futile to base an inflation accounting system on the principle of restoring to HC accounts a significance which they never had.

1 The stationary state

One of the situations in which historical cost accounting has a clear significance is a stationary state,[2] in which all prices are constant through time, and are expected to remain so, and each asset has a single, unambiguous price (i.e. there is no divergence between buying price, selling price and present value in use). The existence of the stationary state ensures that there is no divergence through time between HC and current costs, and that the currency unit in which they are measured maintains a constant value. The existence of only one price for each asset ensures that there is no problem of choice between entry values (replacement costs, which are assumed in these circumstances to equal HC), exit values (selling prices), or value in use, as all are equal. We therefore have a single unambiguous current value which is equal to HC. In these circumstances HC profit will be equal to economic profit, i.e. the increase in net worth measured by HC accounting will equal the increase in the sum of present values of the assets of the firm.[3] Thus, it is not necessary to go beyond HC accounting, as it can provide all of the information provided by these alternative valuation systems.

The assumptions required for this situation to exist are, however, stringent and unrealistic. The requirement that both absolute prices and relative prices remain constant assumes an equilibrium world in which nothing changes. In practice, levels and patterns of both demand and supply change continuously, leading to price changes of both types, so that the value of the currency unit in terms of a standard basket of commodities (such as the consumer price index) changes through time, as do the relative values of different commodities. The assumptions necessary to achieve one price for each asset are equally unrealistic. They include:

(1) Perfectly competitive long-run equilibrium in all markets, with all the assumptions which this entails.[4]
(2) The existence of such a market in all commodities, so that, for example, part-used fixed assets have a market price.
(3) The accrual conventions used in the application of HC are such as to value part-used assets at market prices.

The latter assumption is necessary because, although HC accounting may appear superficially to be objective, the accrual process gives rise to the allocation problem, which has been explored rigorously by Thomas (1969 and 1974), i.e. when services are purchased in a group, only part of which is used up in a period, how do we allocate the cost of the group between costs charged against profits of the period and costs accrued as an asset to be used in future periods? The obvious example of this problem is depreciation, and conventional methods of depreciation, such as straight line or reducing balance, would not necessarily meet requirement (3) above.

The perfect competition assumption ensures that no good can trade for two separate prices, so that replacement costs equal selling prices, and each cost or price is independent of the quantity sold. In combination with the stationary state (a form of long-run equilibrium) it also ensures that there are no excess profits (sometimes called 'pure profits') in the economy, each asset earning only a normal rate of profit (equal to the discount rate, r, of Chapter 2) and present value equalling market price. Complete certainty is not necessary for perfectly competitive equilibrium, but correct expectations are necessary if the equilibrium is to be sustained. If expectations are not fulfilled, the stationary state is likely to be upset, because *ex ante* plans have not been fulfilled *ex post*, causing disequilibrium.

Even in these stringent conditions, it should be noted that HC is not uniquely suited to be the valuation basis of accounting: it merely happens that there is equality between the alternative values. In these circumstances, we would probably select HC as the chosen basis because of its traditional rôle in accounting, which makes it acceptable, familiar and of proven feasibility, and because of its ease of verification and its compatibility with the control function of the firm. HC is readily documented by means of invoices and similar records, and it arises naturally out of the process of recording the physical transactions of the business and controlling the amounts of goods and services under the firm's ownership. This is a central theme in Ijiri's classic defence of HC (Ijiri, 1971).

In reality, the world is characterised neither by stationary state conditions nor by perfectly competitive equilibrium with complete markets. We might hope to deal with the break-down of the stationary state by adjusting HC records by means of indices: general price indices to deal with general price level changes and specific indices to deal with cases in which individual prices diverge from the general index. This would lead us to a form of Constant Purchasing Power (CPP) accounting if general indices alone were used, or to a form of Real Terms accounting when both types of index were applied. However, when the second set of conditions (complete perfectly competitive markets) breaks down, we are faced by a more fundamental problem: that income and value are no longer uniquely defined. Thus, we face a choice between HC, replacement cost, current selling price, or present value in use (and possibly a variety of choices within each of these categories), and we are forced to consider the possibility, discussed in Chapters 1 and 2, that different types of information will serve different purposes.[5] This situation has given rise to the wide range of alternative accounting theories and systems which are discussed in subsequent chapters.

2 Profits on completed projects

An alternative situation in which HC yields an unambiguous measure of profit which might be considered useful is in the case of the lifetime profit on completed projects, starting with an initial cash injection and finishing with completed liquidation, i.e. realisation in cash. If we assume, for illustrative purposes, that such a project extends over two accounting periods, we might demonstrate this result as follows, using the notation of Chapter 2. Assume an initial cash subscription at time t of M_t. The balance sheet equation is then:

$$P_t = M_t \tag{3.1}$$

Assume that, at the end of Period 1 (time $t + 1$), the cash M_t has been exchanged for stocks N_{t+1} and there have been no other transactions. The balance sheet equation is now:

$$P_{t+1} = N_{t+1} \tag{3.2}$$

Because the stocks are valued at HC, $N_{t+1} = M_t$ and $P_{t+1} = P_t$. The profit for Period 1 is therefore:

$$P_{t+1} - P_t = N_{t+1} - M_t = 0 \tag{3.3}$$

At the end of Period 2, at time $t + 2$, the venture is liquidated by the exchange of the stocks N_{t+1} for cash M_{t+2}. The balance sheet equation is now:

$$P_{t+2} = M_{t+2} \tag{3.4}$$

and the profit for Period 2 is therefore:

$$P_{t+2} - P_{t+1} = M_{t+2} - N_{t+1} \tag{3.5}$$

Clearly, the periodic profits depend crucially upon the valuation of stock at the end of the first period, N_{t+1}. If this had been at market value, it is possible that this would have exceeded the HC valuation, so that a positive profit would have appeared in Period 1, but this would have been exactly offset by a lower profit in Period 2, when the stock was written off against profit, leaving total profits for the life-time of the venture unchanged. This latter result is easily demonstrated. The life-time profit of the venture is the sum of the profit for the two periods:

$$P_{t+2} - P_{t+1} + P_{t+1} - P_t = M_{t+2} - N_{t+1} + N_{t+1} - M_t \qquad (3.6)$$

or

$$P_{t+2} - P_t = M_{t+2} - M_t \qquad (3.7)$$

Thus, the intermediate valuation attaching to the assets is of no consequence for the lifetime profit calculation and HC is as accept-able as any other basis for intermediate valuation, if we are not concerned with periodic profits within the full lifetime. However, some important reservations must be made:

(1) The accountant is typically concerned with *going concerns*, not with self-liquidating ventures, and he cannot, therefore, make the convenient 'cash-to-cash' assumption.
(2) Even in the case of a self-liquidating venture, the accountant is usually concerned with *periodic* evaluation of the entity, not with its performance over its lifetime. The intermediate valua-tion N_{t+1} will clearly have a crucial bearing on how the relative performance of the entity is measured within each period.
(3) The equivalence of alternative lifetime profit measurements was obtained by assuming that P_t was to be the capital to be maintained. The importance of the capital maintenance concept was illustrated, in a 'cash-to-cash' business, in Chapter 1. As we saw there, a CPP system would adjust P_t by the change in a general purchasing power index over the relevant period, in order to define capital to be maintained. Thus, in our simple example, CPP lifetime profit would not be $P_{t+2} - P_t$, but would rather be $P_{t+2} - P_t(1 + p_1)(1 + p_2)$ where p_1 is the percentage increase in the general index during Period 1 and p_2 the increase during Period 2.[6] Equally, an entity-based replacement cost measurement system might involve writing up the initial capital by changes in a specific index, s, relating to the type of goods traded by the entity, yielding a lifetime profit of $P_{t+2} - P_t(1 + s_1)(1 + s_2)$.

Thus the 'cash-to-cash' long-run equivalence of HC with other asset valuation systems has little bearing on how the periodic accounts of continuing entities should be drawn up in a period of inflation, since it ignores the essential asset valuation problem of periodic reporting. Furthermore, the problem of measuring the capital to be maintained before recognizing a profit is inadequately dealt with by HC in a period of changing prices.

3 The equivalence of the 'book yield' and the internal rate of return

Another possible defence of HC is that it yields an accounting rate of return (ARR) or 'book yield' which is a good approximation to the Internal Rate of Return (IRR) used in capital budgeting theory. It will be recalled (Chapter 2, note 29, p. 214) that the IRR is that rate of return, r', which, when used as a discount rate, renders the net present value of an investment equal to zero:

$$\text{NPV} = \sum_{t=1}^{n} \frac{Q_t}{(1 + r')^t} - C_0 = 0 \tag{3.8}$$

where C_0 is the initial net cash outlay
Q_t are future net cash inflows
n is the number of periods in the life of the investment.

The ARR is simply the accounting profit for a period divided by the average accounting value ('book value') of the net assets employed to earn that profit. It might be thought that, as accounts are often used for purposes of *ex post* appraisal, it is desirable that the rate of return measured by the accounts (ARR) should equal, or at least approximate, the IRR, which is the 'true' *ex post* yield derived from economic theory, and maximisation of which is, in most cases, consistent with economic decision-making models.

There is a considerable literature on this subject, starting with papers by Harcourt (1965) and Solomon (1966), which demonstrated that wide divergencies were possible between ARR and IRR. A series of papers followed, which served to identify how the relationship between ARR and IRR was affected by various conditions, such as aggregation across numbers of projects (i.e. measurement at the firm level or the project level), additional investment, different periods of measurement (e.g. taking average ARR rather than annual ARR), and different lengths of life of investment. All of this has been neatly encapsulated in an analytical paper by Kay (1976) which demonstrates the general relationship between ARR and IRR. It appears that *over the lifetime* of a project or firm (i.e. from initial flotation to final liquidation), IRR is a weighted average of ARR. Kay demonstrates a method of calculating the appropriate weights. Thus, *over long periods*, average ARR may be a good approximation to IRR. Certain other conditions (such as steady growth of the firm at something close to the rate of profit), which improve the approximation, are also specified.

From the point of view of annual reporting of company performance, this is not encouraging, and certainly does not justify the view that HC accounting is adequate, for the following reasons:

(1) The ARR/IRR equivalence holds only over the complete life-cycle of a firm. Thus, for reporting the performance of a continuing entity, the valuation of assets at the end of a period is crucial, and HC may not prove to be as good a proxy, or 'surrogate', for economic value as some current valuation basis, such as replacement cost.[7] This is another example of the weakness of the 'cash-to-cash' assumption discussed in the previous section of this chapter.

(2) The equivalence holds strictly only for *averages* (weighted in a specific manner) over the lifetime of the firm, or, as an approximation, over long periods. Thus, it is of little use in supporting the use of ARR as a measure of economic return in a single period, which is presumably one of the principal functions of the annual accounts of companies. This deficiency of the ARR is readily conceded by Kay (1976 and 1978) and is another illustration of the weakness of the lifetime 'cash-to-cash' approach.

(3) A fundamental issue, which was raised early in the debate by Vatter (1966), is the appropriateness of the IRR as an ideal standard. The IRR is itself a calculation of the average compound rate of return earned over the lifetime of an investment or venture. It is based upon the assumption of constancy of the rate of return over all periods and does not allow for the fact that the opportunity cost of capital may vary between periods, or for the fact that the returns themselves may be concentrated in various periods. Thus, the IRR is really an expression of rate of return

over the lifetime as a whole. It may, for convenience or for comparative purposes, be expressed as an annual rate, but it does not record the profitability of a particular year or other period shorter than the full life-cycle. In other words, it solves the allocation problem by means of the arbitrary assumption that an equal rate of return was earned in each period. This makes it an inappropriate standard by which to judge the performance of the firm over any period shorter than the full life-cycle.

Another defence of the use of ARR in empirical studies across firms, which is made by Whittington (1979), is that many types of error in ARR (viewed as an approximation to IRR) can be expected to average out in such a way as to impart little or no bias to statistical studies. This argument relates specifically to large-scale studies involving many firms and assumes that the rate of return is averaged over a number of years. It is therefore relevant to certain economic studies of the structure and performance of industries, or larger groups of firms, over fairly long periods, but it does not purport to be a valid defence of ARR as a measure of the performance of an individual firm in a single year. It is thus not of direct relevance to the problem of producing annual financial reports to the shareholders or other interested parties of a particular firm.

4 Smoothed cash flow

An alternative approach to evaluating HC accounting is to take as our model not conformity with the type of valuations proposed by economists but consistency with the 'Hicks No. 3' consumption maintenance approach, defined in Chapter 2. This interpretation emphasises the HC profit and loss account rather than the balance sheet. The profit and loss account is seen as measuring the net cash flow which the firm derives from its operations. Accruals are seen to be necessary in order to eliminate abnormal cash flows, e.g. due to the acquisition of a fixed asset, and the writing off of accruals (e.g. by charging depreciation) is interpreted as a device for smoothing out the impact of the cost of such lumpy items, so that the profit figure is a measure of the maximum sustainable dividend.[8] The balance sheet is interpreted simply as an accrual sheet, recording those cash outlays (at HC) which have not yet been charged to profit and loss. Recent examples of such an interpretation are the Trueblood Report (1973) and Whittington (1974), but this approach has deep roots in the history of accounting thought, e.g. Schmalenbach adopts this interpretation in his *Dynamic Accounting* (1959), which first appeared in 1919, and which justifies the approach by reference to historical precedents.

The main problem with this approach is that we have to make strong assumptions in order for the single year's profit figure to be a useful measure of sustainable future distributions. If everything (demand, output, prices, costs) remained constant we might regard the profit figure as 'standard stream' income which could be divided by an appropriate discount rate to give a valuation of the firm at the end of the period. This, however, is an unreasonably stringent assumption, and it is likely in practice that each period's performance will have unique features which are unlikely to be repeated. Some of these features, such as a build-up of stocks in anticipation of rising sales, will improve the firm's prospects for the future, and others will worsen them. We might hope that some of these changing prospects would be reflected in changing end-of-period asset values (although, as we shall see later, it is unlikely that even current values will correspond with the economist's measure of present value), but accrued historic costs do not seem likely to be appropriate values for this purpose outside the stationary state conditions described earlier. There will be some features of a particular year which have no bearing whatsoever on future prospects but which will affect historical cost profits, unless some highly subjective adjustments are made, e.g. exceptionally low demand leading to low sales and poor capacity utilisation. Thus, it seems unlikely that HC accounting, interpreted as 'smoothed cash flow' can reasonably be used as a measure of standard stream income.

It might seem that the introduction of general and specific price changes would weaken yet further the possible link between HC accounting and standard stream income, but this is not necessarily the case. Much depends upon the precise assumptions made about the future course of general and specific prices. For example, if we were able to accept the view that, in the absence of inflation, HC profit was a good approximation to standard stream income, and if we further assume general price inflation at a constant annual rate with real variables unchanged and a balanced age structure of assets, HC profit under inflation becomes a measure of standard stream income in current prices, or 'real' standard stream income. If we wished to estimate money standard stream income,[9] we would sim-

47

ply multiply by the inflation factor appropriate to a particular future year. Specific relative price changes would give rise to more subtle problems. A crucial factor would be how and when specific price changes were reflected in selling prices: if pricing were always conducted on the basis of recovering HC rather than current costs, then HC accounting would still yield a measure of standard stream profit.[10]

However, the problem of adjusting for price changes is subordinate to the problem of interpreting HC profit as standard stream income even under conditions of constant prices. It seems that, under conditions of uncertainty and market imperfection, it is difficult to sustain this interpretation, although relatively little attention has been paid to the subject by accounting theorists and it is possible that stronger arguments in favour of HC may be found in the future.

5 Objectivity and stewardship

Hitherto, we have been concerned with the extent to which HC accounts match up to some ideal standards derived from economic theory, but it was argued in Chapter 2 that the measurement of such standards usually requires conditions which do not prevail in the real world. It is therefore not particularly surprising that HC fails to *measure* economists' concepts for profit or value, under realistic conditions. However, it can also be argued that HC fails to provide information relevant to the measurement of such concepts, and that current values, reflecting the most up-to-date market evaluation of the firm's assets, would be much more appropriate to the assessment of the economic progress of the business.[11]

There is, however, one other important line of defence of HC accounting which has been put forward trenchantly by Ijiri (1971). The basis of this defence is that the unique property of HC is that it is based on the recording of events which have actually occurred, rather than upon contingent events, such as the price which an asset would obtain in the market were it sold or its cost in the market were it replaced. This gives basic HC data a unique claim to objectivity, although in the actual practice of HC accounting an important element of subjectivity creeps into the operation of the accrual system, since, as Thomas (1969) has shown, the rules for allocation of costs are 'incorrigible' and arbitrary.[12] Ijiri argues that this objectivity gives HC a unique advantage in resolving potential conflicts where there is a problem of dividing claims on the firm between different interested parties (a type of problem which he describes as 'allocation': this is, of course, an entirely different allocation problem from that described by Thomas, and is what economists would describe as a distribution problem, as in the theory of distribution). An example of such a problem is the determination of the corporation tax base. Ijiri also argues that HC records perform a unique control function in keeping a record of the actual external transactions of the business. This is part of the traditional stewardship rôle of accounting. Few would deny the value of HC records in this respect, but the keeping of basic HC records for control purposes does not necessarily rule out revaluation at current values for decision-making or financial reporting.[13]

Conclusion

We conclude, not surprisingly, that HC accounts do not have a clear significance in terms of economic concepts of value and profit, except in closely defined circumstances which are unlikely to be prevalent in the real world. HC accounts do have some value, as records of past events, in fulfilling the traditional stewardship rôle of accounting and this, together with the fact that the system is established in practice, provides some motivation for accountants to wish to retain it. It is with respect to decision-making and valuation, by managers, shareholders and others, that HC is likely to be found deficient. Under stationary state conditions, in which all prices are constant, HC is acceptable as a surrogate for current values, but once prices are (realistically) allowed to change, it is current values rather than HC which will represent economic opportunities available or forgone and which are likely to enter decision or valuation calculations. Of course, it is not obvious which of a variety of current values is likely to be the most relevant: this issue will be taken up in later chapters. What is clear is that HC alone is unlikely to provide adequate information.

The appendix to this chapter gives some simple numerical examples which illustrate the more general algebraic argument used in the main text of the chapter. The next chapter will discuss the nature of inflation, its measurement by the use of index numbers, and the technique of CPP (Constant Purchasing Power Accounting) as a means of measuring the impact of general inflation. Later chapters will deal with the measurement of the effects of specific price changes, by means of current value accounting systems.

Appendix: a numerical example

This numerical example is a variant of that given in the appendix to Chapter 2. We here introduce a depreciating asset and follow the course of the business over a three-period life cycle, in order to illustrate some of the concepts introduced in Chapter 3.

The additional facts for Period 1 are now:

(1) Fred started the period with an additional asset. This was a depreciable fixed asset (a van) purchased for £100 at the start of the period.
(2) This asset is to be depreciated over a ten-period life by the 'straight-line' method (i.e. at $1/10$ of cost per period).
(3) The van was paid for by the proprietor, so that his opening capital is now £150.
(4) The proprietor withdraws £30 for his own use at the end of the period.

The facts for Period 2 are:

(1) 80 pineapples purchased for £1.30 each, half for cash and half on credit, payable in the next period.
(2) 90 pineapples sold for £1.50 each.
(3) 80 of these pineapples were sold for cash and 10 were sold on credit, payable in the next period.
(4) The proprietor spends all of his cash for private purposes, other than what he needs to pay his creditors.

The facts for Period 3 are:

(1) 100 pineapples purchased for £1.80 each on credit.
(2) The creditors from the previous day are paid, and the debtors redeem their debts.
(3) 90 pineapples sold for £2 each, 80 for cash and 10 on credit.
(4) The proprietor spends £10 cash for private purposes.

In Period 4, the proprietor decides to liquidate his business:

(1) The remaining stock of pineapples is sold for £2.20 each.
(2) The van is sold for £120.
(3) The creditor is paid, and the debtor pays, in full.
(4) The proprietor pays off the loan and withdraws the remaining cash for his own use.

Historical Cost Accounts

Balance Sheet at *t* (start of first period)

	£			£
Proprietor's Capital	150	*Fixed Assets*		
Loan (Aunt Mabel)	50	Van (at cost)		100
		Current Assets		
		Cash		100
	200			200

Profit and Loss Account for period 1, *t* to *t* + 1

	£
Sales	120
Less Cost of goods sold*	80
Trading profit	40
Less Depreciation†	10
Profit	30

* Cost of goods sold is purchases £100, less closing stock £20, both at historical cost.
† Depreciation is $1/10 \times £100$ (historical cost).

Balance Sheet at *t* + 1

	£			£
Proprietor's Capital		*Fixed Assets*		
Opening balance (at *t*)	150	Van (at cost)	100	
Add Profit for the period	30	*Less* depreciation to date	10	
	180			90
Less Drawings	30	*Current Assets*		
Closing balance (at *t* + 1)	150	Stock (at cost)	20	
Loan	50	Cash	90	
				110
	200			200

51

Historical Cost accounting

Profit and Loss Account for period 2, $t + 1$ to $t + 2$

	£
Sales	135
Less Cost of goods sold*	111
Trading profit	24
Less Depreciation	10
Profit	14

* On the FIFO (First in, First out) principle: opening stock (20 pineapples at £1 each) £20 + purchases £104 − closing stock (10 pineapples at £1.30 each) £13.

Balance Sheet at $t + 2$

	£			£
Proprietor's Capital		*Fixed Assets*		
Opening balance (at $t + 1$)	150	Van (at cost)	100	
Add Profit for the period	14	*Less* depreciation to date	20	
Closing balance (at $t + 2$)	164			80
Less Drawings	106	*Current Assets*		
	58	Stock (at cost)	13	
Loan	50	Debtors	15	
Current Liabilities		Cash	52	
Creditors	52			80
	160			160

Profit and Loss Account for period 3, $t + 2$ to $t + 3$

	£
Sales	180
Less Cost of goods sold*	157
Trading profit	23
Less Depreciation	10
Profit	13

* Opening stock £13 + purchases £180 − closing stock (20 pineapples at £1.80 each) £36.

Balance Sheet at $t + 3$

	£			£
Proprietor's Capital		*Fixed Assets*		
Opening balance (at $t + 2$)	58	Van (at cost)	100	
Add Profit for the period	13	*Less* depreciation to date	30	
	71			70
Less Drawings	10	*Current Assets*		
Closing balance (at $t + 3$)	61	Stock (at cost)	36	
Loan	50	Debtors	20	
Current Liabilities		Cash	165	
Creditors	180			221
	291			291

Profit and Loss Account for period 4, $t + 3$ to $t + 4$

	£
Sales	44
Less Cost of goods sold*	36
Trading profit	8
Realised Holding Gain†	50
Total Profit	58

* Opening stock (20 pineapples at £1.80 each).
† Sale of van £120, less written down value £70.

Balance Sheet at $t + 4$*

	£			£
Proprietor's Capital			Cash	169
Opening balance ($t + 3$)	61			
Add Profit for the period	58			
	119			
Loan	50			
	169			169

* This balance sheet is drawn up prior to the final payment of £50 to redeem the loan, the remaining £119 being available for the proprietor.

Historical Cost accounting

Illustration of some points made in the chapter

(1) *Equivalence of 'cash-to-cash' income measures* (equations 3.1 to 3.7)

The reported profits in this example are:

	£
Period 1	30
Period 2	14
Period 3	13
Period 4	58
	£115

This is equal to what the proprietor put in, less what he took out, in cash, over the whole period from flotation to liquidation of the business. His drawings were:

	£
$t+1$	30
$t+2$	106
$t+3$	10
$t+4$	119
Total	265
Less capital introduced (t)	150
	£115

If we vary the asset valuation conventions in the intermediate balance sheets ($t+1$, $t+2$ and $t+3$) we will shift profits between periods, but the total profits over the lifetime of the business will be the same.

For example, if we varied the depreciation method, to write off the asset over a 5-period life, we would charge £20 per period rather than £10, so that profit of each of the first three periods would be lower by £10. However, the realised holding gain in the final period would now be £30 higher (£120 less written down value £40 = £80), exactly compensating for the lower profit in earlier periods. A higher depreciation rate in the earlier periods produces a lower written down value in the final period and therefore a correspondingly higher gain when the asset is sold. The change in the depreciation method could also shift the relative profitability of the first three periods, e.g. by employing the reducing balance method which charges the earlier years relatively heavily, but there would always be the same net result over the asset's lifetime. This is because the net cost of the asset from purchase to sale is always original cost, less sale price. Depreciation is merely a device for allocating this total cost between periods.

The choice of stock valuation method could also affect the relative profitability of different periods. We might, for example, use the last-in, first-out (LIFO) method, which assumes that those goods acquired most recently are the ones sold first. This has the possible advantage of more closely approximating a replacement cost charge against profit, and has found favour in the USA, but it can lead to very low valuations of stock, and may not be a very realistic representation of stock movements especially in the case of a perishable commodity, such as pineapples. In our illustration, the alternative stock valuations are as follows:

Time	FIFO	LIFO	
$t+1$	20	20	(20 at £1 each)
$t+2$	13.	10	(10 at £1 each)
$t+3$	36	28	(10 at £1 each, plus 10 at £1.80 each)

Substituting the LIFO values into the calculation of costs of goods sold gives us the following profit figures:

	£
Period 1	30
Period 2	11
Period 3	8
Period 4	66
	£115

The total lifetime profit is unchanged, but the profit in Periods 2 and 3 is reduced (reflecting rising costs of replacing stocks). This is exactly compensated by a higher profit in Period 4, when the stock is liquidated and the cost charged in calculating profit is based on the lower LIFO valuation. This must always be the case over a 'cash-to-cash' life-cycle. The closing stock of one period serves to reduce the cost of sales in that period but will increase the cost for subsequent periods in which the stocks are sold. A lower valuation of closing stocks implies a higher cost of sales for the current period, but a lower cost for subsequent periods. So long as stocks are held, a lower value will imply lower profits to date and a higher value will imply higher profits to date, but when the stocks are finally liquidated the value is their realised cash value, whatever the previous basis of valuation. Thus, accumulated profits were different (by the difference in stock values at the end of each period) under the two valuation schemes, at the end both of Period 2 and Period 3, but in Period 4, when stocks are no longer held, total profits once again become identical.

(2) *Non-equivalence of 'cash-to-cash' income when inflation adjustments are introduced* (p. 43, (3)).

Suppose that there was inflation of 10 per cent in Period 1, 20 per cent in Period 2, 10 per cent in Period 3 and 5 per cent in Period 4. If the proprietor had not withdrawn any money, his capital to be maintained before recognising a profit on final liquidation would be [£150(1.1)(1.2)(1.1)(1.05)] if he were to maintain the purchasing power of his funds, i.e. £228.69p.

In fact, his position is rather more complicated, because he has withdrawn money at each period end. His periodic profit, applying a 'real' capital maintenance concept would be as follows:

Period	Original 'money' profit £	Restated opening capital Calculation	Amount (£)	'Real' profit £
1	30	£150 × 1.1	165	15
2	14	£150 × 1.2	180	−16
3	13	£58 × 1.1	63.80	7.20
4	58	£71 × 1.05	74.55	54.45
Total	115			60.65

The sum of the 'real' periodic profits, £60.65, is substantially below that of the unadjusted 'money' profit measure, as would be expected in a period of inflation. Each period's opening capital is increased in proportion to the rise in the price index during the period. This results in a 'real profit' calculation, based on maintaining capital in 'end of period' £s rather than 'beginning of period' £s, although the unit of measurement is still not strictly comparable between periods, as would be the case with the CPP system, described in the next paragraph. The periodic adjustment of opening capital now means that life cycle profits, even in the 'cash-to-cash' case, will depend upon the valuation scheme: a different valuation scheme will lead to different measurements of opening capital in each period and, therefore, different amounts of re-statement to allow for inflation. For example, suppose that the stock was valued £10 higher at the end of period 1 and that this revalued stock was consumed in period 2, leaving later valuations unchanged. This would imply profit higher by £10 in period 1 and this would be added to opening capital for period 2, which would now be £160. However, at the end of period 2 this capital would be restated (×1.2) to give £192 to be maintained before recognising a profit, an increase of £12 over the previous figure. Thus, the increased profit of £10 in Period 1 would be offset by a £12 reduction in the profit (actually an increase in the loss to £28, in this example) for Period 2, causing a reduction of £2 in total life-cycle profit.

The 'real' profit calculated above is not a full Constant Purchasing Power (CPP) measure such as will be discussed in Chapter 4. The full CPP system would involve an alternative valuation scheme, re-stating the historical costs of assets in terms of £s of constant purchasing power. Furthermore, CPP would require re-statement of the periodic profit figures in constant £s, so that that the total profit for the life-cycle of the firm would be an aggregation of homogeneous units of measurement. At present, the periodic profits are measured in end-of-period £s for each separate period, and a CPP purist would object that these figures are not comparable or aggregable across periods because they are expressed in different units of measurement. A CPP adjustment to restate the 'real' profit figures in current (end of period 4) £s would be as follows:

Period	'Real' profit	Re-statement calculation	CPP profit (end of period 4 £s)
1	15	£15 (1.2) (1.1) (1.05)	20.79
2	−16	−£16 (1.1) (1.05)	−18.48
3	7.20	£7.20 (1.05)	7.56
4	54.44	£54.44 (1)	54.44
Total	60.64		64.31

It should be noted that this re-states the 'real' profit figures without adjusting the underlying valuation scheme (for depreciation and stock valuation) which would also be affected by full CPP adjustment: the full adjustment is illustrated in the appendix to Chapter 4. However, the present illustration is sufficient to demonstrate that we can obtain yet another different life-cycle profit figure if we measure in units of constant purchasing power. We would, of course, obtain a different number for each different CPP measuring unit: for example, if we measured in base-year (t) pounds, lifetime profit would be £42.18 ($= 64.31 \div [(1.1)(1.2)(1.1)(1.05)]$).

(3) *'Book yield' as a measure of the Internal Rate of Return*
The accounting rate of return (ARR), or 'book yield' in the above example is calculated as follows:

Accounting Rate of Return calculation

	Average capital employed		Profit	
Period	Calculation	Amount (£)	(£)	Rate of return (%)*
1	[150 + 180] ÷ 2	165	30	18.18
2	[150 + 164] ÷ 2	157	14	8.92
3	[58 + 71] ÷ 2	64.50	13	20.16
4	[61 + 119] ÷ 2	90	58	64.44
Total		476.50	115	24.13

* Rate of Return is Profit divided by amount of Capital Employed.

We have a choice of two measures of rate of return: the arithmetic average of the rates for periods 1 to 4, which is 27.93%, or the weighted average, obtained by calculating the ratio of the totals over the period, which is 24.13%. The latter corresponds more closely with (but is not identical with), the weighting scheme proposed by Kay (1976).

If we take 24% as our estimate of the Internal Rate of Return (r'), we can test this by the following discounting calculation, based on equation (3.8) in the text:

Discounted Cash Flow Calculation, with $r' = 0.24$

Time	Cash flow (£)	Discount factor $\left(\dfrac{1}{(1+r')^t}\right)$	Present value (£)
t	−150	1.00	−150
$t + 1$	30	0.806452	24.19
$t + 2$	106	0.650364	68.94
$t + 3$	10	0.524487	5.24
$t + 4$	119	0.422974	50.33
Total	115		− 1.30

The cash flows are the actual cash contributions and withdrawals by the proprietor. These are multiplied by the discount factor to yield a present value as at time t. The sum of the final column is the Net Present Value (NPV) of the business to the proprietor at time t, discounting at 24% per period. This is very close to zero, indicating that 24% is a good approximation to r'. The fact that the NPV is negative shows that 24% is an over-estimate of r', since a slightly lower discount rate would increase the present value of the positive cash flows, bringing NPV closer to zero. A precise solution, calculated by a computer programme using iterative methods,[14] shows that IRR is 23.58%.

Despite the relative accuracy of ARR as a measure of IRR in this instance, the example also serves to illustrate the limitations of this property. ARR fluctuates widely between periods and the assessment of the performance of the business within each separate period is one of the main concerns of periodic accounts. If this assessment is based on ARR, then the valuation and allocation methods used to measure capital employed and profit for the individual period become crucial, and correspondence of life-cycle ARR with IRR becomes irrelevant.

It should be noted that the IRR calculated here is unadjusted for inflation, i.e. it is based upon the comparison of nominal cash outlays with nominal future cash flows, no attempt being made to adjust the cash flows for inflation. It is therefore a money rate of return rather than a real rate of return, and is suitable for comparison with the rates of interest actually observed in markets (which incorporate an element to compensate for anticipated inflation), rather than 'real' rates of interest (which attempt to eliminate the inflationary element).

4

Inflation and the general price level

1 The inflationary process

Inflation was defined in Chapter 1 as a decline in the purchasing power of money, due to an increase in the general level of prices. Whilst we may question the precise meaning of 'the general level of prices', this definition does capture the essence of the popular conception of inflation as a decline in the value of money relative to goods. This phenomenon is not new, but it has been particularly acute in the twentieth century, during which the evolution of sophisticated banking systems has combined with high levels of government expenditure to increase both the capacity and the incentive for governments to inflate the currency. The century has witnessed a number of hyper-inflations, notably that in Germany in 1923, which resulted in the complete collapse of the currency.[1] Other countries, notably those in Latin America (Baxter, 1976), have experienced persistent inflation at high levels (often in excess of 50 per cent per annum) for long periods, and more advanced industrial countries have experienced inflation at historically unprecedented levels. Table 4.1 illustrates the recent inflationary experience of the United Kingdom. This table serves to illustrate the relatively high inflation rates experienced in the 1970s, which was also, as a consequence, a period of great activity in the debate on inflation accounting, culminating in the publication of the first British accounting standard on the subject (SSAP16: Accounting Standards Committee, 1980). The table also illustrates the divergences between alternative price indices, a fact which poses important conceptual problems for the measurement of inflation and, therefore, for inflation accounting.

It is beyond the scope of the present book to review the historical evolution of the inflationary process or economists' efforts to explain it. Accessible reviews of the latter will be found in the books by

Table 4.1. *Price indices for the United Kingdom 1955–80;*
Indices, 1975 = 100

Year	Materials and fuel purchased by manufacturing industry		All manufactured products; home sales		All items		Total food	
	Index	% change	Index	% change	Index	% change	Index	% change
1955	31.8	2.9	36.1	2.6	32.0	4.6	30.6	7.4
1956	33.0	3.8	37.7	4.4	33.6	5.0	32.0	4.6
1957	33.2	0.6	38.9	3.2	34.8	3.6	32.8	2.5
1958	31.1	−6.3	39.1	0.5	35.9	3.2	33.5	2.1
1959	31.4	1.0	39.2	0.3	36.1	0.6	33.8	0.9
1960	31.4	0	39.8	1.5	36.5	1.1	33.6	−0.6
1961	31.1	−1.0	40.9	2.8	37.7	3.3	34.1	1.5
1962	31.1	0	41.8	2.2	39.3	4.2	35.4	3.8
1963	31.8	2.3	42.2	1.0	40.1	2.0	36.3	2.5
1964	33.1	4.1	43.5	3.1	41.4	3.2	37.3	2.8
1965	33.6	1.5	45.1	3.7	43.4	4.8	38.6	3.5
1966	34.4	2.4	46.3	2.7	45.1	3.9	40.0	3.6
1967	34.2	−0.6	46.8	1.1	46.2	2.4	41.0	2.5
1968	37.2	8.8	48.7	4.1	48.4	4.8	42.6	3.9
1969	38.7	4.0	50.5	3.7	51.0	5.4	45.3	6.3
1970	40.7	5.2	54.1	7.1	54.2	6.3	48.5	7.1
1971	42.5	4.4	62.1	5.3	63.6	7.3	58.6	11.1
1972	44.4	4.5	62.1	5.3	63.6	7.3	58.6	8.7
1973	58.8	32.4	66.7	7.4	69.4	9.2	67.5	15.2
1974	86.8	47.6	81.8	22.6	80.5	16.0	79.6	17.9
1975	100.0	15.2	100.0	22.2	100.0	24.2	100.0	25.6
1976	127.0	27.0	117.3	17.3	116.5	16.5	120.0	20.0
1977	145.6	14.6	140.5	19.8	135.0	15.9	142.8	19.0
1978	144.6	−0.7	153.3	9.1	146.2	8.3	152.9	7.1
1979	167.6	15.9	172.0	12.2	165.8	13.4	171.3	12.0
1980	200.9	19.9	200.0	16.3	195.6	18.0	191.9	12.0

Source: CSO *Economic Trends* Annual Supplement 1981 Edition, p. 114 and *Economic Trends*, March 1981, p. 42.

Flemming (1976) and Trevithick (1977) and the history of inflation in the United Kingdom is surveyed in Deane (1979). It is sufficient to note that inflation is currently a world-wide problem of historically unprecedented proportions, and there is little sign that either economists' understanding of the inflationary process or governments' power to halt the process are at such a high level that the problem is likely to disappear within the foreseeable future. Thus, accountants need to adopt methods which will deal with the problems which inflation poses for them, and the most fundamental of these is that money is the measuring unit commonly used by accountants. Inflation implies that this measuring unit fluctuates in value through time and might therefore be thought misleading in the case of comparisons over different points in time.

This problem is not, of course, confined to the accounts of businesses. For example, the measurement of national income is also affected by inflation, and economists have long been accustomed to use specific indices to estimate stock appreciation and replacement cost depreciation ('capital consumption') in the calculation of Net National Product, or 'national income' (Stone and Stone, 1977). Thus, the national income statistician's approach to measuring national income is similar to that used by current cost accounting in measuring business income. However, the national income statistics go further than this, using broadly-based price indices to re-state the annual national income figures in 'real' terms, as an aid to inter-year comparison. These 'real' national income figures have much in common with what we described earlier as 'real terms accounting'.

Nor is the problem merely one of measurement. The vagaries of unanticipated inflation lead to arbitrary re-allocation of resources between parties who have contracted in money terms. For example, the more rapid is inflation, the more will those who have borrowed money on fixed terms gain at the expense of those who have lent to them. Equally, if the wage bargain has been set in money terms at an annual pay-round, the more rapid is subsequent inflation, the more will employers gain at the expense of employees. The result of this type of problem in relation to fixed money contracts is not merely inequity, due to the arbitrary impact of unanticipated inflation, but also inefficiency, due to the creation of unnecessary uncertainty by linking real contractual rewards to an uncertain inflation rate. Thus, lenders and borrowers will have to make estimates of the likely inflation rate before they can fix an appropriate interest rate, and wage negotiations will also involve taking a view as to the probable inflation rate during the period of the agreement.

In order to deal with the latter problem, a number of economists have proposed indexation, i.e. adjusting the terms of contracts by a price index to allow for inflation. This would enable the terms of contracts to be fixed in 'real' rather than money terms, insofar as it is possible to construct an appropriate price index. Irving Fisher (1920) was an early advocate of indexation and was also a pioneer in the construction of index numbers. More recently, the case for indexation has been associated with Friedman (1974), who advocates it as a means of speeding the stabilisation effects of controlling the money supply, although this argument depends crucially upon such effects occurring: otherwise indexation might speed de-stabilisation. Recent British advocates of indexation have been Jackman and Klappholz (1975) and Fane (1975), and the case for indexation has been explored thoroughly in Liesner and King (1975) and Carsberg, Morgan and Parkin (1974), although neither book provides a thorough exploration of the contrary case. A review of this work will be found in Whittington (1976).

Apart from academic discussion, indexation has been adopted in practice in a number of countries, notably, in recent years, in Latin America, especially in Brazil and, more recently, Chile, although the range of contracts which are indexed has never been as comprehensive as that contemplated in the theoretical literature. In Britain, an experiment in the partial indexation of wage rates, the so-called 'threshold agreement' of 1973–74[2] was abandoned, presumably in the belief that it was strengthening, rather than weakening, the inflationary spiral. This experience may have been instrumental in motivating the government effectively to reject the accounting profession's proposals for CPP, which can be regarded as a form of indexation of accounts, by setting up the Sandilands Committee in 1974. The terms of reference of the Sandilands Committee required it to examine the wider economic implications of inflation accounting and parts of its Report[3] suggest some anxiety that the indexation of accounts might lead to the indexation of taxes, wages and other transactions and that this in turn might lead to further inflation. The only forms of indexation in Britain at the present time are public sector pension increases, the index-linked Save As You Earn scheme, index-linked Savings Certificates and a restricted government stock issue. The indexation of public pensions is currently being questioned, and investment in the latter three schemes is restricted. It is notable that all are supported by the government, although the issue of indexed stock to pension funds and life assurance companies may enable these bodies to offer indexed contracts in the future.

Inflation and the general price level

2 Index numbers and the measurement of inflation

Implicit in the preceding discussion of inflation and indexation has been the assumption that it is possible to construct a price index which is a useful measure of the changing values of money relative to goods. The type of indices most widely advocated for this purpose are broadly-based indices of retail prices (such as the UK Retail Price Index) or the indices used to obtain 'real' national income figures (such as the GNP deflator in the UK, which measures the price-level of all the components of GNP, or 'national income'). It must be admitted that, for a variety of reasons, no index is likely to be an ideal measure, but, in considering the deficiencies of indices, we must be prepared to balance the deficiencies of indexation against the deficiencies of data which are completely unadjusted for changes in the purchasing power of money.

The literature of index numbers is very large and no attempt will be made to survey it here. We shall concentrate on a brief statement of the elementary principles of index numbers, which are essential for an appreciation of their use in accounting, and a broad outline of their theoretical limitations, which are stated more fully elsewhere in the literature.[4]

A price index is used to measure how the purchasing power of money over goods differs at different times or at different locations. In the context of inflation, we are concerned with the comparison of different times. If there were only one good in the world, the construction of a price index would be very simple: the index at any time would merely be the ratio of the current unit price of the good to its price at the constant reference time chosen as the base of the index. Thus, if time 0 is the base, time 1 is when we wish to measure the index, and p_0 and p_1 represent the unit prices ruling at these times, the index at time 1 is p_1/p_0. However, in this simple situation, we do not really require a price index, because, in a single-commodity world, we can measure wealth, income or whatever other economic attribute is being assessed, in terms of physical units of the good. Measurement in monetary terms becomes essential only when we have more than one good. Monetary measurement is then a device for translating heterogeneous physical measures into a common unit of measurement, the monetary unit.

In this more complicated but realistic situation, we are faced with a set of prices p_i, where i indicates the ith commodity. If these prices change, we may wish to use a price index to reduce such monetary aggregates as income or expenditure over different periods of time to a common 'real' basis of measurement, by eliminating the illusory upward trend caused by the declining purchasing power of money in a period of inflation (or the corresponding downward trend which would be induced by deflation). The problem of reducing the changes in many prices, p_i, to a single index is the essence of index number construction, and it poses difficulties in all but the simplest case, when all prices increase in the same proportion. In the latter case, we can derive the appropriate index by choosing arbitrarily any particular commodity, i, and calculating the ratio of the current price (at time 1) to that of the base period (time 0), p_{i1}/p_{i0}. Alternatively, we could take any combination of other prices (weighted or unweighted) and we would, by definition, obtain the same ratio. However, in the realistic situation in which there are differences in the rate of price change of different commodities, the selection of commodities to be included in the index and the relative weights attached to them in the averaging process are likely to affect the value of the index, and this is the central issue in the debate on index numbers amongst both economists and accountants. However, it should be remembered that, in practice, there is often a great deal of correlation between different index numbers (as demonstrated, for example, in the work of Peasnell and Skerratt, 1976a) and, in discussing the problem of relative price changes, which is central to the specification of index numbers, we should not lose sight of the fact that, in many situations, even an imperfect index number may be of practical use. It is notable that the adjustment of accounts by using broadly-based general indices has been widely practised, and the precise estimation of specific price changes has commonly been ignored, in those countries such as Brazil which have experienced very high rates of general inflation (Baxter, 1976). In this situation, any broadly-based index is likely to capture a large proportion of the change in most prices.

There are two basic approaches to the index number problem. Frisch (1936) in a classic survey of index number theory, classified these as the 'atomistic' and the 'functional' approaches. The 'atomistic' approach is essentially statistical. It assumes that there is a general price level from which individual prices may diverge in a random fashion, so that the purpose of the index number is to average prices across commodities in such a way that the random element is minimised, so that we have the best possible estimate of the general price level. This approach is associated with Edgeworth, the British pioneer of index number theory, and with Irving Fisher, who reinforced the approach by specifying a number of tests of mathematical properties which an index number should possess.

Fisher's allegiance to this approach is particularly important, because his book, *The Purchasing Power of Money* (1911), is referred to by both the first English writer (Fells, 1919) and the first American writer (Middleditch, 1918) on inflation accounting, and his writings are extensively referred to by Sweeney (1936) who can be regarded as the seminal writer on CPP accounting in the English language. Sweeney's work was the model for the American Institute of Certified Public Accountants' Research Study, ARS6, '*Reporting the Financial Effects of Price-Level Changes*' (1963), which subsequently became a model for CPP proposals in both the USA (by the Accounting Principles Board in 1969, and by the Financial Standards Board in 1974, 1978 and 1979), and in the United Kingdom (in the Accounting Standards Steering Committee's *ED8*, 1973, and PSSAP7, 1974). It is notable that Appendix A of ARS6, on the Index Number Problem, takes an overtly statistical (or, in Frisch's terminology, 'stochastic') view of the index number problem, and it therefore advocates the GNP implicit price deflator (a price index covering all of the components of Gross National Product) as the most appropriate index, on the ground that this has the widest coverage and is therefore presumably the best indicator of 'the general price level'.[5] Subsequent advocates of CPP accounting have accepted this argument, sometimes accepting a consumer price index on practical grounds (consumer indices being more frequently published), but always retaining the broader GNP deflator as an ideal. For example, the latest pronouncement of the United States Financial Accounting Standards Board (FASB) on the subject (*Constant Dollar Accounting*, March 1979) states:

> The index to be used in Constant Dollar Accounting in the United States shall be the Consumer Price Index for All Urban Consumers (CPI-U) . . . The Board has designated the CPI-U instead of the Gross National Product Implicit

Price Deflator because the CPI-U has the practical advantages of being calculated more frequently (monthly instead of quarterly) and not being revised after its initial publication. Also, the rates of change in the CPI-U and the GNP Implicit Price Deflator tend to be similar and, therefore, use of the CPI-U will tend to produce a comparable result (Para. 3, p. 2).

This 'atomistic' approach was described as such by Frisch because it ignores the relationship between prices of commodities (p_i) and the quantities consumed (q_i), regarding them as two sets of independent variables. The other approach, labelled by Frisch as the 'functional' approach, is that adopted by economists and regards the relationship between prices and quantities as being one of interdependence. This approach is grounded in the concept of welfare, regarding goods as a means of creating utility for the individual consumer. The economist does not, therefore, attempt to measure the change in 'the general level of prices' as a uniquely defined objective concept but attempts to measure the change in 'the cost of living' defined by reference to the utility function which expresses the subjective preferences of the individual consumer. Thus, the basic approach used by the economist is to define a certain standard of living for the individual consumer (a 'reference indifference curve') and to calculate the cost of attaining this standard under different sets of prices. The ratio of this cost measured at various points in time to its level in the base period provides us with a cost of living index, reflecting how all price changes have affected the cost of living of the individual consumer.

The strength of the economist's approach is that it provides a precise rationale for and definition of 'the cost of living'. It thus provides a framework within which the problems of index number construction can be identified precisely, which is a necessary prelude to dealing with the problems. In particular, the problem of weighting different commodities is clarified: the appropriate weighting is the quantity of each commodity which would be consumed at the set of relative prices existing at the particular times being considered, at the reference standard of living. Thus, where n commodities are consumed, the index is:

$$\frac{\sum\limits_{i=1}^{n} p_{i1} \cdot q_{i1}}{\sum\limits_{i=1}^{n} p_{i0} \cdot q_{i0}}$$

where the q_i are those quantities necessary to achieve the reference standard of living at the prices reigning at the relevant time (1 or 0). The quantities depend on relative prices because a rational, welfare maximising consumer seeks to achieve the maximum benefit from a given budget (and therefore will achieve the reference standard of living at minimum cost), and this will imply that as relative prices change, he substitutes those commodities which have become relatively cheap for those which have become relatively more expensive (except in the extreme case of commodities which have a zero elasticity of substitution, i.e. demand for them is invariant to their relative price).

However, the greater precision of the economist's welfare-based concept of 'the cost of living' as opposed to the statistical concept of 'the general price level' is purchased at the cost of a number of restrictions on its applicability. The more important of these restrictions are as follows:

(1) The measurement of the 'true' economic cost of living index strictly requires full knowledge of the individual's preferences, i.e. his relative rankings of all possible bundles of goods. In practice, this is not available, so we have to infer preferences from actual behaviour.

(2) Unless the individual's utility function assumes a specific form (homothetic indifference curves), which implies that relative preferences for different goods are dependent only on relative prices, and independent of standard of living, the classic 'index number problem' arises, i.e. in measuring a change in the cost of living which results in a change in the standard of living, do we take as our point of reference for the price index the relative weights at the closing standard of living (defined by the indifference curve reached at the closing prices) or at the opening standard of living (defined by the indifference curve reached at the initial prices)?

(3) The economist's approach starts from an individual with stable preferences. In practice, individual preferences can vary through time. This is a serious problem, because the use of indices in practical situations typically involves comparisons through time. This difficulty can be dealt with by making appropriate assumptions, such as stability of preferences through time or by techniques such as 'chaining' (changing the weights through time to reflect changing tastes). The validity of the resulting index will then be dependent upon the accuracy of the assumptions and the precision of the techniques upon which it is based.

(4) In the case of inter-personal comparisons of the cost of living, there is the additional problem that tastes and consumption patterns vary across individual consumers. Furthermore, utility is strictly a subjective concept, and there is no objective method of comparing the pleasure, or 'standard of living', which different individuals derive from consuming even identical bundles of goods (Sen, 1979). Here again, for practical purposes, we can make assumptions which limit the theoretical properties of the index but do provide a basis for measurement which may serve at least as well as any other in yielding an index which is suitable for decision-making, e.g. we can assume 'that for two individuals with identical preferences (i.e. identical behaviour in all circumstances), the same economic constraints give rise to the same welfare' (Deaton, 1980, p. 51), i.e. the same availability of goods and services is assumed to give rise to the same 'standard of living' in two such individuals.

(5) The fact that the economist's approach is based upon individual welfare gives rise to further difficulties when we deal with groups of individuals, e.g. when we measure national income and attempt to construct a price index which can be used to express this in constant 'real' terms across periods when prices are changing. Here we encounter the problem of aggregation over individuals and, in particular, the question of the relative weights to be attached to the different preferences of different individuals in the community. Lest it should be thought that this is somewhat removed from the province of the accountant, it should be pointed out that proprietorship of the typical business firm is a community of individuals (partners or shareholders) and in attempting to construct an index to be applied to pro-

prietors' interest to calculate the amount which, after price changes, is necessary to maintain capital intact, we face precisely this problem, of selecting an index which is appropriate to a community (the proprietors) rather than an individual, if we take the 'proprietary' view of capital.

The use to which the price index is put will often be to devise a measure of 'real income' or 'real capital' by applying the index to unadjusted data measured in monetary units. It is important to note the limitations of the resulting 'real' measure as a reflection of the satisfaction which an individual might derive from the income or capital being measured. The 'real' measure will be a positive *function* of utility but not a cardinal measure of it: a '£15,000 a year man' who has become a '£20,000 a year man' is not necessarily $1/3$ better off than before, although he will be better off to some extent (i.e. 'real' income will be an ordinal measure, giving correct rankings of the individual's preferences for different income streams). The 'real' measure tells us that he is better off, but not by how much. Thus, the individual is left to translate the measure into something which has a more precise but subjective meaning in terms of his feeling of well-offness.[6] 'Real' accounting measures, based upon the use of indices, cannot therefore provide a precise measure of the utility of an income stream or capital sum to the proprietor of a business, but they can potentially provide useful measures of command over goods and services which will assist the individual proprietor in assessing the significance of income in terms of his personal utility.

In summary, economists and statisticians have devised a number of ingenious techniques for overcoming the difficulties of estimating price indices. These techniques typically make assumptions which restrict the theoretical applicability of the resulting indices, but the importance of the restrictions is not necessarily such as to rule out the use of the indices: for practical purposes, we must recognise that perfect measures do not exist and we must select the imperfect but feasible measure whose restrictions seem least important for the particular purpose which we have in mind.[7]

Thus, whether we approach index number construction from the statistical or the economic standpoints, we reach a common area of middle ground. The statistical approach requires some theoretical underpinnings to give a precise meaning to the concept of 'the general price level' and to justify the relative weighting attached to different prices, so that the implementation of this approach naturally draws us towards economic theory. The economic approach, on the other hand, inevitably encounters difficulties in the empirical implementation of measurements based upon so subjective a concept as welfare, so that it necessarily relies on a number of assumptions and approximations which lead it towards measures which can be justified by the statistical approach. The outcome is that neither approach would claim to lead to an index number which is a perfect representation of the effect of price changes on the welfare of an individual with a fixed sum of money to spend, but both would hope to give a better representation of this than would be obtained by making no correction at all. In deciding which index is the best for some particular purpose, we would resort, on a theoretical level, to economic theory, but on a practical level we would also need to know whether the use of alternative indices led to a material difference.

Perhaps there is still a difference of emphasis between the economic and statistical approaches which is not made clear enough in the literature. The statistical approach, at least in the form in which it is employed in arguments for CPP accounting, seems to be arguing for replacing the nominal £ by a unit which has more stable general purchasing power, e.g. the practical origins of CPP were in the German and French stabilisations in terms of gold currency (Sweeney, 1936). This approach does not claim to reflect the consumption pattern of an individual in any particular manner (e.g. it would be an unusual individual indeed who consumed only gold): it is designed to construct a unit of measurement representing constant (or more constant than money) command over those goods and services which are traded in the economy. It thus assumes that it is necessary for the individual to make his own translation from this CPP unit into his own welfare, and it may well be that the rate of exchange of CPP units into welfare will be different at different times.

The economic approach, on the other hand, starts from the much more ambitious position that an ideal measure should reflect individual welfare. In its most extreme form, as expressed, for example, by the Sandilands Committee (1975), it rejects entirely any concept of the general price level. In its more moderate and realistic form, it recognizes that the practical problems of measuring individual welfare are such that any index is bound to be an approximation. Furthermore, in the case of the accounts of a company, it would be impracticable to supply a separate set of accounts to each shareholder, adjusted by his individual price index, or, alternatively, to construct an index based upon some concept of the social welfare of shareholders as a group.[8] However, in adapting to practical constraints, the economic approach retains the essential assumption that the index should ideally reflect the effect of price changes on the individual. Thus, although the statistical and the economic approach may now occupy a common middle ground, they may still be facing in different directions.

This difference may perhaps be discerned in the advocacy of alternative indices for use in CPP accounting. As stated earlier, professional pronouncements on the subject have traditionally preferred a statistical approach and have advocated the use of as broadly-based an index as possible, such as the GNP implicit deflator. Economists, however, tend to prefer a consumer price index (e.g. Scott, 1976), on the ground that command over goods and services should be confined to items which will, potentially at least, be consumed by shareholders. This implies that 'the general price level' should be defined in terms of 'the cost of living' of shareholders. However, both approaches recognise that the shareholder will have to make his own subjective translation of 'real' economic magnitudes into welfare, and it is perhaps surprising that no research has been done to assess whether, in practice, very broad indices, such as the GNP deflator, do help shareholders or other individuals to translate economic magnitudes into welfare judgements, and whether they do this more or less effectively than alternative, narrower indices or unadjusted data. In practice, it is possible that individuals' perceptions of the price level are conditioned by a broader basket of goods and services from that which is contained in the consumer price index, and it may therefore be the case that individuals find it easier to assess their personal cost of living in relation to a more broadly-based index. However, an individual cost of living index would be superior to both of these alternatives, if it were practicable. Equally, the economist's welfare-based approach is the only one which offers a clear rationale for the relative weightings of different prices in an index during periods in which prices and quantities consumed are both changing.

In section 6 of this chapter, we shall return to the issue of index number selection for CPP accounting and discuss, in a pragmatic and practical manner, some considerations which might lead us to accept the use of a general index, despite the unavoidable ambiguities surrounding the interpretation of any particular index.

3 Constant Purchasing Power Accounting

Constant Purchasing Power Accounting (CPP) is a consistent method of indexing accounts by means of a general index which reflects changes in the purchasing power of money. It therefore attempts to deal with the inflation problem in the sense in which this is popularly understood, as a decline in the value of the currency. It attempts to deal with this problem by converting all of the currency unit measurements in accounts into units at a common date by means of the index. We shall concentrate on the *current* purchasing power variety of CPP, i.e. one which uses the current currency as the CPP unit.

Two common criticisms of CPP are, firstly, that general price indices are inappropriate for up-dating the historical costs of specific assets and, secondly, that general price indices cannot reflect the consumption patterns of individual shareholders and are therefore inappropriate for up-dating the amount of proprietors' capital to be maintained intact. We shall return to the second issue later, but the first must be dealt with here, because it indicates a misunderstanding of CPP accounting. CPP is concerned with the measurement unit, not with the techniques used to value assets and liabilities. It is possible to apply CPP methods to any valuation base, whether it be historical cost, replacement cost, net realisable value, or some eclectic combination (as in the Sandilands version of Current Cost Accounting). The 'real terms' approach illustrated in Chapter 1 combined CPP methods with current values. Some important pioneers of CPP, such as Sweeney (1936) and Accounting Research Study No. 6 (American Institute of Certified Public Accountants, 1963) and PSSAP7 (Accounting Standards Steering Committee, 1974) in the UK have been at pains to point out the fact that CPP can be applied to a current value base, although, as a matter of practical expediency, CPP has typically been proposed (e.g. in Accounting

Research Study No. 6 in the USA and PSSAP7 in the UK) as a means of amending traditional historical cost accounting.

A brief illustration of the CPP approach and its applicability to alternative valuation bases is as follows. Suppose a firm has a single asset, £100 in cash, which it holds in a period of 10 per cent inflation. If the sole source of finance is equity, the CPP approach would show a loss of £10 due to the fact that the asset had not risen in monetary value to match inflation: at the end of the period 110 devalued £s would be required to maintain the equity interest in terms of general purchasing power, but the asset would be only worth £100 in the devalued currency. This is an example of 'the loss on holding money' in a period of inflation. Suppose now that the firm was partly financed by an interest-free loan of £40. In this case only 40 devalued pounds would be required to pay the loan, so there would be a 'gain on borrowing' of £4 (10 per cent of £40) to offset against the loss on holding money, the net loss being £6 (which is the loss on money holding financed by the equity stake, 10 per cent of £60). These calculations are common to all CPP systems because it is assumed that the money holding and the loan do not fluctuate in nominal money value, i.e. historical cost and current value are equal in terms of monetary units, although the value of the monetary unit itself fluctuates.

Assume now that, instead of holding money, the firm has held shares which are quoted on the stock exchange and that these rose in market value to £150 at the end of the period. If we revert to the 'all equity' finance assumption, CPP applied to Historical Cost (HC) would show neither a profit nor a loss. The restated closing value of the shares would be £110, their HC in 'opening £s' translated into 'closing £s' to allow for inflation, because shares are a 'real' asset not denominated in fixed monetary units. The equity interest would similarly be restated, by applying the general index, to be £110, leaving no net gain or loss.

If, on the other hand, CPP were applied to a current value base in a 'real terms' system, the closing value of the asset (the share investments) would be £150.[9] This is, by definition, in terms of current (closing) £s, so no further restatement is required. The equity stake, on the other hand, will need to be restated as before: it was £100 in 'old £s' at the start of the period, and this is equivalent to £110 'new £s' at the end. Thus, our closing balance sheet, expressed in 'new £s', shows an asset of £150, equity capital of £110, and a surplus, attributable to equity, of £40.

If we now reintroduce the assumption of loan finance, so that opening capital is £60 equity and £40 loan, the 'gain on borrowing' of £4 will reappear. This will add £4 to the surplus attributable to equity, irrespective of the valuation basis of the non-monetary (or 'real') asset), bringing the total to £4 in the case of HC valuation and £44 in the case of current value.

For the purpose of this chapter, we shall confine the discussion to CPP as a means of amending historical cost accounting, but CPP adjustments will re-emerge two chapters hence as a means of amending current value accounts to produce 'real terms' accounting.

4 A brief history of CPP

The CPP technique owes its origins to the inflation which followed the First World War, particularly in France and Germany. In both of these countries, the paper currency was extremely unstable in value and it became customary to draw up financial accounts in terms of the equivalent gold currency (the gold franc and the gold mark) which was much more stable in value. Thus, in the early days, the parallel which is frequently drawn between currency translation and CPP accounting[10] was an exact one. The European experience was studied by a number of American scholars, such as Wasserman (1931) and Sweeney (1927 and 1928), and there was a significant American literature on the subject in the period 1918–35, much of which is gathered together and reviewed by Zeff (1976). Outstanding among the American writers was H. W. Sweeney, whose book *Stabilized Accounting* (1936) is the classic statement of the case for and the techniques of CPP accounting.[11]

Interest in CPP accounting naturally declined during the depression years of the 1930s, but it revived during the inflationary period following the Second World War. During this period, the American Accounting Association published two influential empirical studies by R. C. Jones (1955 and 1956) which examined the quantitative effect of CPP adjustment, and a brief manual by Perry Mason (1956) on the technique of CPP adjustment, using an HC valuation basis. This work, together with the earlier work by Sweeney, was clearly a powerful influence on *Accounting Research Study No. 6*, published by the American Institute of Certified Public Accountants in 1963. This, in turn, was the basis of the Accounting Principles Board's[12] *Statement No. 3* of June 1969, which recommended a supplementary statement showing the effects of CPP adjustment to traditional (HC based) accounts. Subsequent American proposals by the FASB in 1974 and 1978 were also of this type.[13] In the UK, the professional proposals for CPP accounting, *Exposure Draft 8* (1973) and *Provisional Statement of Standard Accounting Practice No. 7* (1974) resembled *APB3*, and were clearly influenced by the earlier publication, *Accounting for Stewardship in a Period of Inflation* (1968), which, in turn, was influenced by the earlier American work.[14]

Thus, by the early 1970s, CPP adjustment of Historical Cost had emerged as the inflation accounting technique favoured by professional bodies in both the UK and the USA. Professional bodies in Australia, Canada, New Zealand and South Africa followed this trend. CPP was also in use in practice in certain Latin American countries (Baxter, 1976). However, it has failed to be adopted as the only approved technique in any country outside Latin America: in the UK it has been supplanted by Current Cost Accounting, and in the USA the most recent pronouncement by the Financial Accounting Standards Board (FAS33: FASB, 1979) is eclectic, requiring both CCA and CPP information. One possible reason for this is that the professional proposals for CPP have always been based on its application to a traditional, historical cost valuation base. This was presumably done to portray CPP as an evolutionary reform, growing naturally out of traditional accounting and avoiding the subjectivity involved in estimating the current values of specific assets, but it had the effect also of putting CPP in apparent competition with other reforms, such as CCA, although it was potentially compatible with them.[15] Current values may be seen as a more urgent reform of traditional accounting, especially from the point of view of the users of accounts, who are likely to be concerned with the specific current values of the assets of the entity in which they have an interest, rather than with the CPP adjustment of historical costs which are of doubtful relevance to current circumstances.

Another reason for the widespread rejection of the professional proposals for CPP may have been fear of its possible economic consequences. CPP could be seen as a step towards indexation, and there may have been anxiety in government circles that indexation could institutionalise inflation, possibly even reinforcing inflationary spirals by leading to automatic inflation adjustment of wages, tax reliefs and the national debt. Certainly, the move to current cost accounting (CCA) in the mid-1970s was initiated by a series of government reports and interventions such as the requirement of the United States Securities and Exchange Commission (SEC) for replacement cost accounting disclosure, announced in 1975, the United Kingdom's Sandilands Report (1975), the Mathews Report on Taxation in Australia (1975), and the Richardson Committee Report in New Zealand (1976). This 'current cost revolution' initiated by government intervention is described and discussed more fully in the companion volume, *The Debate on Inflation Accounting*.

5 The technique of CPP

The basic technique of CPP is extremely simple. In practice, of course, complications arise, and it is not proposed to explore these here. Many admirable text-books, manuals and case studies have been published which deal with these problems, and some of these are listed in Appendix A at the end of this Chapter, and a numerical illustration is provided in Appendix B.

As stated earlier, the essence of CPP is to translate all measurements in currency units into units at a common date by using the general index as an indication of the purchasing power of currency at different points in time. Thus, the proportionate change in the price index represents the 'exchange rate' between currency units of different dates. The justification for making such an adjustment is that accounting requires a stable measuring unit and an 'unstabilised' (i.e. not indexed) currency unit fails to provide this.

A simple illustration of CPP adjustment is to use the notation of earlier chapters and apply a general price index to the accounts of a period. It will be recalled that the opening balance sheet was defined as:

$$N_t + M_t \equiv L_t + P_t \tag{4.1}$$

where N represents non-monetary assets

M represents monetary assets

L represents liabilities

(assumed to be fixed in monetary terms)

P represents the proprietor's net worth.

The closing balance sheet, rearranged to show proprietor's interest on the left hand side is:

$$P_{t+1} = N_{t+1} + M_{t+1} - L_{t+1} \tag{4.2}$$

If we assume that the valuation of N_t is in £s of that date, either because the assets were acquired on that date or because previous indexation exercises have up-dated historical cost to that date, we can translate the opening balance sheet from £s of t into £s of $t + 1$ by the following adjustment. If the general price index increases by p per cent between t and $t + 1$ the restated opening balance sheet becomes:

$$P_t(1 + p) = N_t(1 + p) + M_t(1 + p) - L_t(1 + p) \tag{4.3}$$

In order to assess profit, we need to compare this with the closing balance sheet, which also has to be restated in £s of $t + 1$. Assume for simplicity that the balance sheet structure of the firm has been un-disturbed during the period, i.e. there have been no transactions.[16] In order to restate the closing balance sheet, we can increase the valuation of the non-monetary asset to compensate for the decline in the value of the £, one historic £ (at t) being equivalent to $(1 + p)$ current £s (at $t + 1$).[17] We cannot, however, alter the valuations of M or L, because they are fixed in monetary units, irrespective of the fluctuations in purchasing power of those units. Thus, a £1 liability at t is still a £1 liability at $t + 1$, albeit the £ has depreciated in value. The closing balance sheet, in $t + 1$ £s is now:

$$P_{t+1} = N_t(1 + p) + M_t - L_t \tag{4.4}$$

Subtracting the price-level stabilised opening balance sheet, (4.3), from the equivalent closing balance sheet, (4.4), gives us CPP profit:

$$Y_{\text{CPP}} = \Delta P = L_t p - M_t p \tag{4.5}$$

$L_t p$ is the 'gain on borrowing', i.e. the gain to the firm due to the facts that the loan is fixed in money terms and the purchasing power of money has declined. $M_t p$ is the 'loss on holding money' (or assets denominated in monetary units), which is the mirror-image of the gain on borrowing: it represents the loss of purchasing power of the monetary units held. Thus, CPP accounting, applied in this manner as a modification of historical cost, recognises only two methods of valuation: restatement of HC to allow for the fluctuating purchasing power of money, which applies to non-monetary assets and to proprietors' net worth (the capital to be maintained before income is recognised), and the fixed value in terms of the monetary units, which applies to 'monetary' assets and liabilities. Clearly when, as in 'real terms' accounting, the valuation base of the accounts being stabilised is some form of current value, there is no need to apply the general index to 'non-monetary' balance sheet items which are stated at current values, as these are, by definition, already expressed in current £s. However, a current value Profit and Loss Account will be stated in terms of values current at the time of transactions *within* the year, and this will require CPP restatement into *end of year* units.

This statement should be qualified, in that it assumes that CPP takes on the current purchasing power form, rather than using some other unit of constant purchasing power. It is also important to note that the above example deals with CPP accounting *within a particular year*, whereas a particularly important use of CPP is for the *comparison of different years*, or series of years: the longer the period, the more important are changes in the purchasing power of money likely to be. In the case of such comparisons, it is necessary to ensure that the same CPP unit is used for all the years being compared, although, if the figures within individual years are based upon consistent CPP units, translation between units is a simple matter, merely involving multiplication of the numbers in the accounts by the appropriate 'rate of exchange'. Thus, if the accounts are expressed in current purchasing power units as of the end of each individual year, in order to make figures for earlier years comparable with those for the current year, we need to calculate the rates of exchange between the £ at the end of the current year and the £ at the end of each preceding year: this rate of exchange is simply the ratio of the current price index to that of the earlier years. We then restate the accounts for each earlier year by multiplying each item by the rate of exchange relevant to the year. This is a purely mechanical process, analogous to the translation of £s into $s at a given exchange rate.

Although, for simplicity and precision, the algebraic illustration in equations (4.1) to (4.5) above was confined to the 'no transactions' situation, it can easily be extended to the more realistic situation in which transactions take place. In general, we can define current purchasing power income, by deducting the opening balance sheet, stabilised in closing £s, from the closing balance sheet, similarly stabilised, as:[18]

$$Y_{\text{CPP}} = P'_{t+1} - P'_t(1+p) = [N'_{t+1} - N'_t(1+p)]$$
$$+ [M_{t+1} - M_t] - [L_{t+1} - L_t] - M_t.p + L_t.p \qquad (4.6)$$

where the valuation basis of N'_t and N'_{t+1} is historical cost restated to the relevant date by application of a general price index. The primes indicate variables which differ from historical cost data because they are indexed to date. If a current value base were used, the primed variables would represent current values as of the respective dates, and these would, by definition, be expressed in currency units as of the valuation date.

This formulation brings out clearly the essential feature of CPP: the use of the general index p to adjust all items in the accounts so that they are expressed in currency units as of a constant date, and therefore of constant value. Opening capital is measured in real, rather than in monetary terms, where real terms is defined in general purchasing power $[P'_t(1+p)]$. Real, or 'non-monetary', assets (N) are assumed to fluctuate in value in terms of monetary units: in this case, using a historical cost valuation basis, they are assumed to retain their real historical values, so that, if the same assets were held throughout the period, there would be no change in the real value of these assets, because N'_{t+1} would be equal to $N'_t(1+p)$. 'Monetary' assets and liabilities (M and L), on the other hand, are assumed to have values fixed in monetary units, resulting, in a period of inflation, in the gain on borrowing ($L_t.p$) and the loss of holding money ($M_t.p$) which are separated out on the right-hand side of equation (4.6). However, this is a correct expression of these two factors only when M and L have remained constant throughout the period (as in our earlier transactionless example). In other circumstances, the only strictly accurate method of calculating the gain on L or the loss on M is to stabilise each transaction individually: examples of this will be found in Sweeney (1935 and 1936) and Ijiri (1976). Strictly, this method requires the availability of an index for each time at which transactions took place. A simpler method, which is quicker and cheaper but less precise, averages transactions over the whole period and assumes that they occurred linearly through time, so that the mid-year index can be taken as the average at which transactions took place. Examples of this approach will be found in *Accounting Research Study No. 6* and *Provisional Statement of Standard Accounting Practice No. 7*. A simple numerical example of CPP adjustment will be found in Appendix B to this chapter, and another will be found in Lee (1980).

The balance sheet formulation of equation (4.6) provides a definition of profit but does not identify the flows of which profit is the net result, and which are reported in the Profit and Loss Account. A fully stabilised CPP accounting system includes a Profit and Loss Account re-stated in units of constant purchasing power. The following simple example should serve to illustrate the principles involved in stabilising the Profit and Loss Account, and the relationship between the Profit and Loss Account and the Balance Sheet.

Assume that a business starts the accounting year with a single asset, £1,000 of stock, which has just been acquired, so that it is expressed in 'beginning of year £s', and which is financed by the proprietor's capital. At the beginning of the year, the general price index stands at 100 and at the end it stands at 120. During the year, with the index standing at 105, the stock is sold for £1,200, which is received in cash, and held in this form to the end of the year.

The historical cost (HC) and constant purchasing power (CPP) accounts are as follows:

Profit and Loss Account

	HC (£)	CPP Adjustment	CPP (end of year £)
Sale	1,200	$\times \dfrac{120}{105}$	1,371
Less Cost of Sale	1,000	$\times \dfrac{120}{100}$	1,200
Trading Profit	£ 200		171
Less Loss on holding money		$1,200 \times \left(\dfrac{120}{105} - 1 \right)$	171
Net CPP Profit			£ 0

Inflation and the general price level

Closing Balance Sheet

	HC (£)	CPP Adjustment	CPP (end of year £)
Asset			
Cash	£1,200	(Fixed monetary value)	£1,200
Financed by			
Opening capital	1,000	$\times \dfrac{120}{100}$	1,200
Add Profit for the year	200		0
Closing capital	£1,200		£1,200

Each HC item is translated into CPP by applying the change in the general index between the date at which the HC value is established and the date of the CPP unit (the end of the year). Sales and cost of sales (and any other revenue and expense items) are therefore restated in CPP units. In this particular example, the loss on holding money entirely wipes out the CPP operating profit, but this is not a general result: a net CPP profit would have remained had the selling price been higher, or had the sales proceeds been reinvested in a non-monetary asset, such as replacement stock, which would be assumed to maintain its real value and would therefore have avoided the loss on holding money. This example uses a precise 'transaction by transaction' indexing method, which is made possible by there being only one transaction. If the sales were spread evenly over the year, the averaging method would suggest using the mid-year index (which may be different from 105) for adjusting the sales and for calculating the loss on holding money.

There are inevitably a number of variations on the CPP method. Sweeney (1936), for example, did not recognise gains or losses on holding money as part of profit (although they did affect the reserves in his balance sheet): this is discussed critically in Baxter (1975). There are also a number of variations on the actual technique. Apart from the choice between the stabilisation of individual transactions and the averaging method, discussed above, and the choice of price index discussed in section 2 and in the following section, there is the question of the date of the currency unit used for stabilisation. As was noted earlier, *Current* Purchasing Power presumes that the latest (closing balance sheet) date will be the date at which the standard currency unit will be measured, but this is not a special case of *Constant* Purchasing Power, which allows stabilisation in any currency unit, provided that the stabilisation is carried through consistently. Sweeney (1936) recommends that, for record-keeping purposes, accounts should be stabilised on a standard unit of a past date, which remains constant from year to year. It is then possible to stabilise transactions before the closing index value is known, and it is a simple matter to translate constant purchasing power figures stabilised on a past date into current purchasing power: this is done by multiplying the constant purchasing power figures by the ratio of the current price index to the index at the base date.

One other technical problem of CPP accounting is the definition of 'monetary' assets and liabilities. Conceptually, this may seem straightforward, 'monetary' implying fixed in value in terms of nominal monetary units, and therefore declining in real value as the real value of the monetary unit declines. In practice, the wide variety of financial assets and claims means that there are 'grey areas' such as holdings of foreign currency and various forms of interest-bearing deposits, which might be classified as either 'monetary' or 'non-monetary' depending upon the precise definition used. This issue is explored thoroughly at a conceptual level by Heath (1972), who compares the definitions used by various writers and professional pronouncements on the subject. A useful case study by Wanless (1976) has demonstrated that this issue is of practical importance. In a case study, applying the provisions of the British provisional accounting standard (ASSC, 1974) to the accounts of the Scottish Wholesale Co-operative Society, she demonstrates that a material increase in reported profit (or reductions in the 'loss on holding money') can be obtained by deliberately interpreting the definition of 'non-monetary' assets as liberally as possible. This problem is, of course, avoided if a comprehensive current value system is adopted, which re-states all assets and liabilities at their current values. However, we then face the problem of choosing between alternative current values, which is discussed in the next chapter.

However, it is not our central purpose to expound the technicalities of CPP accounting: this has already been done elsewhere. We now turn to the important question of the merits and deficiencies of CPP.

6 Criticisms of CPP

The case for CPP adjustment rests primarily on the variability of the value of the currency, which renders it inappropriate as a unit of measurement. CPP claims to produce a stable (or at least a relatively stable) currency unit for measurement purposes. Two broad lines of attack have been mounted against this case: firstly, that general index adjustment of historical cost is an inappropriate method of valuing assets and liabilities, and, secondly, that the general index adjustment does not reflect accurately the change in the cost of living of the individual shareholder, or the cost of the goods which the firm will need to buy in order to maintain its assets intact.

With regard to the first line of criticism, that CPP applied to historical cost produces poor current valuations, we have already seen that this relates only to a limited range of applications of the CPP technique, since CPP can also be applied to current value bases. The discussion in the previous chapter makes it clear that the case for historical cost accounting is rather weak. It is therefore clear that translating historical cost into 'real' terms by means of a general index is not likely to produce figures which are of great utility, despite the fact that this may be a consistent way of dealing with the effects of inflation on historical cost accounts. In particular, this type of adjustment will not produce current market values of assets and liabilities, which are also expressed in current £s, and which are probably of greater relevance to most potential users and uses of accounts. The case for current values will be discussed in the next chapter. This line of criticism is, of course, aimed at the historical cost base rather than CPP itself, and it must be reiterated that the proponents of CPP have typically seen it as complementary to, rather than competitive with, current values. The association of CPP with historical cost has been due to its proposal as an evolutionary reform of traditional accounting, although it must be admitted that not all of its supporters have recognised this, and that its attractions to the accounting profession may have been enhanced by the prospect that its implementation would postpone the day when accountants would have to deal in such subjective matters as the estimation of replacement costs.[19] The possibility of combining some form of current value accounting with CPP adjustment in a system of 'real terms' accounting will be discussed further in Chapter 6.

The second line of attack on CPP rests on the inappropriateness of a general index adjustment as a measure of the loss in purchasing power of money. If we accept the argument of the previous paragraph, that the issue of valuation is (or can be) separate from that of measuring the effects of inflation, then this second line of attack becomes a matter of questioning the appropriateness of using general purchasing power adjustments to measure the capital which is to be maintained intact. This can be demonstrated, in terms of our earlier notation, as follows. Assume that non-monetary assets are valued at some acceptable form of current value, indicated by a double prime (N''). For simplicity, maintain the assumption that all liabilities, L, are 'monetary' and, like 'monetary' assets M, therefore have a current value equal to their face value. The proprietors' interest, at current value, will now be:

$$P''_t = N''_t + M_t - L_t$$

and

$$P''_{t+1} = N''_{t+1} + M_{t+1} - L_{t+1} \tag{4.7}$$

If we now wish to apply an adjustment for general price level changes to bring all items into current purchasing power units, no further adjustment is necessary to the closing balance sheet, as all items are expressed in current currency equivalents. In measuring profit, however, we shall need to bring the opening balance sheets, now expressed in £s at t, up to date, into £s at $t + 1$, to produce a 'real terms' profit measure:

$$Y_{RT} = P''_{t+1} - P''_t(1 + p) \tag{4.8}$$

In the case in which there are no transactions, this can be applied to individual assets and liabilities to separate 'real' gains and losses (in constant £s) from 'fictitious' gains and losses (those due to changes in the value of the £) as follows:

$$P''_{t+1} - P''_t(1 + p) = [N''_{t+1} - N''_t(1 + p)] + [M_{t+1} - M_t(1 + p)] - [L_{t+1} - L_t(1 + p)] \tag{4.9}$$

or, treating the rise in the value of N'' as being due to a rise of s per cent in the specific index of the firm's non-monetary asset values (i.e. $N''_{t+1}/N''_t = (1 + s)$) and separating out the loss on holding money and the gain on borrowing:

$$Y_{RT} = N''_t (s - p) - M_t.p + L_t.p \tag{4.10}$$

where the first term on the right hand side is the real gain (if $s > p$) or loss (if $s < p$) on holding non-monetary assets, the second term is the loss on holding money (a gain if $p < 0$) and the third term is the gain on borrowing (a loss if $p < 0$).

Thus, the general price level adjustment $(1 + p)$ is applied to the opening capital figure to define the real capital to be maintained intact. This adjustment can also be applied to individual assets and liabilities to separate 'real' gains and losses (due to $s > p$ for gains, or $s < p$ for losses) from those which merely reflect a maintenance of 'real' value when the value of the monetary unit is changing (at a rate p). This approach can be attacked from two rather different standpoints.

Firstly, the general index approach embodies a 'proprietary' view of capital maintenance, i.e. the real value of shareholders' funds in terms of their general command over goods and services is assumed to be the central concern. The alternative 'entity' capital maintenance approach, discussed further in the next two chapters, holds that it is the maintenance of the assets specific to the firm which is the object of capital maintenance: this clearly leads to the rejection of a general index for the adjustment of capital, in favour of a specific index, representing the changes in price of the specific assets held by the firm.

Secondly, even if it is accepted that the general purchasing power of the proprietors is that which should be maintained intact before a gain in money value is recognised as income, it can be argued, following the discussion of index numbers in section 2 of this chapter, that a general index does not adequately capture changes in the purchasing power of any particular individual shareholder. This line of argument is particularly associated with Gynther (1966 and 1974) and with the Sandilands Report (1975). Some of the counter-arguments to Gynther were aired by Bromwich (1975b) and a critique of the Sandilands position is provided by Chambers (1976, pp. 5–12). The attitude of the Sandilands Committee (1975) is summarised as follows:

> The term inflation describes a situation where the movement in the average price level of goods and services in a period is upward. However, the average movement of prices and the rate of inflation will vary for different individuals and entities in the country according to the

selection of goods and services which they buy. It is incorrect to assume that a wide-ranging index such as the Retail Price Index can be a measure of the rate of inflation equally appropriate to all individuals and entities (*Sandilands Report*, para. 28).

This argument clearly adopts the 'economic' rather than the 'statistical' view of index numbers, and claims that a general index fails to meet the criteria for measuring the cost of living of individual shareholders. The following counter-arguments can be made to the Sandilands view:

(1) The fact that 'inflation' is not precisely quantifiable is not necessarily a reason for ignoring it. We must compare the value of 'inflation adjusted' information with that of information which is unadjusted, not with some ideal measurement standard which might be possible if no prices changed. This argument is often supported by quoting Keynes' proverbial epigram 'It is better to be approximately right than precisely wrong.' As we saw in the earlier discussion of index numbers, it is impossible in practice to obtain a 'true' index which directly measures the effects of price changes on individual welfare, so some degree of approximation is inevitable, particularly in accounts which are intended for the general use of a wide range of individuals.

(2) Although it is clearly possible that individual prices will change in a different manner, and even in a different direction, from a general index, it is reasonable to assume that the typical consumer purchases a variety of commodities. It is therefore possible that the averaging effect of purchasing a variety of commodities will mean that changes in the cost of the individual's basket of goods will not differ greatly from changes in a general index, this being the result of a process analogous to the averaging out of unsystematic investment risk by holding a portfolio of investments rather than a single investment. Moreover, it is likely that there will be a considerable overlap between most individual consumption patterns and the composition of a general index, since certain basic needs, such as food, clothing and housing are common to all (although of course there may be differences within these broad commodity classes). Finally, if the price of an individual commodity does diverge widely from the general index, we might expect substitution effects to lessen

the inappropriateness of the general index (on the assumption that the weighting of the general index is revised regularly to reflect current consumption patterns). If the commodity becomes relatively expensive, the individual consumer is likely to substitute cheaper alternatives, so that his consumption pattern will tend to revert towards the community average. If, on the other hand, the commodity becomes relatively cheap, the rest of the community will now buy it in greater quantities, in preference to relatively expensive substitutes, and the community consumption pattern, as reflected in the general index, will move closer to that of the individual.[20]

These *a priori* arguments are supported by recent empirical testing by Peasnell and Skerratt (1978), who conclude, on the basis of recent United Kingdom experience, that 'the impact of inflation is remarkably constant across income groups, suggesting that the concept of inflation is meaningful to different individuals'. It should be noted that Peasnell and Skerratt studied income groups rather than individuals, and there is clearly scope for further empirical work at the individual level. However, their results are encouraging for those who support the use of general price-level indices.

(3) In the earlier discussion of index numbers, it was argued that it is not possible to measure directly the welfare of the individual. We can merely hope to measure his command over goods and services. It is arguable that the use of a general index, preferably as broadly-based as possible, such as the RPI or the GNP implicit deflator,[21] will best reflect this, by giving a measure of potential consumption which the individual may be able to translate into his own consumption pattern and welfare. Of course, by restricting ourselves to measuring potential consumption, we are forgoing the right to say anything directly about the individual's welfare, i.e. because his 'real' income has gone up, he is not necessarily better off in the welfare economist's sense (i.e. he is not necessarily on a higher indifference curve). However, if we accept that his utility function can change over time, he is not necessarily better off even if he has increased his command over the specific basket of goods which he chooses to buy.[22] More generally, as we saw in the earlier discussion of index numbers, the precise measurement of welfare is essentially a subjective process, and economic magnitudes, adjusted by index numbers,

should be judged as useful inputs into that process, rather than as direct measures of welfare. In assessing alternative forms of information, it should be stressed that some form of monetary measurement underlies all of the alternatives. If we abandon money we are left with heterogeneous quantities of physical assets, but expressing these quantities in money terms overcomes the heterogeneity problem only if the weighting scheme has some significance for the individual in assessing his potential welfare.

Thus it is arguable that we can hope, by means of a general index adjustment, to produce a useful (but not exact) measure of command over goods and services in general which is of use to an individual in assessing his potential welfare, but we cannot hope to measure the utility which the individual derives from exercising that power, unless we are prepared to tread the difficult, tortuous, and (for accountants) practically infeasible path of exploring individual utility functions. It is up to the individual, who presumably does have knowledge of his own past and present preferences, to establish what his current purchasing power means in terms of utility. It was suggested earlier (in section 2) that one issue for behavioural research, which has not yet been investigated, is whether individuals find it easier to use unadjusted monetary data or 'real' CPP data to establish whether they, individually, feel that they are better or worse off. It is possible that unadjusted data do have an advantage in this respect, because they do represent prices which actually prevailed at particular points in time, whereas a constant general purchasing power unit is an abstract construct which might be more difficult for the individual to relate to his own consumption patterns. On the other hand, memory of past prices may be short and confused, and the general index adjustment does at least give the individual some indication of how prices have moved, although not a perfect one from the point of view of his assessment of his own welfare. It was also suggested in the earlier discussion (section 2) that the form of general index which is most appropriate might also be investigated by behavioural research.

We can summarise the present state of knowledge as follows. Financial accounts are intended to report the economic performance of the firm to the individual shareholder or proprietor. In times of rapid inflation it seems likely that such a report should remind the proprietor of the effects of the change in the purchasing power of the monetary unit. For comparability between firms and consistency in reporting to many individual shareholders it seems likely that a general index adjustment will perform this task at least as well as any feasible alternative. In terms of the problem originally stated, that of defining capital to be maintained, general index adjustment implies recognizing a profit only when the proprietors' interest, P, has been maintained in terms of command over a basket of goods broadly representative of that purchased by the average consumer. In terms of splitting the holding gains into 'real' and 'fictitious', general index adjustment compares movements in the price of the specific assets with movements in the price of a portfolio of commodities contained in the general index. We shall return to this subject in Chapter 6.

7 Some empirical studies

A considerable number of empirical studies of CPP accounting has been carried out in recent years. The object of this brief survey is to convey the broad thrust of this work and to refer the interested reader to some of the main sources. It will not be possible to do full justice to these empirical studies by providing a comprehensive survey.

Early empirical studies, such as those by Sweeney (1936) and Jones (1949 and 1955) in the USA and by Baxter (1959) in the UK, tended to be of the case study type. A useful survey of the earlier work will be found in ARS6 (American Institute of Certified Public Accountants, 1963), Appendix E. This type of work applies CPP adjustments to the accounts of real firms with two broad objectives: to establish the materiality of CPP adjustments and to establish problems of interpretation and application. As an example of the first type of result, Sweeney (1936) has a case in which a significant unadjusted loss becomes an adjusted (i.e. Sweeney version of CPP) gain. As an example of the second type, Wanless' (1976) study of a co-operative society demonstrates some of the difficulties of defining 'monetary' assets and the materiality of the differences which arise from using alternative definitions. This type of research has continued to be pursued fairly widely up to the present time, some examples being the work of Petersen (1973, 1975 and 1978), Davidson and Weil (1975) and Parker (1977)[23] and the FASB's own Field Tests (1977), in the USA, Cutler and Westwick (1973) and Hope (1974) in the UK, and the University of Waikato project in New Zealand (Emanuel, 1976). This type of research has, in general, shown that CPP does in practice lead to materially different results from those of traditional accounting. It has also shown that CPP adjustment is feasible in practice and has served to highlight some of the practical issues which arise in its implementation. An alternative to the case study method is the simulation approach, used by Arnold and El-Azma (1978) which assesses how alternative accounting income measures (including CPP adjusted ones) reflect alternative economic conditions.

More recently, new lines of research have been developed which hope to identify the utility as well as the materiality, of price-level adjustments. One such approach is the behavioural approach, based upon confronting users of accounts with a choice between traditional accounting data and CPP. Dyckman (1969) carried out such a study using investment analysts as subjects and found that CPP data did lead to different decisions. Subsequent studies by Heintz (1975) and McIntyre (1975), using students as subjects, failed to establish such differences.[24] An alternative approach is to look at the predictive power of alternative accounting measures, and there are a number of studies of this type. For example, Buckmaster, Copeland and Dascher (1977) studied the relative self-predictive ability (i.e. the extent to which the past value of a variable can be used to predict its future value) of historical cost, replacement cost and CPP income measures across 42 US companies, and found that historical cost produced the best self-prediction, and CPP the worst. However, the criterion of self-predictability is appropriate only if the future value of the variable has some intrinsic value to a user of accounting information, e.g. as an indication of future dividend potential for the shareholder: prediction for its own sake is of no use. A more obviously useful criterion is the ability to predict directly an event which is relevant to the user's needs. For example, Ketz (1978b) and Norton and Smith (1979) consider the question of whether traditional historical cost or CPP data produce the best prediction of corporate bankruptcy in the USA. CPP data appear to perform as well as historical cost in this respect, but not significantly better (Patell, 1978).

Finally, there is a growing group of studies which attempt to assess the impact of CPP data on share prices. Basu (1977) is a study, based on the COMPUSTAT file of accounting data of North American firms to obtain estimated CPP data. Basu used an efficient markets framework, assuming that all relevant information is reflected in share prices as soon as it becomes available. He failed to find a significant advantage in using CPP rather than conventional data to explain 'unsystematic' returns.[25] He concludes that 'GPL restated measures' (i.e. CPP) 'of risk and return, by and large, do not convey information beyond that transmitted by the basic historical cost alternative' (p. 32). An alternative view could be that sophisticated investors already have access to such measures. Basu's conclusion is based upon studying the possible benefits of CPP reporting at a time when it was not provided. A UK study by Morris (1975), which also uses an efficient markets framework, attempts to assess the market response to the release of estimated CPP data for 132 listed companies by a firm of stockbrokers in 1971. He was unable to detect a significant response and concludes that there is no evidence that the CPP data had any additional value. A more recent American study by Hillison (1979), which, like Basu's study, uses COMPUSTAT data and an efficient markets framework (although the detailed methodology is different) also fails to find any superior returns by using CPP data. A study by Short (1978) finds some evidence that CPP adjustment improves the ability of accounting data to explain market risk, but the conclusions are qualified by serious statistical problems. Another American study, by Devon and Kolodny (1978) claims that CPP earnings are more closely related to stock price changes than historical cost earnings, but this study, unlike the others, does not allow for risk by using the Capital Asset Pricing Model (see p. 217, n. 25).

In summary, it may be said that empirical work in this field is still in its infancy and the results are far from decisive. It is clear that CPP adjustment does produce material changes in reported figures in certain individual cases, e.g. companies which are highly geared show large gains on borrowing, but it is also clear that there is a large common information content in CPP and traditional accounting. It is not proven that the additional information content of CPP is not already taken account of by investors, who obtain the information from other sources or from their own estimates when it is not produced by the company, or that there simply is no information content in CPP. However, the variety of approach, the statistical limitations and the relatively narrow data coverage of the studies referred to is such that they do not provide a firm foundation for forming an opinion as to the merits of published financial accounts incorporating CPP adjustments to traditional historical cost information. Even if investors do take account of CPP adjustments already, by making them for themselves, it could be argued that the company should supply such information as a 'public good' made freely available to all users of the accounts to eliminate the excessive cost of such calculations having to be duplicated by different users of accounts.

8 Summary

In this chapter we have described briefly the history and the method of CPP accounting. Attention has been focussed on the CPP method defined narrowly as general index adjustment of historical cost accounts, but it was pointed out that the CPP method can equally well be applied to current value accounts, in which case a current purchasing power balance sheet for a particular year can be obtained by adjusting only the measurement of opening capital, the assets and liabilities already being recorded in current £s. However, the flows recorded in the Profit and Loss Account will have to be re-stated in current £s. This type of 'real terms' accounting system will be discussed further in Chapters 5 and 6. CPP applied to historical cost deals only with the problem of the changing value of the currency and does not, therefore, provide a general solution to the deficiencies of historical cost, discussed in the previous chapter.

The CPP adjustment of the capital to be maintained intact is controversial but has strong arguments in its favour. The main criticisms of this approach are, firstly, that it does not lead to the maintenance of the specific capital of the firm, and, secondly, that it does not maintain the purchasing power of any particular individual proprietor or shareholders. The first criticism comes from 'entity' theorists, who reject the 'proprietary' capital maintenance concept upon which CPP is based: this will be discussed further in the next two chapters. The second criticism leads us into somewhat pragmatic arguments. If accounts are intended for the use of a whole community of shareholders and others, it is not possible to provide different individual index adjustments for each user, yet, if inflation exists at a significant rate, it seems likely to be useful to remind users of the possible order of magnitude of its effects on accounting measurements, and general index adjustment may be the best practical method of doing this. Furthermore, it is possible that the divergences of the impact of inflation on the cost of living of different individuals are not very great. Finally, the argument for constructing individual indices is suspect, since it is not possible to measure individual utility, without imposing severe restrictions on the assumed form of the individual's utility function. If all that we can do is to measure general command over goods and services, a general index may be as good, or better, than a specific index.

Finally, a brief survey was made of the empirical literature relating to CPP accounting. The 'case study' approach has established that CPP adjustments can lead to material changes and has shown that such adjustments are practically infeasible, as well as highlighting the technical aspects which require close definition. The more recent trend in research is towards establishing the usefulness of CPP data, e.g. by considering its actual or potential impact on stock market prices, or by assessing its value in predicting the future. This type of research is still in its infancy and has yet to yield decisive results.

The two appendices to this chapter provide, respectively, a select bibliography of books describing and illustrating the CPP technique (Appendix A) and a worked example of the CPP technique applied to a historical cost basis (Appendix B), based on the example used in earlier chapters.

Chapter 4: Appendix A Select bibliography on Constant Purchasing Power Accounting

1 Original sources

The classic monograph on this subject is:
Stabilized Accounting, by H. W. Sweeney, Harper, New York, 1936.
    Currently available in a reprint by the Arno Press.
Sweeney's book contains detailed case studies and worked examples, including CPP adjustment applied to a replacement cost (RC) valuation base.

In the mid-1950s, the American Accounting Association published three monographs on the subject, which were very influential in subsequent developments:
Effects of Price Level Changes on Business Income, Capital and Taxes, by R. C. Jones, American Accounting Association, 1956.

This examines the distortionary effect of inflation on accounts in theoretical terms, and advocates CPP adjustment, whilst accepting the usefulness of replacement cost rather than historical cost as a valuation basis, as in Sweeney's system.

Price Level Changes and Financial Statements – Case Studies of Four Companies, by R. C. Jones, American Accounting Association, 1955.

This companion volume provides case studies of four real companies, adjusting their published (historical cost) accounts by the Consumer Price Index to provide CPP restatement in December 1951 dollars. It serves as an illustration of the CPP technique and demonstrates its materiality.

Price-Level Changes and Financial Statements, Basic Concepts and Methods, by Perry Mason, American Accounting Association, 1956.

This is a concise 'how-to-do-it' manual of the CPP technique, illustrated with clear numerical examples.

Much of this earlier work is surveyed and incorporated in:

Reporting the Financial Effects of Price-Level Changes, Accounting Research Study No. 6 ('ARS6'), by the Staff of the Accounting Research Division, American Institute of Certified Public Accountants, 1963.

This became the model for subsequent professional proposals for supplementary CPP adjustment of published (historical cost) accounts, in both the USA and Britain.

The model for subsequent British proposals was:

Accounting for Stewardship in a Period of Inflation, The Research Foundation of The Institute of Chartered Accountants in England and Wales, 1968.

The anonymous author of this pamphlet was W. E. Parker. It provides a concise 'how-to-do-it' blueprint for supplementary CPP adjustment of traditional historical cost accounts, similar in many respects to the Perry Mason pamphlet, listed earlier. It became the model for the subsequent CPP proposals of the Accounting Standards Steering Committee.

2 Publications of standard-setting bodies in the USA and the UK

The first recommendation for supplementary disclosure of CPP-adjusted accounts came from the United States Accounting Principles Board (APB):

Inflation and the general price level

Statement No. 3, Financial Statements Restated for General Price-Level Changes, Accounting Principles Board (APB3), June 1969. This recommended supplementary statements based on CPP adjustment of the main accounts, following the proposals of ARS6. It was a recommendation rather than a requirement and was widely ignored. The statement contains a useful exposition of the technique, with numerical illustrations.

In 1974, the Financial Accounting Standards Board (FASB) which had replaced the APB, issued an exposure draft which largely reiterated the contents of APB3:

Financial Reporting in Units of General Purchasing Power, Exposure Draft, Financial Accounting Standards Board, 31 December 1974.

The FASB also initiated a field study, which provided evidence on problems of application:

Field Tests of Financial Reporting in Units of General Purchasing Power, Research Report, Financial Accounting Standards Board, 1977.

A further FASB exposure draft, published in December 1978, proposed a choice between supplementary CPP and current cost disclosure, but concentrated on expounding the current cost technique. The CPP technique associated with this model was a slightly modified form of that proposed in the 1974 exposure draft (e.g. the choice of index and the definitions of 'monetary' items were modified) and was expounded in another exposure draft (strictly a supplement to the 1974 exposure draft):

Constant Dollar Accounting, Financial Accounting Standards Board, March 1979.

Finally, a standard was issued in September 1979, which proposed certain supplementary CPP restatements (of profit and loss account items and holding gains and losses on assets), some of which were applied to a current cost, rather than a historical cost, valuation basis (notably in measuring real holding gains on certain assets):

Statement of Financial Accounting Standards No. 33: Financial Reporting and Changing Prices, Financial Accounting Standards Board, September 1979.

In the United Kingdom, the first pronouncement on the subject by the Accounting Standards Steering Committee (ASSC) was a 'Discussion Paper and Fact Sheet':

Inflation and Accounts, published by Accountancy on behalf of the
   Accounting Standards Steering Committee, 1971.

This largely followed the argument of the earlier *Accounting for
Stewardship in a Period of Inflation*, proposing supplementary CPP
adjustment of traditional accounts. It provided a worked example,
together with brief details of inflation rates, empirical studies of the
effects of inflation on accounts, and accounting practice in the UK
and abroad. The design of its cover led to its popular title, 'the
Tombstone'. It was mainly drafted by Christopher Westwick, who
has provided a useful first-hand account of the development of inflation accounting standards in the UK (Westwick, 1980).

In 1973, the ASSC produced an exposure draft, which followed
the proposals of 'the Tombstone':

Accounting for Changes in the Purchasing Power of Money, Exposure Draft 8 (*ED8*), Accounting Standards Steering Committee,
   January 1973.

This was supplemented by a two-volume working guide:

*Accounting for Inflation, a working guide to the accounting proce-
   dures, Part 1: Text* and *Part 2: Tables*, Institute of Chartered
   Accountants in England and Wales, General Educational Trust,
   1973.

This provides a very helpful guide, with many worked examples, to
the detailed application of the proposed system.

The provisional accounting standard (PSSAP7) published in the
following year did not differ substantially from ED8:

Provisional Statement of Standard Accounting Practice No. 7
   (PSSAP7), *Accounting for Changes in the Purchasing Power of
   Money*, Accounting Standards Steering Committee, May 1974.

This statement was provisional, because, by the time it was issued,
the Sandilands Committee had already been appointed by the government. This committee recommended current cost accounting in
its *Report*, published in 1975, and since then none of the exposure
drafts or standards of the Accounting Standards Steering Committee
has recommended the use of CPP methods.

3 Text-books

There are many text-book treatments of the CPP method.
Amongst those which can be recommended are:

Inflation and the general price level

Accounting Values and Inflation, by W. T. Baxter, McGraw-Hill, 1975.

Inflation Accounting. A Guide for the Accountant and the Financial Analyst, by S. Davidson, C. P. Stickney and R. L. Weil, McGraw-Hill, 1976.

Accounting for Changing Prices, by J. A. Largay III and J. L. Livingstone, Wiley, 1976.

Income and Value Measurement: Theory and Practice, by T. A. Lee, Nelson, 1974 (2nd edition, 1980).

All of these books deal with the application of CPP techniques to current value bases ('real terms accounting'), as well as to the historical cost valuation basis. Davidson, Stickney and Weil gives the most comprehensive account of the detailed computational techniques of CPP, within the framework of the 1974 American Exposure Draft, and Largay and Livingstone also provide a thorough, but more concise, treatment of this aspect of the subject.

Chapter 4: Appendix B   A numerical example of Constant Purchasing Power Accounting

This illustration is based upon the example of 'Old Fred', using the facts as stated in the appendix to Chapter 3. CPP restatement is applied to the historical cost figures, as used in the earlier illustration. The Appendix to Chapter 6 describes the CPP restatement of current value figures to yield what is described as 'real terms accounting'. CPP will be applied here by translating the accounts for each period into £s as of the end of the relevant period, i.e. we shall use the *current* purchasing power variety of CPP, which is that most commonly advocated for practical use. A wide variety of CPP techniques has been developed and, whilst this illustration indicates the more important alternatives which are available, it does not purport to be a comprehensive demonstration of the available techniques: those requiring such a demonstration should refer to the works listed in Appendix A.

The index

The levels of the general price index, and the corresponding periodic increases, assumed in the appendix to Chapter 3, were as follows:

Time	Index level	Period	Percentage increase
t	100		
		1	10
$t+1$	110		
		2	20
$t+2$	132		
		3	10
$t+3$	145.2		
		4	5
$t+4$	152.46		

Period 1

The first stage of CPP restatement in end-of-period £s is to restate the opening balance sheet in end-of-period £s for comparison with the closing balance sheet. This involves increasing each figure in the opening balance sheet in proportion to the rise in the general index during the period, as the opening balance is, in this example, expressed consistently in beginning-of-period £s. The appropriate rise in the general index is 10 per cent for each item (i.e. multiply by 1.1).

Opening Balance Sheet at t restated in £s of $t+1$

	£		£
		Fixed Assets	
Proprietor's Capital [150 × 1.1]	165	Van (at cost) [100 × 1.1]	110
Loan (Aunt Mabel) [50 × 1.1]	55	*Current Assets*	
		Cash [100 × 1.1]	110
	220		220

Figures in square brackets show the calculations necessary to restate the historical figures at t, given in the Appendix to Chapter 3, into £s as of $t+1$ [historical figure × proportionate rise in the general index].

The profit and loss account may be restated as follows:

Profit and Loss Account for Period 1, t to $t+1$
restated in £s of $t+1$

	£
Sales [120 × 1]	120
Less Cost of goods sold [80 × 1.1]	88
Trading profit	32
Less Depreciation [10 × 1.1]	11
Net Profit	21
Add Gain on borrowing [50 × (1.1 − 1)]	5
Total Profit	26

Inflation and the general price level

The explanation for the profit and loss adjustment is as follows:

(1) *Sales* were assumed in this example to take place at the end of the period, so that they are already stated in current £s. If they had occurred at the beginning of the period, they would have been increased by 10 per cent, to £132, but this increase of £12 would have been offset by a corresponding 'loss on holding money' (£120 × 0.1) due to the fact that the cash received from the sales had deteriorated in purchasing power during the period. Thus, the total profit figure would be unchanged. Large firms with many transactions might find it impractical to make adjustments on the basis of a precise dating of each transaction, and an approximate adjustment which is often proposed is to assume an even flow of transactions throughout the period and adjust by reference to an average index. In this example, if we assume that the rise in the index was linear through time, the appropriate index value would be 105, sales would be restated as £126 [= 120 × 1.05], and the corresponding 'loss on holding money' would be £6.

(2) *Goods sold* were assumed in this example to be purchased at the beginning of the period. Cost of goods sold is therefore increased by the full 10 per cent rise in the index to £88. If the goods had been bought at the end of the period, no restatement of their cost would have been necessary (as in the case of sales) but there would have been a corresponding 'loss on holding money' of £8, due to the fact that the £80 used to purchase the goods had declined in general purchasing power while it was held during the period. As in the case of sales, precise dating of purchases may not be possible in practice and averaging devices may be used to give an approximate adjustment.

(3) *Depreciation* is adjusted by the rise in the general price level since the asset was acquired (10 per cent), so that the depreciation charge represents an appropriate proportion of the cost of the asset expressed in end of period £s (i.e. the charge can be calculated either as [10 × 1.1] or as a proportion of restated cost [110 × 1/10], the two bases being equivalent).

(4) *The gain on borrowing* is one of the most controversial features of CPP accounting. It represents the decline in purchasing power of the loan, which, as explained in the text of the chapter, implies a lightening of the real burden of debt on the firm (Fred)

at the expense of the creditor (Aunt Mabel). There has been a great deal of controversy as to whether the gain on borrowing (and the corresponding loss on holding money) should be regarded as part of profit or merely credited to a reserve, especially when the borrowing is long-term, so that the gain might be regarded as not realisable in the immediate future. When interest is paid on loans, there is a strong case for offsetting the gain on borrowing against the interest payment, as the interest payment should include compensation for any inflationary loss which was anticipated by the lender at the time when the loan was made.

One general aspect of the Profit and Loss Account is that some proposals for CPP accounting advocate restatement in average-for-the-year prices. This has the advantage that sales figures require no adjustment, so that there is a direct correspondence between the figure reported in the profit and loss account and the amount actually realised and, if a replacement cost valuation basis is used, there is a correspondence between the reported cost of goods sold and replacement cost at the time when the goods were disposed of. However, if the closing balance sheet is expressed in end-of-period £s, a profit and loss account in average-for-the-period £s means that the two statements are not expressed in strictly comparable units. This issue is discussed by Edwards and Bell (1961, p. 253).

This restated closing balance sheet is as follows:

Closing Balance Sheet, at $t + 1$, restated in £s of $t + 1$

	£			£
Proprietor's Capital				
Opening balance (at t)		Van (at cost) $[100 \times 1.1]$		110
$[150 \times 1.1]$	165	*Less* depreciation $[10 \times 1.1]$		11
Add Profit for the period				99
(as in restated Profit				
and Loss Account)	26			
	191	*Current Assets*		
Less Drawings	30	Stock (at cost) $[20 \times 1.1]$	22	
Closing balance (at $t + 1$)	161	Cash	90	
Loan	50			112
	211			211

Inflation and the general price level

The restatement is different from that of the opening balance sheet because it distinguishes between monetary and non-monetary items. The monetary items, cash and the loan, are fixed in monetary value, so that it would be unrealistic to state them at the amounts which they ought to assume in order to maintain constant real value (£55 in the case of the loan, but no adjustment necessary in this example for cash, since it is assumed to have been received only at the end of the period). Thus, the closing balance sheet assesses monetary items at their fixed nominal money value, and non-monetary items at their real historical cost, i.e. original cost revised by reference to a general price index. The rôle of the restated opening balance sheet is different: it does not purport to state year-end values, but merely provides a benchmark for comparative purposes, showing the period-end equivalent of the opening position. Thus, the restated opening proprietor's capital in the closing balance sheet (£165) is the same as that in the restated opening balance sheet, and the comparison of the two balance sheets lies behind the calculation of the gain on borrowing (£55−£50).

The non-monetary assets in the closing balance sheet are valued at historical cost adjusted by the change in the general index since acquisition. In the present example, both assets are assumed to have been acquired at time t, so that they are both subject to a 10 per cent adjustment. It should be noted that, in most practical proposals for CPP, an upper limit on restatement of non-monetary assets is imposed by the requirement that they should appear at restated historical cost or current market value, whichever is the lower: this is intended to ensure prudent valuation.

The proprietor's capital, as already noted, starts with the beginning-of-period balance, restated in end-of-period £s. To this is added the profit from the restated Profit and Loss Account, which is already expressed in end-of-period £s. Drawings are deducted and do not require restatement in this case because they were assumed to take place at the end of the period. If the transaction had taken place at the beginning of the period, drawings would have been restated as £33 [=30 × 1.1] and there would have been a corresponding reduction in the loss on holding money, had there been a money balance out of which drawings could have been paid.

Period 2

The same basic procedures are adopted for Period 2, and for sub-

Inflation and the general price level

sequent periods, although certain details assumed in the example for
these periods, but not for Period 1, make it worthwhile following the
example through to the end of Fred's career ($t + 4$).

Firstly, the closing balance sheet for Period 1, expressed in £s of
$t + 1$, becomes the opening balance sheet for Period 2 and is restated,
for comparative purposes, in £s of $t + 2$:

Opening Balance Sheet, at $t + 1$ restated in £s of $t + 2$

	£			£
Proprietor's Capital		*Fixed Assets*		
Closing balance (at $t + 1$)		Van (at cost) $[110 \times 1.2]$		132.00
$[161 \times 1.2]$	193.20	*Less* accumulated deprecia-		
		tion $[11 \times 1.2]$		13.20
Loan $[50 \times 1.2]$	60.00			118.80
		Current Assets		
		Stock $[22 \times 1.2]$	26.40	
		Cash $[90 \times 1.2]$	108.00	134.40
	253.20			253.20

Inflation in Period 2 is at a 20 per cent rate, so that the proportionate
increase in the various items is 1.2, but otherwise the procedure is
identical to that adopted in Period 1.

The Profit and Loss Account is then re-stated, again using the
same basic technique as for Period 1:

Profit and Loss Account for period 2, $t + 1$ to $t + 2$
restated in £s of $t + 2$

		£
Sales		135.00
Less	Cost of goods sold $[(22 \times 1.2) + (91 \times 1.2)]$	135.60
	Trading Loss	.60
Add	Depreciation $[10 \times 1.32]$	13.20
	Net Loss	13.80
Less	Gain on net monetary items $[64 \times 0.2]$	12.80
	Total Loss	1.00

The individual components of the profit and loss account are subject to the same assumptions and limitations as were described above
for Period 1. The following additional features should be noted:

103

Inflation and the general price level

(1) Cost of goods sold now has two components: opening stocks and purchases during the period (less closing stocks, adopting the First-in-First-out convention). Each of these components should be adjusted separately, as they will, in practice, typically involve different time lags and therefore different adjustment factors. In the present example, both elements are subject to the same adjustment factor (1.2) because opening stocks have already been restated in beginning-of-period £s and it is (artificially) assumed that purchases were made at the very beginning of the period and are therefore also denominated in £s of this date.

(2) The depreciation charge has been expressed as the historical cost written off (£10), adjusted proportionately to the rise in the general price index since the date at which the historical cost occurred (1.32). It could equivalently be expressed as an appropriate proportion ($^1/_{10}$) of the historical cost of the asset expressed in end-of-period £s in the balance sheet (£132).

(3) The gain on net monetary assets is the gain on borrowing (calculated on the same basis as for Period 1), less the loss on holding monetary assets, which is the mirror-image of the gain on borrowing. The borrowings which give rise to the gain are the long-term loan (from Aunt Mabel) of £50, and the £52 credit given by the supplier of purchases, both of which existed throughout the period and therefore gave rise to gains of £10 [$=50 \times 0.2$] and £10.40 [$=52 \times 0.2$] respectively. The loss on holding money is on the £38 [the £90 opening cash balances, less £52 paid for purchases at the beginning of the period] which was held throughout the period: the loss of purchasing power is £7.60 [$=38 \times 0.2$]. Since all of the monetary items were held for the full period and therefore have a common inflation factor applied to them, we can calculate the net gain of £12.80 [$=£10.00 + £10.40 - £7.60$] more simply by applying the inflation factor to their net amount, a net loan of £64 [$=£50 + £52 - £38$].

The adjusted closing balance sheet for Period 2 is as follows:

Inflation and the general price level

Closing Balance Sheet at $t + 2$ restated in £s of $t + 2$

	£			£
Proprietor's Capital		*Fixed Assets*		
Opening balance (at $t + 1$)	193.20	Van (at cost) $[110 \times 1.32]$		132.00
Less Total loss for Period	1.00	*Less* accumulated deprecia-		
		tion $[20 \times 1.32]$		26.40
	192.20			
Less Drawings	106.00			105.60
	86.20	*Current Assets*		
Loan	50.00	Stock $[13 \times 1.2]$	15.60	
Current Liabilities		Debtors	15.00	
Creditors	52.00	Cash	52.00	82.60
	188.20			188.20

The proprietor's capital in the balance sheet starts with the opening balance in £s of $t + 2$, as shown in the restated opening balance sheet. The loss which is deducted is taken from the restated profit and loss account and the drawings are assumed to be made at $t + 2$, so that no restatement is required. The 'monetary' items (the loan, creditors, debtors and cash) all appear at their fixed monetary amounts and do not require restatement. The non-monetary items, stock and the van, are restated by reference to the change in the general price index since their date of acquisition: in the case of the van, this is equivalent to cost, less depreciation, in the restated opening balance sheet, less the additional depreciation for the period, charged in the restated profit and loss account.

One point of general interest is that, if comparison is required with earlier periods, the figures for earlier periods should be restated in current £s. When the earlier figures are expressed consistently in £s of a given date, this is merely a matter of multiplying all the figures by the proportionate rise in the general index from that date to the present, as was done with the $t + 1$ balance sheet when it was restated in $t + 2$ £s. For example, this procedure could be adopted for the restated Period 1 profit and loss account, all of the figures being multiplied by 1.2, in order to express it in £s of $t + 2$.

Period 3

The closing balance sheet for Period 2, at $t + 2$, is the opening balance sheet for Period 3, and is restated in £s of $t + 3$ for comparative

Inflation and the general price level

purposes, and the profit and loss account and closing balance sheet for Period 3 are derived on the basis of the same techniques as were used in Periods 1 and 2.

Opening Balance Sheet, at $t + 2$ restated in £s of $t + 3$

	£		£
Proprietor's Capital		*Fixed Assets*	
Closing balance (at $t + 2$)		Van (at cost) [132 × 1.1]	145.20
[86.2 × 1.1]	94.82	*Less* accumulated deprecia-	
Loan [50 × 1.1]	55.00	tion [26.40 × 1.1]	29.04
			116.16
Current Liabilities		*Current Assets*	
Creditors [52 × 1.1]	57.20	Stock [15.60 × 1.1] 17.16	
		Debtors [15 × 1.1] 16.50	
		Cash [52 × 1.1] 57.20	
			90.86
	207.02		207.02

Profit and Loss Account for period 3, $t + 2$ to $t + 3$ restated in £s of $t + 3$

		£
Sales		180.00
Less	Cost of goods sold [(15.6 + 144) × 1.1]	175.56
	Trading Profit	4.44
Less	Depreciation [10 × 1.452]	14.52
	Net Loss	10.08
Add	Gain on net monetary items [215 × 0.1]	21.50
	Total Profit	11.42

Note: Net monetary items held during the period were creditors £180, plus loan £50, less cash £15, a net borrowing of £215. With 10 per cent inflation, this gives rise to a net gain on borrowing of £21.50.

Closing Balance Sheet, at $t + 3$ restated in £s of $t + 3$

	£			£
Proprietor's Capital		*Fixed Assets*		
Opening balance (at $t + 2$)	94.82	Van (at cost) $[100 \times 1.452]$		145.20
Add Total profit for the		*Less* accumulated deprecia-		
period	11.42	tion $[£29.04 + £14.52]$		43.56
	106.24			101.64
Less Drawings	10.00			
		Current Assets		
Closing balance (at $t + 3$)	96.24	Stock $[36 \times 1.1]$	39.60	
Loan	50.00	Debtors	20.00	
		Cash	165.00	
Current Liabilities				224.60
Creditors	180.00			
	326.24			326.24

Period 4

Opening Balance Sheet, at $t + 3$ restated in £s of $t + 4$

	£			£
Proprietor's Capital		*Fixed Assets*		
Closing balance sheet		Van (at cost)		
(at $t + 3$)		$[145.20 \times 1.05]$		152.46
$[96.24 \times 1.05]$	101.05	*Less* accumulated deprecia-		
Loan $[50 \times 1.05]$	52.50	tion $[43.56 \times 1.05]$		45.74
				106.72
Current Liabilities		*Current Assets*		
Creditors $[180 \times 1.05]$	189.00	Stock $[39.60 \times 1.05]$	41.58	
		Debtors $[20 \times 1.05]$	21.00	
		Cash $[165 \times 1.05]$	173.25	
				235.83
	342.55			342.55

Note: All figures are rounded to the nearest penny.

Profit and Loss Account for period 4, $t + 3$ to $t + 4$
restated in £s of $t + 4$

	£
Sales	44.00
Less Cost of goods sold [39.60 × 1.05]	41.58
Trading Profit	2.42
Add Gain on net monetary items	
[(50 + 180 − 20 − 165) × 0.05]	2.25
	4.67
Add Realised holding gain	13.28
Total Profit	17.95

Note: The realised real holding gain arises on disposal of the van. Its written down value at the beginning of the period (in $t + 4$ £s) was £106.72 and it was sold for £120, the difference being the gain, expressed in $t + 4$ £s (i.e. it is a 'real' gain).

Closing Balance Sheet, at $t + 4$ restated in £s of $t + 4$

	£		£
Proprietor's Capital		*Current Assets*	
Opening balance (at $t + 3$)	101.05	Cash	169.00
Add Total profit for the			
period	17.95		
	119.00		
Loan	50.00		
	169.00		169.00

Note: This balance sheet is drawn up after the liquidation of the assets but prior to the repayment of the loan and the final withdrawal of the proprietor's funds.

Life-cycle profitability

The total profits of the business over its lifetime, on three different bases, are reported below. Firstly, we show historical cost profits, as reported in the appendix to Chapter 3. Secondly, we report total CPP profits, expressed in £s of the end of each individual period, as reported above, and thirdly we restate the CPP profits in terms of constant £s of $t + 4$. The comparison of the totals of the three columns shows that the different methods yield different aggregate profits, and comparison of the figures for different years shows that the different methods give a different view of the relative profitability of operations in different periods.

Period	Historical Cost Profit (£)	CPP profit in end of period £s	Adjustment factor	CPP profit in £s of $t + 4$
1	30	26.00	(1.2)(1.1)(1.05)	36.04
2	14	(1.00)	(1.1)(1.05)	(1.15)
3	13	11.42	(1.05)	11.99
4	58	17.95	1.0	17.95
Total	115	54.37		64.83

Note: Brackets indicate loss.

5

Current value systems 1: valuation

1 The problem of valuation

The earlier discussion has shown that it is possible to separate the problem of valuation from that of inflation, if we accept that inflation implies a decline in the general purchasing power of money.[1] Even in the absence of general inflation, it is possible that individual prices will change, and in the presence of inflation it is possible that individual prices will not move directly in line with the rate of inflation, as measured by a general index. Thus, in the first case, historical cost will not be an accurate representation of current value, and, in the second case, neither historical cost nor historical cost adjusted by a general index (CPP) will give an accurate representation of current value. Therefore, if some indication of current value is considered to be an important feature of accounts assets and liabilities (liabilities being negative assets) will require revaluation.

The case for reporting current values is strong, but not overwhelming. If accounts are supposed to give information relevant to decisions about the allocation of assets and liabilities or claims on them (such as the proprietor's net worth) then current values are relevant information because they represent the value of opportunities which are currently available, whether it be replacement (in the case of replacement cost, RC), sale (in the case of net realisable value, NRV) or value in current use (discounted present value of future cash flows, PV). This immediately raises the problem of whether to choose any single current valuation method and, if so, which one. Alternatively, it would be possible to choose different valuation methods for different assets (as in the case of Value to the Owner, which is discussed later in this chapter), or a variety of current values could be reported for each asset in the balance sheet. This topic will be discussed further in a later section. The question of aggregation and the converse problem of allocation also arise, but the main practical objection to current valuation is usually the subjectivity involved. This has been an important issue in the recent world-wide debate on Current Cost Accounting, particularly in relation to estimating value in current use (PV).

The above argument relates to the reporting of current values in the balance sheet. There could also be benefits to be obtained from income statements based on current values. However, we saw in Chapter 2 that current-value income is equivalent to ideal economic income only under very restrictive conditions, and Revsine's (1970) demonstration that, under certain conditions, current value holding gains on assets would measure windfall gains, whilst current operating profit would measure sustainable income, serves to demonstrate the restrictive nature of the conditions, rather than to encourage the belief that it is possible to measure economic income under realistic conditions. A less compelling but more plausible reason for basing income measures on current values is that advanced by Edwards and Bell (1961), that current values provide a means of providing an *ex post* account of the economic progress of the firm to date, using the latest available market-validated information (Tippett, 1979, provides an elaboration of this point of view). An assessment of economic income, or the economic value of the firm as a whole, requires taking a view as to the prospective cash flows of the firm. Current values may be a relevant input in forming such a view. This will lead to an assessment of the value of the firm by discounting the prospective cash flows, and the excess of this over the sum of the current value of the assets of the firm is subjective goodwill.

An alternative case for current value based income measures might be in terms of the maintainable consumption or 'standard stream' (Hicks No. 3) concept of income. This type of concept has often seemed to underlie the recent debate on current cost accounting (one possible form of current value accounting), especially in the discussions of 'distributable profit' or 'distributable operating flow', which can be interpreted as being close to Hicks' idea of maintainable consumption (e.g. Sale and Scapens, 1978), although the Sandilands Report (paragraphs 100 to 103) based its central concept of income on the 'Hicks No. 1' capital maintenance model. However, if current value income measurements are to be justified on consumption maintenance grounds, the precise assumptions necessary to sustain the case need to be explored more thoroughly than is typically the case in published work on the subject. It seems probable that a precise measure of 'Hicks No. 3' income will emerge only under fairly restrictive assumptions about the future course of individual asset prices, the general price level, and interest rates and will therefore rely heavily on subjective expectations. The most thorough attempt to apply the standard stream model to business accounting is by Scott (1976): this demonstrates clearly the importance of expectations in this approach, e.g. the appropriate treatment of real holding gains on stocks depends upon the extent to which the increase in the real cost of stocks will be passed on in the selling price.

If the case for current value accounting is based upon its usefulness as an approximation to the 'Hicks No. 1' capital maintenance measure of income, an important issue is the definition of the capital to be maintained intact. This is also an important issue if we regard current value accounting as a set of relevant data rather than a set of precise measurements of economic variables. There are three broad definitions of capital maintenance which tend to be associated with current value systems, money capital, real proprietory capital and entity capital. Money capital is the value of capital in monetary units, irrespective of fluctuations in the value of money, as in a historical cost system. Real proprietory capital implied the adjustment of money capital by an index reflecting changes in the proprietor's purchasing power. A general index is usually advocated for this purpose, in which case, if assets are valued at current prices, we have a form of 'real terms' accounting, as described briefly in the previous chapter and discussed more fully in the next chapter. Entity capital implies the adjustment of money capital to reflect changes in the price of the specific assets held by the firm. It is thereby intended to maintain the accounting entity intact in its specific form. In an extreme approach, this can amount to maintaining the identical physical assets of the entity intact, but this is often moderated, to allow for technical progress and factor substitution due to changing prices, by defining the maintenance of 'operating capacity' as the object of capital maintenance. Another variant of the entity capital maintenance approach is to introduce a proprietory element by means of a 'gearing adjustment'. These alternative concepts of capital maintenance will be discussed in more detail in the next chapter. For the remainder of this chapter, we shall concentrate upon the basic technique of current value accounting, and the choice of valuation base.

2 Basic methods of current value accounting

Current value accounting requires the periodic up-dating of asset values. In terms of book-keeping entries, this implies debiting the asset account, to record the increase in value, and crediting the holding gain. If the holding gain is regarded as a profit, it is transferred to the credit of the Profit and Loss Account, but if it is regarded as a growth of the capital to be maintained intact (as in the case of the entity approach to capital maintenance, described above) it is transferred to the credit of proprietor's capital, as an increase in capital reserves. The latter transfer can be carried out via a Statement of Gains, as in the Sandilands Report's proposals, so that the proprietors are made aware of the gains despite the fact that they are not recognised as profit.

In terms of the algebraic notation used in earlier chapters, the current value balance sheets are as in (4.7) of the previous chapter:

$$P''_t = N''_t + M_t - L_t$$

and

$$P''_{t+1} = N''_{t+1} + M_{t+1} - L_{t+1} \tag{5.1}$$

where N'' indicates current value of non-monetary assets at the relevant date, M and L are of fixed money value, and P'' is the proprietor's net assets under current valuation. When some liabilities, such as long-term loans, are 'non-monetary', fluctuating in money value, they should be revalued and deducted in calculating N'', which should strictly be defined as *net* non-monetary assets. The profit measure under current value accounting, assuming money capital maintenance and no dividend distributions or introductions of new capital, is:

$$Y_{\text{CVA}} = P''_{t+1} - P''_t \tag{5.2}$$

In the transactionless case in which each asset is held throughout the period, we can re-define the closing balance sheet as:

$$P''_{t+1} = N''_t(1 + s) + M_t - L_t \tag{5.3}$$

where s is a specific index measuring the value change of the specific bundle of assets N''_t. Maintaining the nominal money value of capital, and abandoning the accountant's traditional reluctance to recognise gains on holding assets until they are realised, the profit then becomes:

$$Y_{\text{CVA}} = N''_t . s \tag{5.4}$$

If we substitute an entity capital maintenance concept, the holding gain $N''_t . s$ will be regarded as an accretion to capital, and profit will be zero. This is analogous to the current cost accounting measures of operating profit, proposed by the Sandilands Committee, so we can call it Y_{CCA}.

$$Y_{\text{CCA}} = P''_{t+1} - (P''_t + N''_t . s) = 0 \tag{5.5}$$

More generally, if we drop the assumption of the transactionless interval, we can define current value income, on a money capital maintenance basis, as:

$$Y_{\text{CVA}} = P''_{t+1} - P''_t$$
$$= (N''_{t+1} - N''_t) + (M_{t+1} - M_t) - (L_{t+1} - L_t) \tag{5.6}$$

This is broadly what the Sandilands Committee proposed as the basis of its Statement of Gains.[2] The current cost profit proposed by Sandilands uses the entity concept of capital maintenance and is based upon[3] the following model:

$$Y_{\text{CCA}} = P''_{t+1} - (P''_t + N''_t . s)$$
$$= [N''_{t+1} - N''_t(1+s)] + [M_{t+1} - M_t] - [L_{t+1} - L_t] \tag{5.7}$$

$N''_t . s$ is the total net holding gain. Since the composition of N can now change through time, this holding gain should be calculated by reference to changes in the value of each specific asset over the period for which it is held. Thus s is now not merely an index of the change in value of the asset held during the period expressed as a proportion of the initial assets. The appropriate computational procedure would be first to calculate the total net holding gains on all non-monetary assets held during the period. This sum is defined as $N''_t . s$ and divided by N''_t to yield a measure of s. Thus s is the end product of the calculation rather than an ingredient in making it, and in practice it would be unnecessary to carry the calculation so far as the calculation of s, because the total net holding gain, $N''_t . s$, rather than s, is the centre of interest. This procedure enables entity capital maintenance to be based upon maintaining the value of a shifting population of capital assets, rather than being tied rigidly to assets held at the beginning of the year.

There are, of course, alternative concepts of capital maintenance. There are variants upon the entity approach, and there is the competing concept of maintaining real proprietory capital, which was broadly defined, in algebraic terms, in equations (4.8) and (4.9) of the previous chapter. The alternative concepts of capital maintenance will be discussed in the next chapter. We now turn to the alternative definitions and interpretations of what we have hitherto defined broadly as 'current value'.

3 The choice of current values

The choice of current valuation base is a very complex issue. Not only are there three basic types of value available (RC, NRV and PV, as defined earlier), but within each type a number of variations is possible. In choosing between valuation bases we may face the problem that one basis is appropriate for valuing assets in the balance sheet but another basis is appropriate for assessing changes in assets and capital for the purposes of the profit and loss account (Macdonald, 1974). Thus, if we insist on having articulated accounts[4] prepared on a single consistent valuation basis, we may be unable to implement our preferred valuation basis for each statement. Alternatively, we may wish to prepare a variety of statements on different valuation bases: this will eliminate the first problem but may raise a new problem of complexity, since the user of accounts will now be faced with a choice of different balance sheets and profit and loss accounts prepared on different valuation bases (Chambers, 1972).

Another approach is to use a valuation rule, such as value to the owner, which selects the valuation of a particular asset according to such circumstances as the relative values arising from the alternative bases. This does allow more than one valuation basis to be used in the accounts, whilst avoiding the complexity arising from having alternative values of the same asset, but it does not avoid the articulation problem, i.e. the problem of having the balance sheet and the profit and loss account value the same assets on the same basis. It may also introduce an aggregation problem, since the aggregate value of assets now represents a collection of values using different bases.

As a prelude to the discussion of the choice of valuation bases, we shall briefly describe the three broad bases and the case for each of them, in turn.

Current value systems 1

(i) Replacement Cost

Replacement cost is probably the basis favoured by the majority of writers on current value accounting and it has found most favour in practice. Early advocates of replacement cost were Schmidt (1921 and 1930) in Germany and Limperg in Holland. Schmidt and other members of the German school influenced Sweeney (1936), who advocated replacement cost valuation as the ideal base upon which to implement his system of stabilised accounting (a form of CPP adjustment). Schmidt's ideas were also influential in shaping recent proposals for a form of Current Cost Accounting in West Germany (Coenenberg and Macharzina, 1976). The Dutch school was influential in the adoption of a form of replacement cost accounting by some companies in the Netherlands, notably by Philips of Eindhoven, whose system of accounting was designed by Limperg's pupil, Goudeket. Replacement cost was also favoured as a valuation base by Edwards and Bell (1961) and later by Revsine (1973) in the United States and has been proposed in recent pronouncements by the Securities and Exchange Commission (1975) and the FASB (1979b).[5] In Australia, Mathews and Grant (1958) and Gynther (1966) have been notable advocates of replacement cost accounting, although recent professional and official proposals in Australia (e.g. Institute of Chartered Accountants in Australia, 1975, and Mathews Report, 1975) and New Zealand (Richardson Committee Report, 1976) have tended to follow the 'value to the owner' approach, as advocated by Baxter (1967 and 1975) and others (including Wright, 1970, in Australia) and adopted in the Sandilands Report (1975) and subsequent professional proposals for reform in the UK.[6] Value to the owner leads to replacement cost in most cases in practice (Gee and Peasnell, 1976) but it is based upon different reasoning and will be discussed separately.[7]

In view of the wide range of writers who have supported replacement cost accounting, and the wide variety of their proposals, it is impossible to do justice to all of their arguments. However, it is clear that, to the individual firm, replacement cost is a cost rather than a value, although it might, under certain circumstances, be equal to a value (such as 'value to the owner', in many cases), i.e. replacement cost represents the cost of acquiring an asset (which Edwards and Bell describe as an 'entry' value), not the value attaching to an asset already held. It thus has an obvious relevance to the assessment of

116

costs in the profit and loss account. If we adopt a 'Hicks No. 1' capital maintenance approach to income measurement, it seems intuitively reasonable that replacement cost should be charged to profit because this allows for replacement, and hence for capital maintenance, although more thorough investigation raises the problem of defining what is meant by 'replacement'. If, alternatively, we adopt a 'Hicks No. 3' consumption maintenance approach, it again seems intuitively reasonable that we will maintain consumption levels in future if we replace whatever was used up in creating the output, but again the concept of replacement requires closer definition.

There is, in fact, a variety of concepts of replacement. At one extreme, there is the concept of physical replacement (favoured, for example, by Edwards and Bell (1961) and aptly described by Bell (1971) as 'reproduction cost') which charges against profit the replacement cost of the assets actually used up in the course of the period. Where there is technical progress or where changes in relative factor prices have caused a change in the optimal productive method (a case discussed by Petri and Gelfand, 1979) there is a divergence between the cost of physical replacement and the cost of replacing the equivalent service. Furthermore, in such conditions, it is quite likely that the firm will not wish to replace the equivalent service, if demand for the product is declining in favour of a substitute product. 'Value to the owner' attempts to deal with the latter problem by substituting alternative values (the higher of present value in use or net realisable value on disposal) when replacement is not justified.

If we follow this line of argument very far, we shall arrive at a point at which replacement cost is used merely as a surrogate for economic value, a position explored by Revsine (1973 and 1976), Barton (1974) and Cook and Holzmann (1976). This implies that replacement cost depreciation or appreciation (holding gains) is a measure of the change in the discounted present value of the firm resulting from owning the asset or assets in question. This equivalence will hold only under highly restrictive conditions and is not, therefore, a sound basis for a practical accounting system.

The alternative approach is to adhere strictly to one of two broad concepts: replacement of the physical object ('reproduction') or replacement of the physical service. Both of these approaches avoid the fundamental difficulties involved in imputing an economic value to services, which would lead inevitably to some attempt to assess

117

economic income. If we adopt the cost of reproduction, the profit and loss account will be charged with the current cost of production under the techniques actually employed (by way of the depreciation charge, and the charge for stocks). Under changing conditions (of prices or technology) this will have poor predictive ability, but it will fulfil Edwards and Bell's objective[8] of providing an *ex post* description of the activities of the firm based upon market purchase prices prevailing at the time of each transaction. It will also lead to a 'holding gain', indicating the difference between historical purchase price and price at the time of use. Thus, the year-end balance sheet will show unrealised holding gains (or losses) representing the excess (or deficiency) of replacement cost over (or under) historical cost of assets carried forward for future use. There is, of course, no reason to believe that these assets will be put to a use which justifies current replacement cost, or that replacement cost will remain the same until the time of use. The uncertainty surrounding future replacement cost at the time of use is one reason which has been advanced for separating unrealised holding gains from realised holding gains.[9]

With regard to the choice of the reproduction cost of the service as the basis of replacement cost, the replacement of the service seems to be most appropriate in the calculation of an operating profit which reflects current costs. If the 'reproduction' and the 'service' bases are not identical, this implies that the assets currently used by the firm are not those which it would use were it to seek to purchase the services at their lowest current price in the market place. Thus, the physical assets used by the firm have ceased to be 'best current practice' assets and the firm has sustained a holding loss which should be reported when it occurs, the assets being written down to the lower cost of replacing the services embodied in them. Subsequent use of the assets should be charged to profit or loss on the new, lower 'replacement of service' valuation. In assessing the cost of replacement of the service, an appropriate allowance should be made for changes in the cost of other productive factors which are associated with the use of the asset. For example, if the alternative asset economised on the use of fuel and labour, an estimate of the present value of these savings should be deducted from the cost of the new asset in calculating the replacement cost of the service embodied in the existing asset.

At this point, it might be objected that the physical asset might, in such a case, have maintained its market value because of its value in alternative uses, so that the 'holding loss' is due merely to the firm's mis-management of its resources. Such mis-management might reasonably result in a 'holding loss', but the balance sheet will show the asset at a lower value than it might command in the market. It would clearly be of value to shareholders and other external users of accounts to know that the market value is higher than the balance sheet value of the asset in such a case. For example, in calculating a rate of return on capital employed, it would seem appropriate to include in the denominator (capital employed) the asset at its full market value: this represents the revenue forgone by retaining the asset rather than disposing of it in the market.

Two aspects of this argument should be noted. Firstly, it is not an argument about the basis of assessing replacement cost, but about the greater relevance of an alternative valuation basis, net realisable value. Secondly, it illustrates the possibility of a divergence between the valuation basis appropriate to a balance sheet and that appropriate to a profit and loss statement. This is because we have imputed different uses to the two statements, but these uses do seem to be plausible. The replacement cost profit and loss statement calculates operating profit after charging for replacement of the services used at current costs, and the holding gains (or losses) show how the firm has gained (or lost) by buying assets before the time of their use. The replacement cost balance sheet shows the accumulated, unexpired replacement costs of assets. In a continuing business, this has some meaning because this balance sheet records the current replacement cost of future services which have been bought in advance of use and which will be charged against future revenues when realised. However, the example of choice between reproduction of the asset and replacement of the service produced an instance in which we might also like to know the net realisable value of the asset (which Edwards and Bell call an 'exit value') in order to measure the opportunity cost of retaining a specific asset for use in the firm rather than selling it. The general merits of net realisable value will be discussed later. For the present, it should be observed that a replacement cost balance sheet by itself fails to provide some important information about the value of the firm's assets. Such information would be of value to any user who wishes to assess the potential returns to making alternative uses of the firm's assets, rather than assuming that retention and replacement in the present activities of the firm are inevitable.

Whatever the measure of replacement cost used, we are likely, in practice, to encounter the twin problems of allocation and aggregation (Thomas, 1974). Allocation arises in the valuation of individual assets both across assets and through time. Across assets, we have the problem of attributing jointly incurred costs to individual assets: this is likely to arise most obviously in the case of work-in-progress. Through time, we have the problem of allocating the capital cost of a durable asset across the individual periods during which it is used. In both cases, the problem could be avoided if there were markets for all of the items for which replacement cost was being estimated, but in practice it is likely to be difficult to establish a market purchase price for part-processed work-in-progress or part-used capital assets. The problem of aggregation also arises when assets are interdependent; replacement cost of one asset individually might be either more or less expensive than if we were to replace it together with all of the other assets with which it is associated in the productive processes.[10] Thus, if we were estimating the replacement cost of a whole factory, as we might for insurance purposes, we would probably use different asset prices from those which would be applied to estimate the replacement cost of those assets which need to be replaced as a result of normal wear and tear in an accounting year. The latter level of aggregation is more likely to meet the needs of users of a profit and loss account based on replacement cost, as it indicates the level of replacement cost which is likely to be incurred in the maintenance of the present level of productive activity.

Another difficulty in implementing certain forms of replacement cost accounting (particularly the Edwards and Bell form) is in making the distinction between 'holding gains' and 'operating gains'. More precisely, the problem is one of establishing the exact meaning of replacement cost, particularly with respect to timing. Since production takes time it is extremely difficult to define a precise moment of 'use' at which replacement cost can be established, particularly in the case of stocks and work-in-progress. The precise definition of replacement cost does, of course, determine the division of realised gains between operating profits (against which replacement cost of assets used is debited) and holding gains (to which the difference between historical cost and replacement cost at the time of use is credited). Moreover, the value of the dichotomy between operating gains and holding gains has been questioned[11] on the ground that production and asset holding are essentially joint decisions in many instances. Whether or not these criticisms invalidate the usefulness of the dichotomy depends partly upon materiality (how important is the arbitrary timing element in replacement cost) and partly upon fact (whether the decisions are in fact separate or joint). A further issue, which is also one of fact, is the question as to whether the dichotomy improves the ability of users of accounts to predict the future course of events.

In conclusion, there are two types of basic approach to replacement cost accounting. One sees it as providing surrogates for economic value (in the balance sheet) and income (in the profit and loss account). This relationship has been demonstrated to hold only under very restrictive circumstances. The alternative approach regards replacement cost accounting as providing data relevant to the assessment of the economic progress of the firm and the estimation (but not the precise calculation) of economic value and income by the users of accounts. This approach is probably best characterised by the work of Edwards and Bell. The 'relevant data' provided by the replacement cost profit and loss account are a statement of the operating profit based on current replacement costs and a statement of both realised and unrealised holding gains, due to the change in purchase prices between the time of purchase of assets and the time of use (or, in the case of unrealised gains, the closing balance sheet). The operating profit assesses the *ex post* profitability of operating activities and will be of direct use in predicting the future only if prices, costs and level of activity are expected to remain the same. The precise definition of replacement cost presents a number of conceptual problems, as does the dichotomy between holding gains and operating gains. The replacement cost balance sheet shows the current replacement cost of assets held for future use by the firm. Here also there are conceptual problems, but a more important limitation of the replacement cost balance sheet is that its valuations are based upon the continuity of the business in its present form and do not show the market value of the assets which might be realised by their disposal. Even if we accept the continuity assumption, replacement costs do not indicate the value which the firm will realise from the use of the assets: this will depend upon the operations of future periods.[12] Thus, a replacement cost balance sheet has the advantage over a historical cost balance sheet that it is based upon contemporary rather than historical values, but it shares with it the limitation that, taken by itself, it is based upon costs rather than values and gives no direct indication of the amounts for which the assets of the firm could be sold.

Current value systems 1

(ii) Net Realisable Value

One system which remedies this problem, at the price of raising new problems of its own, is net realisable value accounting. In many ways, net realisable value is an intuitively appealing valuation basis for accounts. If accounts purport to report values, then a natural interpretation of value is the amount of money for which an asset can be exchanged in the market place (net realisable value being selling price, less selling costs). The balance sheet lists assets and attributes values to them, and it is not surprising that unsophisticated users tend to assume that its valuations are based on selling prices (Tweedie, 1977, refers to net realisable value as an 'intuitive concept', and reports an empirical study which supports this view).

This is not to say that all advocates of net realisable value in accounts are unsophisticated. On the contrary, amongst academic writers, those who have advocated net realisable value have tended to argue with greater-than-average sophistication and at a higher-than-average theoretical level.

One of the earlier advocates of the incorporation of net realisable values in accounts was Canning (1929), who made the first systematic critique of accounting practice from the standpoint of economic theory. Canning proposed that assets should be valued at net realisable values when, as in the case of inventories, a 'direct valuation' is possible. In other instances (as in the case of fixed plant and machinery held for future use) Canning proposed 'indirect valuation' methods based upon 'opportunity differences', which are essentially similar to the 'value to the owner' rules developed by subsequent writers, and discussed later in this chapter. Canning was not, therefore, a single-minded advocate of net realisable value, his main concern being to change the orientation of accounting from backward-looking historical cost to forward-looking measures which are more compatible with rational economic decisions. He was aware that different information might serve different purposes and might be subject to different degrees of uncertainty, and he was willing to use a variety of valuation bases, including the use of alternative valuations for the same asset. However, Canning was certainly a pioneer in proposing the incorporation of market selling prices in accounts. In this context it is relevant that Canning shared his contemporaries' pre-occupation with the balance sheet as 'the major end-product of accounting' (Canning, 1929, p. 179), although he was true to his

122

Fisherian economic theory in recognising that, even on a current value basis, the sum of the net assets of the firm will not equal the economic value of the firm as a whole (the discounted present value of future net returns), the difference being goodwill.[13]

Perhaps the best-known early advocate of current market value was Kenneth MacNeal, whose *Truth in Accounting* (1939) has achieved classic status as a polemic in favour of current value accounting. He approached the problem as a practical accountant, rather than a theorist, but his proposals have many features which have been supported by subsequent theoretical writers, notably Chambers (1966). It is notable that MacNeal was financial controller of an investment trust company, and subsequently a property company, both types of activity being associated with investment in durable assets which are held with a view to possible re-sale, not with a presumption that they will be used up in the productive activities of the business. Indeed, the inspiration for MacNeal's work was his (successful) attempt to persuade the auditors of his investment trust to accept accounts based upon current market values of the investments. The background to MacNeal's work has been thoroughly explored by Zeff (1981), who points out that MacNeal stopped short of advocating net realisable values, preferring middle market prices (between buying and selling price) when buying and selling prices differed.

Of contemporary accounting theorists, the two most closely associated with the advocacy of net realisable value are Chambers (1966) and Sterling (1970), although Ross (1969) has provided a practitioner's view of the case for current values, including net realisable values in some cases. Chambers has been a particularly prolific writer on the subject, much of his work being listed, with a commentary, in Chambers (1977). He calls his system Continuously Contemporaneous Accounting, and this has been dubbed CoCoA, to differentiate it from the replacement-cost-oriented Current Cost Accounting (CCA). Net realisable value was also considered as a possible valuation base by Edwards and Bell (1961, Chapter 3) who propounded a model of 'realisable profit' on this basis. Their final choice was to favour replacement cost (a decision defended by Edwards, 1975), as incorporated in their model of 'business profit', as preferable to net realisable value (which they refer to, somewhat imprecisely, as 'opportunity cost') for general purposes, but they emphasise that both measures are of potential usefulness.

Although these various writers emphasise different reasons for using net realisable values, the broad case can be summarised as follows. Firstly, and probably most important, is the usefulness of current net realisable value as an indication of an important opportunity facing the firm, that of disposing of the asset. Chambers refers to this as the 'current cash equivalent' of an asset, and correctly emphasises that this is a relevant value in making a wide range of decisions and appraisals, although he is perhaps at fault in neglecting the merits of alternative valuations: rational economic decisions are usually based upon a *comparison* of values of alternative dispositions of assets, not on the absolute amount of one value in isolation (Whittington, 1974). Edwards and Bell ascribe similar merits to net realisable value by describing it as 'opportunity cost', although in doing this they also are over-stating its merits: opportunity cost uses the *best* alternative revenue forgone, whereas net realisable value represents one of several alternatives which may represent the best (see p. 219, n. 23).

Secondly, there is a group of arguments surrounding the measurement properties of net realisable value. These arguments are particularly associated with Chambers (1966) and Sterling (1970). It is claimed that net realisable values have properties of additivity and objectivity which conform with the requirements of measurement theory better than do alternative measures. Powerful support for net realisable values has come from Thomas (1969 and 1974), whose incisive work on the allocation problem leads him to the conclusion that net realisable values are the only values which avoid completely the allocation problem.[14] However, Thomas does not accept that net realisable values avoid the aggregation problem: the market value of a group of assets valued together is not necessarily equal to the sum of that of the individual assets. Some of the other arguments surrounding the measurement properties of net realisable values are somewhat abstruse (Chambers, 1966), and sometimes appear to involve the imposition of apparently arbitrary criteria for assessing accounting measurements (Chambers, 1978).

Finally, it can be argued that net realisable value has greater intuitive meaning to users of accounts (Tweedie, 1977), and is therefore more likely to communicate more useful information to them, than are various alternative valuation bases. This raises the difficult issue of the extent to which accounts should attempt to accommodate the needs of relatively unsophisticated users. On the one hand, it might be argued that the intuition and common sense of an unsophisticated user should be respected as *prima facie* evidence of the relevance and usefulness of the information. On the other hand, it could be maintained that sophisticated users, such as investment analysts or financial journalists, are the real opinion formers, who influence the less sophisticated users through their advice and comment and who help to make the market share price by their control of institutional investment. Thus, for example, a subscriber to the Efficient Markets Hypothesis[15] would be inclined to regard the information needs of the unsophisticated investor as immaterial: he should accept the ruling stock market price as the best indication of a share's worth and select his portfolio merely with a view to obtaining the desired spreading of risk.[16]

The case against net realisable values as a valuation base is usually based upon its apparent lack of relevance to a continuing business, when continuity is assumed either to be axiomatic, or to be the most profitable option open to the firm. In such a case, net realisable value does not represent the consequences of a course of action which will be taken. It was the continuity assumption which led Edwards and Bell (1961) to prefer replacement cost to net realisable value. Where fixed assets are held for use in the firm, they may have very low net realisable values, because of the heavy transaction costs involved in sale, but they may also have high replacement costs which are, nevertheless, justified by the high prospective returns to be earned by using them in the business, so that replacement would be worthwhile. In the extreme, 'non-vendible' assets may have a zero (or negative) net realisable value but be essential to the profitable operation of the firm. This type of argument has been used by Baxter (1967) in a review of Chambers' (1966) book, and by Weston (1971) in a commentary on a paper by Chambers (1971a). Chambers originally (1966) dealt with 'non-vendible' assets by valuation at replacement cost but has since (1970) hardened the consistency of his approach by advocating that they should be valued on the net realisable value basis, even if this requires a zero value.

Edwards and Bell also claim that, for the continuing business, 'realisable profit' (based on net realisable value) is an essentially short-run measure, since it does not indicate the firm's ability to stay in business by covering the costs of replacement, which must be met if the firm is to stay in business in the long term. This is not an entirely satisfactory argument because the incentive to make replacement

125

investments must depend upon future prospective returns, and Edwards and Bell are concerned with *ex post* performance. Anthony (1976) has suggested that the measure of profit which best indicates the long-term capacity of a steady state firm to survive in an inflationary environment depends upon the firm's pricing policy, replacement cost being an appropriate accounting base only when it is used as the basis for setting selling prices.

Another argument against net realisable value is based upon its contravention of the realisation principle (Edwards, 1975). Traditionally, accountants have been reluctant to recognise selling prices before a sale is actually made. However, this reluctance is based upon the doctrine of conservatism, the belief that it is prudent to under-estimate rather than to give as accurate as possible an estimate of value, and this has no obvious theoretical justification. Furthermore, replacement cost accounting recognises cost increases before the costs are actually paid in the market place, reporting them, in Edwards and Bell's system, as holding gains, so this argument does not seem to favour either of the two current market valuation bases.

Edwards (1975) has suggested that 'exit' values (net realisable values) should not be used when they are derived from markets in which the firm is normally a buyer rather than a seller. This is really an extension of the basic argument that, for assets bought for use rather than re-sale, the proceeds of realisation represent the outcome of an unlikely event, so that replacement cost is probably more relevant to describing the value put on the assets in the usual type of transaction which the firm undertakes. This line of argument leads Edwards to concede that net realisable values might be appropriate in valuing stocks of finished goods. It therefore leads us into the area of multiple valuation bases, which will be discussed later.

The estimation of net realisable values as 'current cash equivalents', in Chambers' system, gives rise to important conceptual difficulties. Chambers has emphasised the importance of realisation in the ordinary course of business as being the rule for assessing current cash equivalents. This avoids some of the excessively low valuations which might arise if stock were assessed at its immediate selling value (a problem which led Chambers (1966) to use a cost basis for calculating stock values, for which he was subsequently criticised by Baxter (1967)). However, especially in the case of certain longer-lived assets, realisation in the ordinary course of business is difficult to apply, without venturing into the difficult and highly subjective area of estimating the present value of future receipts. In such cases, the Chambers system has to use the values which would obtain in an orderly disposal (rather than immediate liquidation), and there is a definitional problem in distinguishing between a current cash equivalent (which Chambers advocates) and discounted present value (which Chambers rejects). Chambers' answer to this is that he is concerned with current market values, not with estimating future returns (Chambers, 1970), but if this rule is strictly enforced it is difficult to justify current cash equivalents as *realisable* values or as opportunity costs.

In summary, net realisable value clearly has relevance to a wide range of potential uses of accounting data. It is particularly appropriate in the balance sheet, the total of which represents the 'current cash equivalent' of the firm's assets on orderly disposal, although there may, in some instances, be an aggregation problem and there may be problems in valuing assets which are 'non-vendibles' in the short term. Furthermore, the value of the firm's goodwill will not be included in this total, so that the value of the firm as a going concern will not normally be equal to the total value of the assets recorded in the balance sheet.[17] However, the sum of net realisable values does represent the value of one important opportunity which is open to the firm. The relevance of this opportunity and the problems of measurement will depend partly on the type of business concerned: a firm whose main business consists of holding durable assets as investments is likely to find net realisable values relevant and relatively easy to implement.

The profit and loss account derived from a net realisable value system is less satisfactory, particularly in the case of a continuing manufacturing business. In the case of a commodity trader (such as Sterling's (1970) dealer in wheat) the problem of substantial fixed assets held for use in the business rather than resale may not arise, so that a measure such as Edwards and Bell's 'realisable profit' might be a particularly appropriate measure of the firm's performance. However, when fixed assets are held for use in the business, the depreciation charge on such assets in a net realisable value system will not reflect the current replacement cost of the asset services used during the period. If we accept Thomas' argument that all depreciation allocations are arbitrary and incorrigible, and that this is sufficient reason to abandon attempts at making such allocations, we may be unimpressed by the case for replacement cost depreciation.[18] However, we may still harbour some anxiety about the alternative offered by net realisable value, if this involves the writing-off of the total cost of a new item of plant in its year of installation, even when its replacement cost is rising and its prospects for profitable use are good, but its selling costs are high. Such a treatment may be consistent with the aims of CoCoA accounting system (as Thomas, 1974, concedes, in contrast with his earlier critical stance as the author of the 1969 Accounting Research Study No. 3), but those aims clearly do not encompass the description of the progress of the business as a going concern.

Finally, it is notable that the principal advocate of the net realisable value basis, Chambers, has defended net realisable value in financial accounting to the exclusion of alternative measure (Chambers, 1972). It seems from the earlier discussion that net realisable value is one measure which is relevant in a wide range of situations but is not the only relevant measure: in many cases, we will wish to compare alternative measures. It may be that promoting net realisable values as the only measures which should appear in financial accounts has impeded the acceptance of the view that net realisable values are widely relevant and therefore deserve a place in accounts, even if it is not the primary or exclusive place.

(iii) Present Value

The third basic method of valuation to be considered is economic value or present value, i.e. the discounted present value of the future receipts to which an asset may give rise. This might be thought to be the 'true' value of an asset or a firm, but, as was apparent from the discussions of Chapter 2, this would only be an appropriate description under restrictive conditions which do not hold in the real world in which accountants operate. Present values require two essential pieces of information, the amount of the future cash flows and of the appropriate rate of discount. In a world of uncertainty we would need to have knowledge of the probability distribution of the cash flows,[19] and the degree of uncertainty which this represented would affect the discount rate. If the economy consisted of a set of complete markets in a state of perfectly competitive equilibrium, we would be able to obtain present values by observing prices in these markets, but a more realistic scenario for the accountant is a disequilibrium economy with imperfect and incomplete markets, in which one rôle of accounts is to provide information on which individual subjective estimates of present value will be made (Beaver and Demski, 1979, Bromwich, 1977a, and Peasnell, 1977).

In practice, the measurement of present values by accountants is regarded as too subjective to provide a reliable basis for accounting. Although it has been adopted as one ingredient in the 'value to the owner' rules, which have been adopted for practical application in a number of countries, present value has been the most controversial component of these rules and has been discarded in some practical applications. However, this has not prevented 'economic value' from being presented as an ideal to which practical measures should conform as closely as possible. The 'surrogate' argument for replacement cost (discussed earlier) is an example of this approach, although it has, in fact, failed to demonstrate that replacement cost can be used as a surrogate for present value under realistic conditions. The work of Canning (1929) is another example of economic value being used as an ideal. Each of Canning's eclectic range of valuations was chosen to reflect, as nearly as possible, the economic value of a particular type of asset. For short-term assets this led him to a net realisable value approach and for fixed assets his 'opportunity difference' approach was similar to the 'value to the owner' basis.[20] Staubus (1971) is a modern representative of this approach, seeking to identify the appropriate valuations of particular assets in particular situations which are consistent with the fundamental assumption that 'the most useful meaning of asset and liability quantities is the item's incremental effect upon the net discounted amount of the entity's future cash flow' (p. 50).

Another possible criticism of the Staubus approach is that the different valuations which he uses are not additive, i.e. we cannot add together the replacement cost of one asset and the net realisable value of another without violating the criteria for homogeneous measurement, upon which Chambers rests part of his case for net realisable values. This is dismissed convincingly by Staubus on the ground that his measurements are not to be treated as realisable values or replacement cost *per se*, but rather as surrogates for present values, so that in this sense they are homogeneous measurements. However, there is a more difficult problem arising out of the addition of the Staubus surrogates for incremental net realisable value, in the form of the familiar aggregation problem. We have no guarantee, unless we impose severe restrictions such as constant returns to scale,[21] that the sum of incremental present values will equal the present value of the whole firm. Thus, even if we accept the Staubus surrogates as being acceptable estimates of the incremental present value of individual assets, which may be of some use in making decisions about the disposition of those assets, the balance sheet total may not give us a useful measure of the present value of the whole firm,[22] and the related profit and loss account will not give us an estimate of economic income. Furthermore, the twin problem of allocation also arises, if we work from an estimate of the aggregate present value of the firm and try to achieve consistency in aggregation by allocating the total (or the aggregate cash flows from which the total present value is derived) between individual assets.

Finally, if a present value basis is applied, either by direct estimation or by means of surrogates, to the complete exclusion of other methods of valuation, another familiar difficulty arises. For many economic decisions or *ex post* evaluations a standard of comparison is required. This may consist of past periods' performance or forecast data using the same valuation basis, but it might also involve comparison of data for the same time or period using a different valuation basis. In this situation, present value data will be useful only in conjunction with other types of data, so that the relationship between alternative valuation bases becomes one of complementarity rather than competition. It should also be noted that, in some circumstances, more than one estimate of present value may be relevant, e.g. if we wish to compare the present use with an alternative use. In such a case, the present value of the asset (or a group of assets) in the best alternative use within the firm will constitute the relevant standard for comparison, if it exceeds net realisable value and the assets are already owned by the firm. If the assets are not already owned, the opportunity cost calculation will use the highest of replacement cost, net realisable value, and present value in the best alternative use, as the standard for comparison.[23]

In summary, present value or 'economic value' is potentially useful information for the purpose of a number of decisions and appraisals. It is difficult to measure, being highly subjective, and various surrogate measurements have been suggested, although the justification for using these, except in very closely defined situations, is purely pragmatic. Moreover, there may be a serious aggregation problem in interpreting the sum of incremental present values or their surrogates, and a serious allocation problem in attributing present value of the whole firm to individual assets.

A common feature of the three 'pure' valuation bases discussed above is that each is of potential relevance in particular circumstances, and that in some cases we might wish to compare values derived from alternative bases. This raises the important issue of whether it is feasible to produce multiple-column accounts which incorporate alternative valuation bases, and this will be discussed in the final section (section 5) of this chapter. However, before doing so we must consider an important valuation basis which makes use of all three 'pure' valuation bases, selecting according to their relative values for the particular asset concerned. This basis, 'value to the owner', is important because it has become part of accounting practice, as well as receiving considerable attention in the literature.

4 Value to the Owner

Value to the owner, 'opportunity value' or 'deprival value' is an eclectic valuation technique: it can value an asset at either net realisable value (NRV), replacement cost (RC) or discounted value in present use (PV). Its basic method is to establish the minimum loss which a firm would suffer if it were deprived of an asset: this is taken as a measure of the value of the benefits conferred by ownership of the asset. Replacement cost therefore sets a ceiling on deprival value in those cases in which it would be possible and worthwhile to replace the asset (cases 1, 2, 4 and 5 in the table below), so that the deprival value argument is often used to justify replacement cost as a general asset valuation basis (e.g. Parker and Harcourt, 1969).

The origins of 'the value to the owner idea' appear to be in the United States in the 1920s, although a single original source has not been established. It is customary to attribute the idea to Bonbright (1937), but Bonbright had been working in the field of asset valuation for some years before the publication of his classic work. Sweeney (in his 1933 paper on Capital) cites Bonbright (without reference to any particular publication) as the source of the argument that replacement cost (of the service rather than the specific asset) is normally the appropriate valuation of an item of capital 'under conditions of intelligent free competition'. However, Canning (1929) had also devised rules of the value to the owner type for the valuation of fixed assets, basing his reasoning upon 'opportunity differences'. His work influenced that of Wright (1964, 1965, 1968 and 1970), who developed the application of 'opportunity value' rules in the context of depreciation (1964 and 1968), stock valuation

(1965), and financial accounting generally (1970). The writers who acknowledge direct allegiance to Bonbright are the LSE triumvirate, Baxter (1967, 1971 and 1975), Edey (1974) and Solomons (1966), and also Parker and Harcourt (1969) and Stamp (1971). Of these, Solomons was the first to set out the value to the owner rules in the familiar inequality form, later popularised by Parker and Harcourt (1969) and adopted by numerous other writers. This is reproduced in the table below, using the format adopted by Ma (1976).

Value to the owner

Case	Interrelationship	Value to the owner
Asset in use		
1	PV > RC > NRV	RC
2	PV > NRV > RC	RC
3	RC > PV > NRV	PV
Asset in trade		
4	NRV > PV > RC	RC
5	NRV > RC > PV	RC
Asset in divestiture		
6	RC > NRV > PV	NRV

The first column of the table classifies the cases according to three broad categories of asset-holding activity. 'Asset in use' describes the three cases in which a rational, profit-maximising decision would imply that the asset be held for use in the firm, because PV in use in the firm is the most profitable opportunity: it should be noted that in case 3 PV is less than RC, so that the asset would not be replaced after use, but PV is the most profitable opportunity available, given that the asset is already owned by the firm, the two opportunities being hold for use (PV) or sell (NRV). 'Asset in trade' describes an asset which, in a profit-maximising firm, would be held for re-sale, since the re-sale value (NRV) exceeds value in use (PV), but which would be replaced, since selling price (NRV) exceeds buying price (RC), i.e. it would be profitable for the firm to trade continuously in the asset. The final case, 'asset in divestiture' is one in which sale is the most profitable use of an asset held by the firm (NRV > PV), but replacement is not worthwhile (RC > NRV), i.e. once-for-all sale rather than continuous trade is appropriate. It will be observed that the six cases listed exhaust all of the possible relationships between the three values, so that the rules deal with all possible contingencies.

Baxter's (1967) advocacy of value to the owner in an influential review of Chambers (1966) led to considerable controversy, especially in the pages of *Abacus*. Chambers (1970) attacked value to the owner as referring specifically to a situation in which the firm was deprived of the asset, a situation which he felt was appropriate to an insurance valuation (which was one of the purposes which Bonbright had in mind) but not to the general problem of financial reporting. He also objected to the subjectivity involved in calculating PV. Chambers was taken to task by Wright (1971) for seeming to identify PV with value to the owner, whereas PV would be the relevant 'value to the owner' only in relatively rare circumstances (case 3 in the table). Stamp (1971) proposed that PV could be dispensed with even in this case by measuring 'netback' (the higher of PV or NRV)[24] as NRV. Stamp's rule was subsequently criticised by Yoshida (1973) on the ground that PV is relevant in determining the final value even when it does not emerge as the final value, so that subjective PV does help to determine the choice of measure under Stamp's system despite never being reported. It was also criticised by Wanless (1974) who maintained that the situation in which PV is the value to the owner might be quite common.[25]

Chambers (1971b) replied to Wright, acknowledging that value to the owner was not always equal to PV, but still maintaining that the use of PV introduced an unacceptable degree of subjectivity and also objecting to the hybrid nature of value to the owner, which was alleged to violate the criteria for homogeneous measurement.[26] Chambers also demonstrated certain ambiguities in Bonbright's definitions, but, as has already been explained, Bonbright was not the exclusive source of the value to the owner principle.[27] Ma (1976) also entered this debate, emphasising the ambiguity of PV when the asset is part of a joint productive process, so that the problem of allocation arises. This criticism seems to be inappropriate: as Edey (1974) points out, if the asset concerned is essential to a joint operation, the PV of the whole operation *will* be relevant to the asset holding decision, and RC will become the 'deprival value' ('deprival value' being the description of value to the owner favoured by Baxter and Edey). It might be argued that deprival value is specifically designed to prevent the attribution of an excessive value in such a case.

In 1975, value to the owner (referred to as 'value to the business') was adopted by the Sandilands Committee and since then it has been the asset valuation base of all British proposals for current cost accounting, including the current SSAP16 (issued in March 1980).[28] It was also proposed by the Richardson Committee Report in New Zealand (1976) and by the 1975 Australian Preliminary Exposure Draft,[29] both of which adopted Stamp's proposal for avoiding the calculation of PV as value to the owner.[30] These developments gave further impetus to theoretical work exploring the rationale of value to the owner.

Two statements from the LSE school of the use of value to the owner in financial reporting, by Baxter and by Edey, were published in the year preceding the Sandilands Report. Baxter's case is essentially pragmatic ('such a standard is grounded in common sense', Baxter (1975), p. 125), stressing that 'deprival value' avoids certain apparently anomalous valuations which would result from applying a single valuation method (RC, NRV or PV) in all circumstances (hence the apparent irrelevance of Ma's criticism). Edey (1974) deals particularly with the problem of aggregation and concedes that, for collections of inter-dependent assets, the only satisfactory method of applying deprival value is in aggregate, i.e. to calculate PV, NRV or RC for the group of assets, which may imply valuing the firm as a whole, a formidable task in practice.

Following the publication of the Sandilands Report, Gee and Peasnell (1976) provided 'A Pragmatic Defence of Replacement Cost' in the context of the Sandilands system. They explore each of the six possible relationships between PV, NRV and RC (given in the earlier table) and appraise them in terms of their likely frequency, the circumstances under which they might arise, and the valuation problems arising from those circumstances. They conclude (with some reservations about case 6, RC > NRV > PV) that RC is likely to be a satisfactory valuation basis in most cases, and that the simplicity resulting from having a single valuation basis is likely to compensate for any consequential loss of accuracy. As this is an extension of Stamp's 'netback' method of simplifying value to the owner, it might be dubbed the Lancaster method.[31] Gee and Peasnell do not produce empirical evidence in support of their assumptions as to the likely frequency of the various cases, and this is an area which deserves empirical investigation.

A second theme in the Gee and Peasnell paper is the problem of aggregation, a problem stated earlier by Edey (1974). They concede the difficulty of interpreting the sum of the RC of individual assets, bearing in mind that this might well exceed the PV of the whole firm, but they point out that this problem of 'over-imputation' of individual values can arise equally under the conventional 'value to the owner' rules, and so does not invalidate the case for their simplified approach. The theme of aggregation is explored further in Peasnell (1978). This uses Thomas' (1969 and 1974) arguments concerning the 'incorrigibility' of allocation rules to demonstrate that the total value of a firm's assets under the conventional 'value to the firm' rule (as used in Current Cost Accounting) is rendered arbitrary when there are interaction effects between assets, which make the allocation of PV dependent upon the precise definition, and level of disaggregation of deprival. This paper also considers interactions due to risk. The author concludes that the valuation of intangible assets and their separation from the valuation of other assets require urgent consideration in Current Cost Accounting. However, he does not discuss the fundamental issue of what the total value of assets in a 'value to the owner' system *ought* to mean: he appears to believe that it should sum to the PV of the whole firm, but the author's own work elsewhere (Peasnell, 1977) suggests that accountants 'do not have a comparative advantage in calculating PV' and should not attempt it. A related question is that, if the aggregate of value to the owner of individual assets is an arbitrary sum of dubious significance (as Baxter (1975), Edey (1974) and Peasnell (1978) all suggest), what can be the significance of an aggregate income measure derived from the same valuation?

A paper by Bromwich (1977b) has explored another aspect of value to the owner: its claim to be rooted in the economist's concept of opportunity cost. Bromwich demonstrates that this claim is valid only in closely defined circumstances, when the best alternative is that defined by the deprival situation, or when value to the owner is numerically equal to (and therefore a surrogate for) the value of the best alternative. Thus, the connection between 'value to the owner' and the opportunity cost concept is not as strong as is sometimes suggested. Even if the connection were stronger, there would be a need to specify more clearly why the opportunity cost of individual assets should be relevant to financial reporting.

In conclusion, the 'value to the owner' concept has been advocated and explored by a number of British writers. It has had the distinction of being adopted as a basis for reforms of accounting practice, and there is no denying its intuitive appeal as a pragmatic compromise between competing valuation methods. However, it is to some extent still a practical technique in search of a theoretical justification, and it requires further analysis and development. The aggregation problem is serious, and the connection with opportunity cost is both tenuous and of dubious relevance.[32] The more fundamental problem is, however, that value to the owner has never been demonstrated to arise out of a particular information requirement of a potential user of financial reports, other than that of an insurer. We need to know whether it is intended, in aggregate, as a surrogate for PV or merely as a set of piecemeal valuations of individual assets and, if the latter, how it is to be used. We also need to know more about the properties of the income measures to which it gives rise and why these are to be preferred to income measures based upon replacement cost, net realisable value, or even historical cost.

However, as a practical technique, value to the owner has proved to be acceptable to the accounting profession and is currently being applied in the United Kingdom as the valuation basis of the supplementary current cost accounts, required as a result of the publication of SSAP16 on 31 March 1980. Looked at from a pragmatic standpoint, it is 'replacement cost or recoverable amount, whichever is the lower' (where 'recoverable amount' is the higher of market re-sale value or value in present use, i.e. Stamp's 'netback'). This avoids some of the potentially misleading valuations which might result from the universal application of replacement cost, even in situations in which replacement would not be worthwhile. By providing an acceptable means of introducing current values into accounts on a systematic basis, value to the owner has undoubtedly led to the availability of data which provide a much more realistic picture of the current state of the business, as portrayed by the balance sheet, than is provided by historical cost data.[33] The depreciation and cost of sales adjustment, on the current cost basis, also provide valuable supplementary information, although the capital maintenance concept embodied in SSAP16 (which has no necessary connection with value to the owner) is unsatisfactory and is discussed further in the next chapter, as part of the section on the gearing adjustment.

5 Some tentative conclusions on valuation

In section 3 of this chapter, three basic methods of valuation (RC, NRV and PV) were discussed. Each was considered as a single valuation basis, to be applied to the exclusion of other values (except where other values could be used as surrogates for the preferred basis), because this is, for the most part, how their advocates have presented their cases. In section 4 we considered value to the owner as the most popular eclectic valuation basis available, selecting one of the three bases according to the particular configuration of the three values.

In the discussion of single valuation bases, each was found to have some merits and some disadvantages. This is hardly surprising in view of the variety of uses to which accounting data are put and the variety of circumstances which can prevail. For example, it is not surprising that a valuation basis which produces a balance sheet which gives a useful description of the present financial resources and liabilities of a firm will not necessarily be equally effective in producing a profit and loss statement which gives a useful description of the firm's production and trading operations over a period of time. Equally, the type of asset valuation which we would use in appraising a firm's suitability for an 'asset-stripping' take-over bid would not necessarily serve equally well in appraising the profitability of its current productive operations with a view to making a synergic take-over bid.

One possible means of overcoming this difficulty might be to select whichever of the alternative valuations was most relevant to the circumstances by means of some algorithm such as the 'value to the owner' rules. Unfortunately, this particular set of rules does not appear to have a strong theoretical foundation, although it may be a useful pragmatic method if the choice is constrained to reporting only one value for each individual asset. Furthermore, it seems unlikely that any such algorithm is likely to prove satisfactory, given the variety of uses to which a particular value is likely to be put. Value to the owner can discriminate according to the relative amounts of the different values but by no other criterion. Any alternative algorithm would face a similar problem: in making a choice of one value out of three it is possible to satisfy only one choice criterion (as in the 'value to the owner' case) whereas in fact we might wish to have information which will satisfy several different criteria which will lead to alternative values. For example, many economic decisions involve the comparison of alternative values, such as a buying price, a value in use, or a selling price, or variant of these in alternative uses or markets.

In such a situation, the only approach which can provide the relevant information is the provision of multiple values for the same asset or transaction, sometimes referred to as 'multiple column reporting'. This has been the subject of a fierce debate, particularly between Chambers (1972) and Stamp (1972 and 1979). Chambers claims that multiple column accounts, by communicating an excessive quantity of information, would lead to confusion in the minds of users. Stamp, on the other hand, stresses the relevance of alternative values. To some extent, this becomes an empirical argument about who are the users of reports, what are the uses to which the reports are put, what is the capacity of users to absorb information about alternative values, and what is the practical feasibility of producing alternative values. This is an important area requiring empirical research.

Although much empirical work needs to be done on the subject of current value accounting, a certain amount has been done and Appendix A to this chapter provides a brief survey of this work. Finally, Appendix B provides simple numerical examples of one form of current value accounting, to supplement the algebraic exposition given earlier. In the following chapter we shall deal with the controversial issue of the definition of capital for the measurement of income: this, in combination with the valuation basis, is fundamental to the design of any financial accounting system, and the existence of inflation renders the choice particularly important.

Chapter 5: Appendix A Some empirical studies of current value accounting

There is a growing empirical literature on current value accounting. In many ways it is parallel to that relating to current purchasing power accounting, although research on current value accounting suffers from the important handicap of requiring additional data for valuation purposes, i.e. current values, which are not readily available, whereas CPP studies can make use of widely published general indices (together with assumptions about acquisition dates) for valuation purposes.

The earliest and most common types of current value study, as with CPP studies, are of the case study variety, seeking to estimate current values, typically concentrating on replacement cost estimates of depreciation and stock appreciation. Some early studies of this type, such as Dean's pioneering studies (1951 and 1954) for the United States and Baxter's (1959) study of British steel companies are summarised in Appendix E of American Institute of Certified Public Accountants (1963). An Australian case study of replacement cost accounting is Gress (1972). Similar studies have been carried out to test Chambers' net realisable value-based system of continuously contemporaneous accounting, for example McKeown (1971) and Gray (1975 and 1976). Manuals explaining how to prepare alternative forms of current value accounts have been produced by the University of Waikato project (Hume 1976, Craswell 1976). Hope (1974) is a British study comparing six different systems for two companies. These studies have served to demonstrate the feasibility of current value accounting systems and to demonstrate that they can yield results which are materially different from traditional, historic-cost-based accounts.

There have also been a number of aggregative studies which attempt to estimate the effects of current value accounting. These have usually been concerned with adjusting conventional profit for replacement cost depreciation and stock appreciation. They are often the work of economists whose concern is with the adequacy of profits to finance replacement investment, and are related to the question of whether company taxation allows adequately for replacement costs. Early examples of this type of work are Harcourt (1958) for the UK and Mathews and Grant (1958) for Australia. There was a burgeoning of this type of work in the United Kingdom during the 'profits crisis' of the mid-1970s (immediately prior to the publication of the Sandilands Report and the granting of stock appreciation relief), good examples being Meeks (1974), King (1975), Flemming *et al.* (1976),[34] Merrett and Sykes (1974 and 1980), and Moore (1980) which was quoted extensively in Chapter 1, section 6. A view of the implications for the reported profits of leading UK quoted companies of the various current cost accounting proposals has been provided in a series of papers published by Philips and Drew under the direction of Martin Gibbs (listed in Gibbs and Seward, 1979). The results of these studies have lent support to tax reforms, such as the introduction of stock appreciation relief, by demonstrating the importance of the divergence between replacement cost and historical cost in periods of rapid inflation.

Another type of research relating to the feasibility and materiality of current value accounting is the work on index numbers done by

Peasnell and Skerratt (1976a, 1977a and 1977b) and Bourn, Stoney and Wynn (1976 and 1977). Both of these teams of investigators set out to establish the materiality of divergences from general indices of special indices of fixed asset prices. The methodology of their approaches differs and there has been controversy as to the correct interpretation of the results. However, both groups conclude that a single index can capture a significant amount, but by no means all of the movements in special indices, i.e. there is some validity in using general indices as proxies for special indices, but this process introduces a degree of inaccuracy. There also seems to be agreement that indices specific to the type of plant capture information different from that captured by indices specific to the industry, i.e. if current cost accounts are to make use of specific indices as alternatives (or supplements in intermediate years) to direct valuations, different results will be obtained by using plant-specific indices rather than industry-specific indices. Peasnell and Skerratt claim that the plant-specific indices are superior, but Bourn, Stoney and Wynn assert that they are merely different. Despite the controversy about the interpretation of the results, this is a useful area of research, and more effort might be devoted in the future to researching the extent to which there are material divergences between alternative methods of valuation. There have been other studies in this field, such as the studies by McDonald (1968) and Sterling and Radosevitch (1969), both of which compared different accountants' estimates of historical cost and market value of a single item of equipment. The evidence of these studies is not decisive, and remarkably little effort has been expended on them relative to that devoted to theoretical arguments, whose relevance often hinges on the practicalities of valuation methods.

A more sophisticated extension of the case studies, described earlier, is to assess the materiality of differences between accounting methods by statistical tests rather than by relying on the description of absolute differences in individual cases, whose general significance is difficult to assess. The statistical approach requires more data than the case study method, so that the scarcity of current value data has inhibited its development. An example of this type of study is by Kratchman, Malcom and Twark (1974, 1975 and 1976) who compared four alternative income measures (including current value income and current value adjusted to real terms) for real estate investment trusts in the USA, finding high correlations (so that the measures were good surrogates for one another) in some cases. Their methodology has been subect to criticism (Liao, 1975, and Picur and McKeown, 1976), and their data are of limited scope, so there is clearly room for much more work of this type. This work may be helped by the increasing availability of current value data, for example replacement cost data were required by the USA Securities and Exchange Commission 10-K reports from 1976 onwards, and by the Hyde Guidelines in the United Kingdom from 1977 onwards.

Statistical studies can also be devised in order to assess the utility of accounting information. As with the materiality studies, these have hitherto been limited in number and in scope. Examples are the predictive ability studies by Frank (1969) and by Buckmaster, Copeland and Dascher (1977) (referred to in Chapter 4), which assesses the self-predictive ability of alternative accounting income models, on the assumption that predictive ability gives rise to utility. A potentially rich field for empirical research on the utility of accounting information is its impact on share prices: this has clearly been inhibited so far by lack of published current value data. A study of this type is by Abdel-Khalik and McKeown (1978), which attempts to estimate the impact on share prices and risk measures of estimates of replacement cost holding gains. Much more research of this type should be possible as current value disclosure increases. A recent example is a symposium on the impact of the 1976 SEC '10-K' replacement cost disclosure requirements in the USA (Watts and Zimmerman, 1980). The three studies in the symposium each had methodological limitations, but were designed and conducted independently, and it is therefore impressive that all three reached the common conclusion that the replacement cost disclosures had no impact on share prices. This suggests either that replacement cost information was already available to the stock market or that it was not considered relevant.

Another approach to empirical research is the behavioural study based upon experiments. Tweedie's (1977) study has already been referred to in Chapter 5: this was based on an experiment which used first-year accounting students as subjects and the results suggested that unsophisticated users of accounts tend intuitively to choose net realisable values as balance sheet measures and cash flows (with no accrual adjustment) as flow measures. Another study, by Benston and Krasney (1978), uses a set of 'sophisticated investors' (life assurance company investment officers) as subjects, and concludes that there is little demand for current value data, although the discussants of the study (Adkerson, 1978, and Buzby and Falk, 1978) disagree with the interpretation.

Although this brief survey has not attempted to be comprehensive or to wrestle with the detailed issues of interpretation which are inevitably associated with empirical work, it seems reasonable to hazard the conclusion that most of the empirical studies to date have been based on limited data and have yielded indecisive results. However, it is also true that an impressive variety of studies has been attempted and that the greater availability of data should facilitate future studies. It is also true that empirical studies are a crucial complementary activity to theoretical work: empirical studies without theory lapse into mere description and theoretical studies which have no empirically testable assumptions or implication give rise, at best, to unverifiable normative assertions and, at worst, are totally irrelevant to accounting as a practical activity. Hitherto, much more attention has been given to theory than to empirical testing, and it is important, for the development of the subject, that this imbalance be redressed.

Chapter 5: Appendix B   A numerical illustration of current value accounting

Introduction

In this appendix, the algebraic statements (5.1) to (5.7) are illustrated by a numerical example, based upon the facts of 'Old Fred's' business, used in the previous chapters. It should be clear from the text of Chapter 5 that there is a great variety of current valuation bases, of associated capital maintenance concepts (which will be discussed and illustrated in the next chapter), and of formats for presenting them. In the illustration which follows, replacement cost is used as the valuation basis and two different capital maintenance concepts are employed: an 'entity' approach which is used to strike the balance of operating profit, and a money capital approach which is used in the calculation of holding gains. This conforms with the current cost accounting model expressed in equation (5.7) of the text.

It should be emphasised that this is a simplified example of a specific form of current value accounting and does not conform even with the current cost accounting model, as it is currently implemented in the UK. Three particularly important divergences are:

(1) CCA, as required by SSAP16, has a different capital mainten-ance concept involving gearing and monetary working capital adjustment, which are discussed in the next chapter. The pre-sent example is closer in spirit (but does not conform in precise detail) to the capital maintenance models of the Sandilands Committee. The two main profit measures which it reports (cur-rent cost operating profit, based upon an entity capital mainten-ance concept, and total gains, based upon a proprietary concept) are summarised, and compared with historical cost profit, at the end of the numerical example.

(2) The example uses only replacement cost valuation (RC), whereas SSAP16 (and the earlier Sandilands Report) requires the use of value to the firm. We can, however, regard this exam-ple as being an application of value to the firm, if we assume that in every instance either NRV or PV or both exceed RC of the asset.

(3) In practice, the application of CCA to complex businesses with many transactions involves a degree of estimation in the early stages of application, when CCA is a supplementary adjustment to traditional (HC) accounts. The SSAP16 proposals, for example, provide for an averaging method of calculating the cur-rent cost of goods sold. Our numerical example is based upon very simple facts and it is assumed that precise information is available, so that no estimation methods are necessary.

A thorough exposition of the application of current cost account-ing as embodied in SSAP16, will be found in Mallinson (1980). The Chambers method of CoCoA accounting is precisely defined in an appendix (in the form of the exposure draft of a proposed standard) to Chambers (1977) and in Hume (1976), which contains detailed work-sheets and numerical examples. Lee (1980) contains clear numerical illustrations of a variety of forms of current value account-ing.

Facts assumed in the illustration

The facts assumed are those made in the appendix to Chapter 3. It is further assumed that the replacement cost of goods subsequently

Current value systems 1

incurred when re-stocking was the replacement cost of goods at the time of sale, e.g. replacement cost of sales in period 1 is assumed to be the cost of purchases at the beginning of period 2. In periods 3 and 4, during which no re-stocking took place, we assume a replacement cost of £1.90 per stock unit. A further assumption is made with respect to the replacement cost of the van: it is assumed that the cost of an equivalent van rose by one half early in period 3, but that otherwise the depreciation rate chosen presented a realistic view of the decline in the van's replacement cost over time.

Current Cost Accounts

Period 1

Balance Sheet at t

	£		£
Proprietor's Capital	150	*Fixed Asset*	
Loan	50	Van (at cost)	100
		Current Asset	
		Cash	100
	200		200

This is unchanged from the historical cost case (Chapter 3), since the fixed asset has only just been acquired, so that its historical cost represents its replacement cost, and the other assets and claims are of fixed monetary value.

Profit and Loss Account for period 1, t to $t + 1$

	£
Sales	120
Less Current cost of goods sold	104
	16
Less Depreciation	10
Current Cost Operating Profit	6
Add Holding Gain on Stocks	30
Total Gains	£ 36

The current cost of goods sold is 80 items at £1.30 each, whereas historical cost was £1 each. The difference between the two, £24 (=£104 − £80), is the realised holding gain on stocks sold during the period. The gain on closing stocks, £6 (=£26 − £20), is calculated on the same basis, and this represents an unrealised holding gain. In this illustration, the two types of holding gain have been added together (£30 = £24 + £6), but, if realisation is considered important, they could be reported separately (as, for example, advocated by Edwards and Bell, 1961). Depreciation is unchanged from the historical cost case, because replacement cost is assumed to equal historical cost in this example.

The format adopted here is basically consistent with current cost accounting as advocated by the Sandilands Committee, although the Sandilands format would separate the information into two statements, a current cost Profit and Loss Account (ending with Current Cost Operating Profit) and a Statement of Gains (which would end with the Total Gains figure). The Sandilands proposals would also ignore the unrealised holding gains on stocks. In terms of the algebraic notation used in the text, Current Cost Operating Profit shown here conforms with Y_{CCA} in equation (5.7), measuring profit after maintaining the specific assets of the entity. Total Gains shown above corresponds with Y_{CVA} in equation (5.6), which maintains the capital of the entity in monetary terms.

Balance Sheet at $t + 1$

	£		£	£
Proprietor's Capital		*Fixed Assets*		
Opening balance (at *t*)	150	Van (at cost)	100	
Add Total Gains for the		*Less* Accumulated		
period	36	Depreciation	10	
	186			90
Less Drawings	30	*Current Assets*		
Closing balance		Stock (at current cost)	26	
(at *t* + 1)	156	Cash	90	
				116
Loan	50			
	£206			£206

The only difference between this balance sheet and the historical cost version given in the Appendix to Chapter 3 is that the current cost value of stocks is £6 higher and this is reflected in a £6 increase in Proprietor's Capital. A further difference would arise if it were assumed that the replacement cost of the van was different from its written down historical cost. Total gains have been added to Proprietor's Capital: a more sophisticated system of reporting might distinguish between distributable profits and capital maintenance reserves to which would be credited gains due to asset appreciation (holding gains) which could not be withdrawn by the proprietor without eroding the physical substance of the business. In the above example, of the £36 Total Gains, £6 would be distributable profit and £30 (the holding gain) would be credited to the capital maintenance reserve.

Period 2

Profit and Loss Account for period 2, $t + 1$ to $t + 2$

		£
Sales		135
Less	Current Cost of Goods Sold	162
	Trading (Loss)	(27)
Less	Depreciation	10
	Current Cost Operating (Loss)	(37)
Add	Holding gains on stocks	50
	Total Gains	£ 13

Cost of goods sold is calculated at the replacement cost (£1.80) of the 90 items sold (£162). This represents a realised holding gain of £51 of which £6 had been recognised in the previous period as an unrealised gain on stock, and there is an unrealised holding gain of £5 ($= £18 - £13$) on stocks held at the end of the period, bringing total holding gains on stocks to the £50 reported above. The detailed calculations are as follows:

Realised Holding Gains:

Current Cost of Goods Sold (charged to Profit and Loss)	£162
Less Historical Cost of Goods Sold (as in appendix to Chapter 3)	£111
Realised during the period	£ 51

Unrealised Holding Gains:

Current cost of closing stocks (10 at £1.80)	£18	
Less Historical cost (10 at £1.30)	£13	
Unrealised gain on closing stock (10 at £0.50)	5	
Less Unrealised gain on opening stock, realised during the period	6	
Net change in unrealised gains		(1)
Total Holding Gains accruing in the period		£ 50

Balance Sheet at $t + 2$

	£			£	£
Proprietor's Capital			*Fixed Assets*		
Opening balance (at *t*)	156		Van (at cost)	100	
Add Total Gains for the period	13		*Less* Accumulated depreciation	20	
	169				80
Less Drawings	106				
Closing balance (at $t + 2$)	63		*Current Assets*		
			Stock (at current cost)	18	
Loan	50		Debtors	15	
Current Liabilities			Cash	52	
Creditors	52				85
	£165				£165

Current value systems 1

Period 3

Profit and Loss Account for period 3, $t + 2$ to $t + 3$

		£
Sales		180
Less Current Cost of Goods Sold		171
Trading Profit		9
Less Current Cost Depreciation		15
Current Cost Operating (Loss)		(6)
Add Holding gains: On stocks	11	
On fixed asset	40	
		51
Total Gains	£	45

The calculation of cost of goods sold is based upon a current replacement cost of £1.90 each for 90 items. The holding gains on stocks are calculated as follows:

Holding Gains on Stocks:

	£	£
Realised gains:		
Current cost, charged to Profit and Loss	171	
Less Historical cost	157	14
Realised gain		
Unrealised gains:		
Current cost of closing stock (20 at £1.90)	38	
Less Historical cost (20 at £1.80)	36	
Unrealised gain on closing stock (20 at £0.10)	2	
Less Unrealised gain on opening stock, realised during the period	5	
		(3)
Total holding gains on stocks accruing during the period		£11

At the beginning of this period, a holding gain accrues on the fixed asset, the van. It was assumed that the replacement cost of the van rose by 50 per cent, and that the depreciation pattern is still appropriate. The revised values are therefore as follows:

	Opening value	Revised value	Increase
Cost	100	150	50
Less Accumulated depreciation	20	30	10
Written down value	80	120	40

The treatment adopted here is to show the revised values in the balance sheet (a net debit to the asset accounts of £40) and a corresponding net holding gain (a net credit of £40) in the final section of the Profit and Loss Account. Some would argue that the net gain should be split into two components, a gross gain (on original cost) of £50, and an increased charge for accumulated depreciation, of £10. This latter charge is known as 'backlog depreciation' and it is sometimes argued that it should be charged at an earlier stage in the profit calculation, rather than merely being offset against the gross holding gain on the cost of the fixed asset. This attitude (which is discussed further in the following chapter) springs from an 'entity' view of the firm and from the view that the depreciation charge should somehow represent an allocation of liquid funds for replacement, rather than merely being an indication for profit computation of the cost of using the asset during the period. This attitude has not been adopted here, and the depreciation charge against profit represents the current cost of using the asset during the period, where current cost is assumed to be one tenth of the current replacement cost of the asset.

Balance Sheet at $t + 3$

	£		£	£
Proprietor's Capital		*Fixed Assets*		
Opening balance (at $t+2$)	63	Van, at replacement cost	150	
Add Total gains for the period	45	*Less* Accumulated depreciation	45	
	108			105
Less Drawings	10	*Current Assets*		
Closing balance		Stocks, at current cost	38	
(at $t + 3$)	98	Debtors	20	
Loan	50	Cash	165	
Current Liabilities				223
Creditors	180			
	£328			£328

As compared with the historical cost balance sheet, shown in the appendix to Chapter 3, this current cost balance sheet shows the fixed asset and stocks at higher current cost values, and this is reflected in the proprietor's capital on the other side of the balance sheet.

Period 4

Profit and Loss Account for period 4, $t + 3$ to $t + 4$

	£
Sales	44
Less Current cost of goods sold	38
Trading profit	6
Add Realised Holding Gain	15
Total Gains	£21

The current cost of goods sold is merely the current cost of opening stocks, no further price changes being assumed before realisation. The realised holding gain is the excess of the sale price of the van (£120) over its written-down value (£105) at the start of the period: it is assumed that realisation took place before any further depreciation occurred.

Balance Sheet at $t + 4$

	£		£
Proprietor's Capital		Cash	169
Opening balance (at $t + 3$)	98		
Add Total gains for the period	21		
	119		
Loan	50		
	£169		£169

Apart from the division of proprietor's capital between the accrued balance and the gains for the period, this is identical with the historical cost closing balance sheet. This is because, as was demonstrated in Chapter 3, lifetime 'cash-to-cash' profit is the same, irrespective of the valuation method, which merely serves to shift profits between periods within the life-cycle. However, this results holds only if a common capital maintenance concept is adopted, i.e. if the current value system uses a money capital concept identical to that used in the historical cost system. In the present case, this implies that we use Total Gains, rather than Operating Profit as our profit measure. This is demonstrated in the table below. The choice of capital maintenance concept is discussed more thoroughly in the following chapter.

Life-cycle profits

	Current Cost			Historical Cost
Period	Operating Profit	Holding Gains	Total Gains	Profit (Ch. 3)
1	6	30	36	30
2	(37)	50	13	14
3	(6)	51	45	13
4	6	15	21	58
Total	£(31)	£146	£115	£115

Note: Brackets indicate a loss.

6

Current value systems 2: capital maintenance concepts and real terms accounting

1 Introduction

The previous chapter concentrated on the question of the choice of basis for valuing assets, but it was apparent that there is another important question to be discussed, the definition and measurement of the capital which is to be maintained intact before a profit is recognised. This question is of the greatest importance for the definition of profit and loss account, but it also affects the division between capital and retained profits in the section of the balance sheet which describes the proprietor's interest. The questions of valuation and capital maintenance are separate but not entirely independent, as they are both essential ingredients of an income measure, and the choice of a particular income measure will therefore require answers to both questions.

The choice of capital maintenance concept hinges on whether we wish to take a 'proprietary' or an 'entity' view of the firm. The former approach regards the equity interest in a company as being central to the purpose of financial reporting, so that it is the value of the firm to the proprietor which must be maintained intact. It is assumed that this implies some measure of the proprietor's command over goods and services in general, rather than over the type of asset which the firm holds. The proprietary approach is therefore consistent with maintaining the money amount of proprietor's capital, or, when money is changing in value, with maintaining the real value of proprietor's capital, as defined by applying a general purchasing power index to the historical money amount. The entity approach, on the other hand, regards the maintenance of the substance of the business entity as being the central assumption of the capital maintenance concept. It therefore requires that the amount of capital to be maintained should equal the current cost of the net assets of the firm, i.e.

money capital, as recorded in the opening balance sheet should be adjusted to allow for changes in the prices of the specific assets held by the firm. Such an adjustment will be necessary whenever the relevant specific price changes, and irrespective of changes in the general price level.

The proprietary and entity approaches represent two self-consistent alternative systems of capital maintenance. An eclectic approach, which combines elements of both, is the so-called 'gearing adjustment'. This has been adopted as the basis of standard accounting practice in the United Kingdom (SSAP16: ASC, 1980), and has been debated vigorously, so it will be discussed after the two 'pure' bases.

In the previous chapter, multiple-column reporting was discussed as a possible solution to the dilemma posed by the fact that more than one valuation basis may be relevant for the same asset. In the case of capital maintenance also, there may be a case for reporting the results of applying more than one concept. In this case, however, it is necessary to have only a multi-row income statement rather than a multi-column set of accounts, and this possibility will be discussed in a later section.

Before embarking upon a more detailed discussion of capital maintenance concepts, it is important to recall some of the fundamental principles discussed in Chapter 2. In particular, it is important to remember that only one of Hicks' definitions of income (Hicks No. 1) was based directly on capital maintenance. The others (Hicks No. 2 and Hicks No. 3) involved *ex ante* consumption maintenance. The maintenance deduction made from receipts in such a definition would be that amount considered necessary to maintain expected future consumption levels and would therefore depend upon expected future prices, costs and rates of return. Where there is certainty and interest rates are not expected to change, this approach could be described as net present value maintenance, i.e. the preservation of the economic value of the equity.[1] In more realistic conditions of uncertainty, however, consumption maintenance will have no obvious capital maintenance counterpart. The subjective nature of this approach, involving as it does the estimation of future returns, has led to a preference for a capital maintenance approach by practical accounting reformers (e.g. the Sandilands Committee), the only explicit exploration of consumption maintenance being that by Scott (1976). However, the idea of consumption maintenance does seem to be implicit in some of the arguments of those who advocate current cost accounting with an entity base (e.g. Merrett and Sykes, 1974 and 1980) and the gearing adjustment, particularly in its split-level form (Gibbs and Seward, 1979).

2 Proprietary capital

Perhaps the simplest and most obvious concept of capital is a sum fixed in historical money units. It will be recalled that this was the basis of historical cost accounting (Chapter 3), in which it had an obvious rationale, representing the amount contributed by the proprietor, either in the form of capital subscriptions or retained profits.

In the context of current value accounting, as described in Chapter 5, the maintenance of money capital implies the recognition of the nominal amount of holding gains as part of profits. In terms of the Sandilands proposals, this implies that the profit would be the total gains, derived from the Statement of Gains. This has already been defined in Chapter 5 (equations (5.2), (5.3), (5.4) and (5.6)). It will be recalled that, in the case of a transactionless period, current value income was defined as:

$$Y_{CVA} = P''_{t+1} - P''_t = N''_t . s \qquad (6.1)$$

where $N''_t . s$ represents the nominal holding gain on (i.e. rise in money value of) the 'non-monetary' assets held during the period. In the more general case, where there are transactions, current value income becomes:

$$Y_{CVA} = P''_{t+1} - P''_t$$
$$= (N''_{t+1} - N''_t) + (M_{t+1} - M_t) - (L_{t+1} - L_t) \qquad (6.2)$$

In this case, unrealised holding gains are included in N''_{t+1} and realised holding gains are included in the value of the assets purchased with the proceeds of realisation.

In times when inflation does not exist, i.e. when the general price level is stable, this definition of capital in money terms is an adequate description of proprietors' past capital contributions which they would wish to maintain intact before recognising income. In times of inflation, however, the general price level adjustment (CPP) described in Chapter 4 might be more appropriate, on the ground that proprietors will wish to maintain the real value of their capital, where 'real' is taken to imply measurement in terms of general command over goods and services rather than a monetary unit which fluctuates in value. It will be recalled that 'real terms' income was defined in Chapter 4 (equations (4.8), (4.9) and (4.10)), in the transactionless case, as:

$$Y_{RT} = P''_{t+1} - P''_t(1+p)$$
$$= [N''_{t+1} - N''_t(1+p)] + [M_{t+1} - M_t(1+p)]$$
$$- [L_{t+1} - L_t(1+p)]$$
$$= N''_t(s-p) - M_t.p + L_t.p \qquad (6.3)$$

In the more general case, in which transactions do take place, this formulation is still adequate, provided that we can interpret p and s as chain indices (of the general price level and specific asset prices respectively) in the manner described in Chapter 5, p. 114: the latter two definitions in (6.3) will then give an accurate attribution of the gains and losses to their various sources. The first definition does not rely on any assumption of this type, as it is merely concerned with the definition of total income.

The final definition in (6.3) is the most revealing in the sense that it shows the nature of the gains recognised by a real terms system. The first term $[N''_t(s-p)]$ is the real holding gain on non-monetary assets. Thus, the nominal holding gain $N''_t.s$ is no longer recognised in full, as was the case when money capital was maintained, but is instead reduced by the rise in the general index, p. When the rise in price of the specific assets (s) fails to keep pace with inflation (p), a real holding loss is deducted from profit $(p>s$, so that $N''_t(s-p)<0)$. The second term is the loss on holding monetary assets in a period of general inflation, and the third is the gain on having loans which are of fixed monetary amounts. The explanations of the latter two items are the same as those given in their explanation in the context of CPP accounting in Chapter 4, section 5 (pp. 78–9): this is hardly surprising, in view of the fact that the 'real terms' approach is the application of CPP adjustment to a current value base rather than the historical cost base.

Although the 'real terms' approach has the possible merit of providing an income measure which is expressed consistently in current pounds,[2] and which is unaffected by the rate of inflation during the reporting period, this property is not always desirable. Indexation is relatively uncommon, outside certain Latin American countries, so that accounting income numbers will often be evaluated by comparison with un-indexed data. Hence, Edwards and Bell (1961, Chapter VIII) regard the real terms adjustment of capital as less important than the current valuation of assets. In particular, rates of interest observed in markets are money rates rather than real rates. Thus, if we wish to value a company's shares by discounting its prospective returns to shareholders, or by some related procedure such as the application of a Price/Earnings ratio to its current earnings, we require money returns or earnings, with no 'real terms' adjustment. This has been demonstrated elegantly by Kennedy (1976). Because of the difficulty of estimating the expected inflation rate, which is necessary in order to derive the real interest rate from observed market rates, it will generally be preferable to compare nominal rates of interest (as observed in the market) with expected money rates of return, rather than comparing estimated real rates of interest with expected real rates of return. However, financial accounts are typically used for *ex post* appraisal, and the real interest rate is known *ex post* and can be compared with 'real terms' rates of return. Furthermore, the calculation of 'real terms' rates of return and profit figures might be relevant to inferring the future performance of a firm in an inflationary environment, when the firm's market position and pricing policy make maintenance of its real rate of return or income the likely course of future events. Thus, there are potential uses for proprietary income measures based on both money capital maintenance and real capital maintenance. There is no conflict between these requirements, as it is quite possible to draw up a profit and loss account which reports the 'real terms' adjustments (the *p* adjustments in equation (6.3)) separately, so that both monetary and real profit measures can be derived from the same statement. This will be discussed in a later section of this chapter.

An important modification of the 'pure' proprietary real income measure, which is made by a number of leading writers on the subject, is to distinguish between realised and unrealised gains. Edwards and Bell (1961) for example, propose a measure of 'realised profit' which includes realised holding gains (those on fixed assets consumed in use, by depreciation, and stocks realised by re-sale) and a measure of 'business profit' which includes, in addition, unrealised holding gains (gains on fixed assets not yet consumed and stocks not yet sold).[3] This distinction is consistent with the objective of providing a useful set of information about the economic progress of the firm: it has already been emphasised that unrealised holding gains are of a different quality from those which have been realised, especially when they are assessed at replacement cost of the gain, because their ultimate realisation will depend upon the future course of costs and prices. Sweeney (1936, Chapter 1), in his pioneering work on real terms accounting, insisted on the strict division of the profit and loss account into realised and unrealised sections. His system 'consists, first, in using a realised-income section the contents of which are identical with those in the ordinary profit and loss statement. Second, an unrealised income section is added because of the helpful information that it contains. Finally, at the very bottom of the profit and loss statement the total of the realised and unrealised income is shown. This total is called, "Final net income for the period"' (Sweeney, 1936, p. 21).

Sweeney's approach is adopted notably by Baxter (1975) among later writers, although Baxter rejects Sweeney's somewhat strict view of realisation, which is carried to the extent of not recognising gains or losses on any monetary liabilities or assets, including cash, until they are exchanged in a transaction (Baxter, 1975, p. 47). Baxter is, however, more cautious than Sweeney in that, whereas Sweeney reported total income in his profit and loss statement, merely using the realisation criterion to segregate different types of gain, Baxter's income statement (Baxter, 1975, Chapter 15, appendix) excludes unrealised gains, confining their reporting to the proprietors' equity interest in the balance sheet.[4] Thus, Baxter's income measure is not based on current values, as it excludes the unrealised real holding gains (or losses), which are implicit in the closing balance sheet values. The result of this is that Baxter's income measure yields an identical total to that of CPP-adjusted historical cost income, although his method of arriving at the total is more informative than CPP, isolating the realised real holding gains (Baxter, 1975, pp. 190–191).[5]

Thus, adherents of the 'real terms' approach to accounting have proposed several income measures which are not on a pure proprietary capital maintenance basis, i.e. maintenance of capital in terms of real purchasing power. Following the realisation principle, unrealised holding gains sometimes appear 'below the line' and are not included in the initial income number, but are added to the calculation of alternative income measures (Sweeney (1936), Edwards and Bell (1961)) or to capital reserves in the balance sheet

(Baxter, 1975). In the latter case, the capital maintenance principle being applied in the profit and loss account is the real purchasing power of opening capital, plus the unrealised real holding gains of the period, and less unrealised real holding losses of the period. This is an important modification of the capital maintenance basis of real terms accounting, if we attach particular weight to a single number measuring real income. If we adopt the broader approach of regarding real terms accounting as producing a set of useful information, we shall be less concerned about the precise format in which the information is presented, provided that it is all accessible. In this case, both the capital maintenance concept and the method of reporting unrealised gains and losses will be less important, although we might prefer a statement such as Sweeney's profit and loss statement, which reports unrealised and realised gains separately, rather than Baxter's system, which forces us to search the balance sheet to discover unrealised gains.

3 Entity capital

The entity view of capital maintenance is invariably linked with the advocacy of some form of replacement cost accounting.[6] The reason for this is that the entity approach assumes the continuity of the business as a fundamental environmental factor in financial reporting, and replacement cost is a particularly appropriate valuation basis if we contemplate continuity, and therefore the replacement of assets which are used up. An early pioneer of the entity approach was Schmidt (1930 and 1931).[7] More recent advocates of this approach are Gynther (1966), Mathews (1968) and Merrett and Sykes (1974 and 1980). Professional recommendations incorporating this view were made by the Institute of Cost and Works Accountants (1952) and by the Association of Certified and Corporate Accountants (1952), and an entity approach is applied in practice in the Netherlands, notably by Philips N. V. (Goudeket, 1960). There are, of course, a number of detailed variations on the basic entity principle, but all approaches have in common a capital maintenance concept which is designed to compensate for the price changes of the specific assets of the firm (a 'special index' approach), rather than for changes in the value of money (a 'general index' approach).

The consequence of this approach is that holding gains on assets are never recognised as part of profit, whether they are real (i.e. due

158

to the price of the asset appreciating more rapidly than the general price level) or fictitious (i.e. due to asset price rises which merely compensate for changes in the general price level). Instead, the holding gain is regarded as an accretion of the firm's capital. In double entry terms, the asset is debited with the appreciation in value, and capital (e.g. in the form of a revaluation reserve) is credited, whereas, in a system which recognised appreciation as profit, the profit and loss account would be credited. The reason for this, given by Schmidt (1931), is as follows:

> Some theoretical explanation of the reasons why appreciation cannot be profit is needed at this point. For this purpose we must consider the enterprise as a part of the national production machine. It will then be clear that a maintenance of total productivity as of a certain moment will only be possible, if the productive instrumentalities of all individual enterprises concerned are preserved intact. The maintenance of productive power as a whole is not possible if accounting is based on an original value basis. The reason is that pure appreciation would then appear as profit whenever a change of value has taken place between the purchase and selling dates for the materials and wages that compose a product.

Gynther defends this point of view from the standpoint of the individual shareholder, as follows:

> if it is believed that the whole or prime purpose is to assist the entity (the firm) in its daily struggles (and that only in this way will the interests of shareholders be looked after in the long term), then it is almost certain that the use of specific indexes will be favoured, i.e. so that the physical assets of the business will be maintained during the period of changing prices.

This plea for maintaining the specific assets of the business intact is intuitively appealing, but further analysis suggests weaknesses in the argument. If the concept is to be useful in accounting it must lead to a measurable and justifiable capital maintenance concept. Schmidt's 'productive power as a whole' is difficult to define clearly or measure precisely. If it implies a physical quantity of output, we meet the problem that output may have a different value per unit (in either real or nominal terms) at different times, so that the maintenance of physical output might not be in the interests of the shareholders, the entity, or the community (e.g. when the product is becoming obsolete). If we resort instead to maintaining the total value of output, irrespective of its composition, we meet the difficulty that varying profit margins might mean that different types of output are of different value to the entity and its shareholders: in the extreme, maintenance of sales of a product which makes a loss is clearly undesirable. We might then resort to maintenance of the profit stream earned by the entity, but this takes us away from notions of capital maintenance and into the area of standard stream income (Hicks No. 2 and No. 3), which is essentially a proprietary approach (maintaining consumption of shareholders or proprietors), although it might be consistent with the entity approach under certain circumstances, e.g. when the profitability of a certain physical output was expected to remain constant in the future.

Gynther's proposal for maintaining physical assets can be criticised on similar grounds. If there is technical progress, relative factor price changes, or product price changes, the value of the physical assets of the firm will change, and the optimal replacement policy will not involve identical replacement of the assets currently held. If we overcome this difficulty by resorting to the maintenance of the value of the assets rather than a physical quantity, we are once more in the realm of the proprietary approach rather than the entity approach.

Thus, if we assume a realistic world in which relative prices change and there is technical progress, it seems unlikely that we can justify the maintenance of an entity in physical terms, whether output or assets. Once we concede the case for defining capital maintenance in monetary terms, without reference to a specific collection of assets, we have conceded the case for a proprietary approach to capital maintenance. This regards the capital of the firm as a fund of general purchasing power which can be switched to its most profitable use, rather than being tied to the preservation of a particular physical activity.[8] It also allows appreciation of asset values to be treated as profit. Thus, a 'real terms' proprietary approach treats real holding gains as profits, and real holding losses as losses.[9]

Proponents of the entity approach (such as Merrett and Sykes, 1980)[10] sometimes object that asset prices can rise without product prices rising, so that the holding gain on the asset recognised by the proprietary approach is illusory. In order to examine this argument, we shall consider the three possible alternative relationships between asset prices and product prices:

(i) *Prices immediately compensate for cost increases.* In this case, replacement cost can be passed on immediately in price rises without loss of sales volume, and the holding gain resulting from the rise in replacement cost of assets already held will be realised when the output is sold, so that it is indisputably accurate to describe this as a realisable gain.

(ii) *Prices compensate for cost increases after a time lag.* In this case, the firm may pass on increased replacement costs as price increases when the output being sold has involved the use of assets purchased at the new replacement cost. In the meantime, it may price on the basis of historical cost, so that the holding gain on assets held at the time of the cost increase will not be realised. In this case, the entity approach will charge enhanced replacement cost against revenue immediately, irrespective of whether the assets used to earn the revenue were purchased at that cost, and will not recognise a holding gain.[11] The proprietary approach will also charge current replacement cost, but it will recognise the holding gain which occurs because the replacement cost being charged now (and, in the case of unrealised gains, in the future) is in excess of the historical acquisition cost of the assets being used. Thus, the proprietary approach recognises a holding gain which is realised or realisable; the realisation takes the form of a charge against profit when the asset is used. The entity approach charges the realisation against profit but does not credit the holding gain, i.e. it treats appreciation and depreciation asymmetrically.[12] In a period of rising prices, this results in an ultra-conservative profit figure, profit being charged with depreciation of holding gains which have not been recognised as profit.

(iii) *Prices never compensate for cost increases.* This case might seem to be one which favours the entity approach. However, the argument of the preceding paragraph can still be invoked in support of a proprietary approach. Although profits, after charging replacement cost, will be reduced permanently by the cost increase, during the transitional period the firm will still benefit, to the extent of the holding gain, by having capital

161

goods in stock which were bought at the lower historical cost, rather than the higher current replacement cost. The proprietary approach will recognise this, and the entity approach will not. To take a simple example, suppose that a firm purchases stock at the beginning of each period and sells and replaces at the end. It has been trading, up to time t, with stock costing £100 and selling at a mark-up of 50 per cent. The profit calculation for periods ending not later than t will be:

	£
Sales	150
Less Replacement Cost of Sales	100
Profit	£ 50

This will be the same on both the proprietary and the entity basis, if we assume that all prices have remained constant. Now, assume that replacement cost at time $t + 1$ rises by 20 per cent but selling prices remain constant. The proprietary approach would report profit for the period ending $t + 1$ as follows:

	£
Sales	150
Less Replacement Cost of Sales	120
Operating Profit	30
Add Holding Gain	20
Total Profit	£ 50

The entity approach, on the other hand, would report profit as follows:

	£
Sales	150
Less Replacement Cost of Sales	120
Profit	£ 30

In this case, the holding gain of £20 would be credited to a capital reserve. Thus, the proprietary approach would maintain a capital of £100 and the entity approach a capital of £120. Both systems recognise the enhanced asset value, so the question of the possibly lower economic value of the assets due to the decline in profit margin is irrelevant to the choice between systems. Equally, the operating profit figure in the proprietary system conveys the same information as that in the entity system. The essential difference between the systems is that the proprietary approach regards the gain as profit, whereas the entity approach regards it as being a necessary part of maintaining existing capital. Again, the entity approach is asymmetrical in its treatment of gains and losses, excluding the holding gain from profit but charging the enhanced stock value (including the gain) against profit, as cost of sales.

In this context, the argument about lower profit margins can be turned against the entity approach, because it is questionable whether the maintenance of existing stocks is justified when margins have declined. If replacement did not take place, but the company instead liquidated its investment, the proprietary approach undoubtedly gives a more informative profit figure: the total profit of £50 does represent the surplus of the cash which the proprietors would have on liquidation, over the value of their capital interest at the beginning of the period, if the stock were not replaced.

Thus, the entity approach has questionable foundations, although it may be relevant in producing a sub-division of income which is useful. The concept of operating profit, for example, may be found useful, and the separation of this from holding gains can be regarded as reconciling the entity approach (profit after charging replacement cost but excluding holding gains) with the proprietary approach (holding gains added).[13] The Sandilands Committee's proposals for current cost accounting could be interpreted as an example of this approach, their operating profit before deducting interest being an entity measure of income,[14] and total gains being a proprietary measure. It should, however, be noted that, for implementation in a world characterised by general inflation, the gains would have to be abated by a general price level adjustment (strongly opposed by Sandilands) in order to produce a 'real terms' proprietary measure. The Sandilands Committee emphasised that its measure of operating profit is not based on physical capital maintenance (Sandilands Report, 1975, para. 129): the capital which it preserves is based upon the 'value to the business' rather than the replacement cost of the assets of the firm. However, 'value to the business' is assessed

163

according to the characteristics of the specific assets of the firm, and it may typically be expected to equal replacement cost (Gee and Peasnell, 1976), so that it does not seem unreasonable to classify the Sandilands operating profit as an entity measure: certainly, its exclusion of all holding gains precludes it from being regarded as a proprietary approach.

To conclude the discussion of the entity approach, we shall briefly consider two details of its application about which its proponents differ in their preferred method. These are, respectively, backlog depreciation and the treatment of monetary working capital.

4 Backlog depreciation

Backlog depreciation arises when the accumulated depreciation provision is inadequate to cover the cost of replacement, the gap being backlog depreciation. A simple example is as follows:

Assume that an asset cost £100 and is to be written off over 5 years on the straight line basis. After 2½ years, the replacement cost of the asset rises to £150, and remains at this level until the end of the fifth year. Replacement cost depreciation would be provided as follows:

Mid-year basis

Time	Annual Provision	Accumulated Provision
1	20	20
2	20	40
3	25	65
4	30	95
5	30	125

End-year basis

Time	Annual Provision	Accumulated Provision
1	20	20
2	20	40
3	30	70
4	30	100
5	30	130

The backlog depreciation is £25 (=£150 − £125) in the case of the 'mid-year' basis and £20 (=£150 − £130) in the case of the 'end-year' basis. This is because the provision made for the period before the cost rise was based on a cost lower than that at which replacement ultimately takes place. Strictly, there are two distinct backlog problems, the between-year problem, and the within-year problem. The former is the problem of under-provision for past years (years 1 and 2 in the example), whereas the latter is the problem of under-provision for the current year, which arises if we charge depreciation on the basis of cost at the time of use (the mid-year basis). The end-year basis bypasses the latter problem by charging on the basis of end-year costs, although this is difficult to justify if we regard depreciation as reflecting cost at the time of use.

The backlog problem arises from regarding depreciation as a fund for the replacement of specific assets. If we regard depreciation as merely an allocation of costs, no problem arises. We are no longer concerned with the total accumulated provision but merely with the charge for the relevant period: if that charge was adequate to cover cost at the time of use, no problem arises. However, even if we are concerned with the total accumulated provision, this raises no problems for the proprietary theorist, because any increase in depreciation will be offset by a holding gain. Suppose, for example, we wished to provide backlog depreciation in period 3, and we were using the mid-year method, which best reflects cost at the time of use. We would revalue the asset at replacement cost, crediting a holding gain:

	Debit	Credit
Cost of Asset	£50	
Holding Gain		£50

We would provide backlog depreciation, debiting this to the holding gain

	Debit	Credit
Holding Gain	£25	
Accumulated depreciation		£25

The net effect would be to record the revaluation of the undepreciated portion of the asset as a net holding gain. An entity theorist would not, however, treat the holding gain on the asset as part of income, whereas he would charge normal depreciation to income. He is thus faced with a choice of charging the backlog depreciation against income, without any offsetting holding gain, or of treating backlog depreciation differently from current depreciation, debiting it to capital rather than income. The latter procedure is the most commonly adopted (e.g. by Gynther, 1966, and by the Sandilands Committee, 1975, para. 606). It can be justified by assuming that accounts are concerned with periodic income, rather than with the life-cycle of asset ownership. It is therefore sufficient that the depreciation for the period should measure the replacement cost of assets used up during the period. It may further be argued that depreciation should only meet the cost of replacement at the precise time when the asset was used up: this would justify the 'mid-year' rather than the 'end-year' method.

Income measurement is concerned with charging the cost of the asset at the time of its use, not with providing funds, so that the concept of depreciation as a fund for replacement is not relevant to income measurement. Even if it were, nevertheless, considered important[15] that current depreciation charges should reflect the current burden of replacement on the funds of the firm, it should be noted that charging replacement cost depreciation would not necessarily achieve this, because the replacement requirements of a period will typically differ from the replacement cost of assets used up during that period. Domar (1953) demonstrates that, with a growing stock of fixed assets and rising replacement prices, historical cost depreciation can be adequate to cover the replacement requirements of a period, because it is the oldest (and, with a growing stock, the least numerous) assets which require replacement.

5 Monetary working capital

The treatment of monetary working capital also lends itself to a variety of alternative interpretations under the entity capital maintenance convention. Under the proprietary approach, the treatment is simple: we either maintain money values, in which case the nominal value of M_t and $-L_t$ are maintained, or we maintain real values, in which case we apply general index adjustment, $M_t(1 + p)$ and $-L_t(1 + p)$). Both of these are adopted by certain adherents of the entity aproach, e.g. the Sandilands current cost system uses the money basis and the Philips system uses the real basis. However, other entity theorists, such as Gynther (1966), advocate a specific index approach, and this type of approach is embodied in the current British accounting standard (SSAP16: ASC, 1980).

The specific index approach is entirely consistent with the spirit of the entity capital maintenance approach. It attempts to extend the concept of the entity beyond its physical assets to its monetary working capital. Physical working capital, in the form of stocks and work-in-progress, is already included as part of the physical capital to be maintained, and it is a natural step to argue that it is just as necessary for the smooth running of the business to hold cash and give trade credit to customers as it is for it to hold stocks. This, if we can define a specific index, s, which reflects appropriately the change in the firm's need for monetary working capital arising from price changes during the period, in order to maintain its level of output, we can define the monetary working capital to be maintained as $M_t(1 + s)$ and $-L_t(1 + s)$.

Of course, many problems arise when we try to define s precisely, and consequently there are many practical variations on this basic theme. For example, we might have different indices for trade debtors (whose needs presumably reflect product selling price) and trade creditors (which presumably reflect the purchase price of inputs), although some writers, such as Gibbs (1976), prefer to regard trade credit net, rather than gross, regarding an increase in creditors as a natural offset to an increase in debtors as the money value of output rises. There are also difficult conceptual and practical problems involved in separating monetary working capital from other forms of monetary capital held by the firm. This is most obvious in the case of cash and deposits, which may be necessary to meet the normal flow of payments (the transactions motive), or may be held in reserve to meet unforeseen fluctuations in payments (the pre-cautionary motive) or may be held as an investment (the speculative motive). Equally, bank overdrafts and short-term liabilities may be held for a variety of motives and are, to some extent, substitutes for long-term liabilities, which are not usually regarded as part of monetary working capital. Even trade credit is not exempt from ambiguity: the concept of the level of trade credit necessary for the maintenance of output cannot be defined in absolute terms, independently of financial conditions. Giving and receiving trade credit entails costs and brings benefits to the firm, and the amount which it is appropriate to give and receive will depend not only on the level of output, but also on the level of interest rates, the financial state of the firm, its suppliers and customers, and the competitiveness of the markets in which the firm operates.

Thus, the maintenance of a specific level of monetary working capital is consistent with the entity approach and brings with it the ambiguities inherent in that approach. Once we move away from concepts of money or general purchasing power, it is extremely difficult to define clearly and measure precisely what is meant by the entity and therefore what is required in order to maintain it intact.

6 The gearing adjustment

We now turn to a capital maintenance concept which has both proprietary and entity elements, that which uses the gearing adjustment. This is of great practical importance because it is a feature of the UK's standard on current cost accounting (SSAP16: ASC, 1980). The gearing adjustment is an eclectic capital maintenance concept. In its purest form, it involves the entity approach to maintaining equity capital but a proprietary approach (using money, rather than general purchasing power) to long-term borrowing. The argument for this usually starts from an entity view of the profit of the firm but then points out that there is an additional profit accruing to equity shareholders[16] in a period of inflation due to the fact that the ownership of the firm shifts from those providers of long-term capital with a fixed money claim ('gearing') to the residual claimants, the equity shareholders. Thus the gearing adjustment is an adjustment indicating how the equity shareholders have gained at the expense of gearing: it indicates changes in the allocation of profit and claims to capital amongst these groups, but does not tell us anything about the firm's profitability in trading and dealing with outsiders.

The gearing adjustment was originally a German creation, the basic idea being the creation of Schmidt; his 1930 and 1931 papers are an accessible account of his ideas for English readers.[17] His work was the main source of inspiration for the 1975 recommendation by the German Institute of Chartered Accountants, which was the first professional pronouncement to advocate a form of gearing adjustment. The German recommendations, and their relationship to the work of Schmidt, are described in Coenenberg and Macharzina (1976).

However, the gearing adjustment was reinvented, apparently independently, by a group of British writers, Godley and Cripps, Kennedy, and Gibbs in a series of articles published in *The Times* between 1974 and 1976. This literature has been surveyed by Kennedy (1978a). It was clearly influential in the thinking behind the *Submission on ED.18* by the London Society of Chartered Accountants (May 1977), which was in turn influential in the move towards the adoption of the Hyde Guidelines (Accounting Standards Committee, 1977), and SSAP16 (ASC, 1980).

The origins of the gearing adjustment in the UK lay in the corporate liquidity crisis of 1974 and Merrett and Sykes' articles about this

(1974). Merrett and Sykes observed a situation in which wage inflation combined with price controls had depressed operating margins but taxable and distributable profits were swelled by stock appreciation, and interest rates were high so that external finance could not be substituted for internal funds. This led them to advocate a measure of profit which was based on the entity capital maintenance principle: the specific assets of the firm must be maintained before any distribution could be made to shareholders or to the tax authorities. Their article was influential in the introduction of stock appreciation relief, which removed stock appreciation from the tax base, in the Autumn of 1974, lightening the tax burden, and therefore easing the liquidity problem. The entity principle of eliminating holding gains in the calculation of operating profit was followed by the Sandilands Report (1975).[18]

Godley and Wood (1974) objected to Merrett and Sykes' entity approach in the case of a loan-financed business, showing by means of numerical examples that the shareholders of such a business did make a distributable profit from stock appreciation and should therefore be taxed on this gain. Day (1974) pointed out that this applied only to a loan-financed business.

The gearing adjustment, proposed by Godley and Cripps (1975)[19] reconciled these two views. Holding gains on assets should be treated as profit to the extent that they were loan financed. Therefore, a proportion of holding gains should be credited to profits, the proportion being the gearing ratio of the firm. As Kennedy (1978a) points out, this implies that, insofar as assets are loan financed, the holding gain recognised is the same as that under 'real terms' accounting (as, for example, proposed by the CCAB, 1975), although the latter would divide the gain, in a period of general inflation, into a gain on borrowing and a real holding gain. Insofar as assets are equity financed, however, the gearing adjustment leaves holding gains 'below the line' and they are not recognised as part of profit, because equity capital is effectively up-dated by the index appropriate to the specific assets of the entity. Thus, insofar as there are real holding gains in an equity financed firm, they will not be included in profit under the gearing-adjustment system, and this profit will therefore be less than 'real terms' profit.[20]

In algebraic terms, the Godley/Cripps/Gibbs/Kennedy gearing adjustment is as follows.

To opening money capital, we add the following:

169

$$N''_t . s \left[1 - \frac{L_t - M_t}{L_t - M_t + P''_t} \right]$$

where $N''_t . s$ is the 'entity' adjustment necessary to provide fully for the replacement of non-monetary assets. If a monetary working capital adjustment is made, its components should be classified as part of N''_t, rather than M_t or L_t.

$$\left[\frac{L_t - M_t}{L_t - M_t + P''_t} \right]$$

is the proportion of opening non-monetary assets [21] which is financed by gearing (since $L_t - M_t + P''_t = N''_t$).

Thus, geared income is:

$$Y_G = P''_{t+1} - \left[P_t + N''_t . s \left(1 - \frac{L_t - M_t}{L_t - M_t + P''_t} \right) \right]$$

$$= (M_{t+1} - M_t) + (N''_{t+1} - N''_t)$$

$$- N''_t . s \left(1 - \frac{L_t - M_t}{L_t - M_t + P''_t} \right) - (L_{t+1} - L_t) \qquad (6.4)$$

This is the simplest and most self-consistent form of gearing adjustment. Apart from the dating problem already noted, SSAP16 and its predecessors have the peculiarity of arbitrarily restricting the holding gains which are recognised, by applying the gearing adjustment only to realised holding gains, i.e. the gearing adjustment is applied as an abatement of depreciation, the cost of sales adjustment (stock appreciation removal) and the monetary working capital adjustment, but is not applied to the appreciation of fixed assets which are still held at the end of the period. This ultra-conservative approach has been condemned by proponents of the gearing adjustment, such as Kennedy (1978a) and Gibbs and Seward (1979), and will not be discussed further. When the gearing adjustment is applied to a system with an adjustment for monetary working capital (as in SSAP16), the definition of gearing has to exclude the monetary working capital elements of M_t and L_t.

It is possible to question the usefulness of profit calculations based upon the gearing adjustment, and their superiority to 'real terms' accounting based on the proprietary approach. The 'entity' valuation of equity capital, which excludes real holding gains from profit seems to imply that the firm must remain intact in its present form, and that no profit results even when the current value of that form rises in real terms. The difficulties of justifying and implementing the entity approach were discussed earlier in this chapter. Kennedy (1978a) describes operating profit, less interest and after the gearing adjustment, as 'proprietary profit'. This *is* a proprietary concept insofar as these two adjustments have been made to reflect profit attributable to equity, but the method of *measuring* equity for capital maintenance purposes is *entity* based, reflecting the values of the specific assets of the firm which are assumed to be maintained,[22] rather than proprietary, reflecting the general purchasing power of shareholders. It is therefore possible to contest Kennedy's view that his 'proprietary profit' is 'the most suitable figure for use as a *base* for dividend distribution policy'.[23]

A second deficiency of the gearing adjustment system is the failure to separate the gain on borrowing from holding gains on assets. To anyone who accepts the proprietary approach with constant purchasing power as the ideal measurement standard (such as Sweeney (1936), Edwards and Bell (1961), and Baxter (1975)), this involves a serious loss of information, pooling gains on financing (the borrowing gain) with gains on investment (asset gains). Kennedy proposes a system which should combine this information with the gearing adjustment.[24]

Finally, the relationship of the gearing adjustment to particular uses is ill-specified. Merrett and Sykes (1974) were clearly concerned with a liquidity crisis rather than a profits crisis (holding gains do not give rise to a cash flow even when they can be regarded as an economic gain which is of the nature of a profit). A concern with liquidity has remained throughout the debate, particularly in the writings of Gibbs (1975, 1976 and 1979), and it is not entirely clear whether the central concern is with profit or with cash flow. Taxation appears to be a central concern of Godley and Wood (1974) and Godley and Cripps (1975), although Kennedy (1978a) avoids any commitment on this issue.

7 Eclectic income statements

Kennedy (1978a) has proposed a 'simplified income statement' which would record 'real terms' proprietary profit in addition to

Current value systems 2

various income measures suggested by proponents of the gearing adjustment and of the entity approach. It is difficult to quarrel with this eclectic approach to the income statement, which seems to be one way to achieve the reporting of 'different incomes for different purposes'. This would have the benefit of reducing the emphasis on a single income number, and would be an application of the 'useful information' approach (or what the Sandilands Report, para. 540, describes as a 'building block' approach) exemplified by the work of Edwards and Bell (1961). It is possible to incorporate a variety of capital maintenance concepts in the same set of accounts because capital maintenance affects only income measurement, and can therefore be dealt with in the profit and loss account. It will be recalled that reporting a variety of asset valuation bases was more difficult because this would entail re-stating individual assets in the balance sheet, as well as various components (such as depreciation) of the profit and loss account. Thus, the valuation problem entails multiple-column accounting, whereas the capital maintenance problem involves only multiple rows in the income statement, since it merely requires alternative statements of a single item, the income number.

For illustrative purposes, Kennedy's (1978a) proposal will be discussed, although many alternatives exist in the literature. Kennedy's 'simplified income statement' is as follows:

		£
	Current cost operating profit	X
plus	Interest received from net monetary assets	X
minus	Adjustment for maintenance of real value of net monetary assets	(X)
equals	*Entity profit*	X
minus	Interest paid on monetary liabilities	(X)
plus	Geared holding gains	X
equals	*Proprietary profit*	X
plus	Ungeared holding gains	X
equals	*Total proprietary gain*	X
minus	Inflationary element of ungeared holding gains	(X)
equals	*Inflation-corrected proprietary gain*	X

Each of the italicised rows represents a different profit concept. We start with current cost operating profit, which uses an entity capital maintenance concept based upon the replacement of the value to the owner of physical assets: $P''_t + N''_t . s$. After the addition of financial income (which could include dividends as well as interest), there is an entity adjustment to allow for the maintenance of net monetary assets in real terms, i.e. a monetary working capital adjustment. This adjusts opening capital to be maintained by $(M_{c,t} - L_{c,t}) . s$, to give a total of $P''_t + N''_t . s + (M_{c,t} - L_{c,t}) . s$, where the subscript c indicates M and L items which are part of working capital. It should be noted that s is a specific index which may vary with asset type. The result of this adjustment is a full-blooded entity profit figure, based on maintaining the business intact. It suffers from the conceptual problems discussed earlier; the precise nature of what is being maintained is not as clear as might be wished.

The next step involves a move to 'proprietary profit', using a gearing adjustment. Interest paid is deducted, since this is an apportionment of entity profit to the non-proprietary element of net worth (the geared element). Geared holding gains are then added back: as explained earlier, this represents an abatement of the capital maintenance concept to allow for the fact that the gearing element is fixed in monetary terms, so that there is a net gain to proprietors (equity). If we define long-term borrowing (for fixed capital) as L_f and short-term borrowing (for working capital) as L_c, the entity capital maintenance concept was $P''_t + N''_t . s + (M_{c,t} - L_{c,t}) . s$ and Kennedy's proprietary capital maintenance concept becomes:

$$P''_t + \left(1 - \frac{L_{f,t}}{L_{f,t} + P''_t}\right)(N''_t . s + [M_{c,t} - L_{c,t}] . s) \qquad (6.5)$$

where the term $L_{f,t}/(L_{f,t} + P''_t)$ is the gearing ratio.[25] The effect of this adjustment is that a money capital maintenance concept is applied to geared capital but equity capital (P''_t) is still maintained on an *entity* basis, i.e. applying an index, s, which is specific to the firm. This becomes obvious in the ungeared case, when the term in the first bracket becomes unity. This is not, therefore, a proprietary concept in the sense in which this was defined earlier in this chapter, but is rather a product of the gearing adjustment which was discussed critically in the previous section. It should be noted that this form of gearing adjustment embraces all holding gains: the SSAP16 form would exclude unrealised holding gains.

The next stage is to add back to profit the ungeared holding gains

173

(the product of the two brackets in (6.5) above), to apply the simple capital maintenance concept, P''_t. This is proprietary capital in money terms, as discussed earlier, and the proprietary profit measure which it yields is described by Kennedy as Total proprietary gain.

Finally, an adjustment is made to derive 'real terms' proprietary profit, which Kennedy describes as the Inflation-corrected proprietary gain. The correct method of doing this is to add to the capital maintenance concept (i.e. deduct from profit) the general price adjustment of equity, $P''_t . s$, to give a total capital to be maintained, $P''_t . (1 + p)$. Kennedy makes an arithmetic slip here in deducting from profit the 'Inflationary element of all holding gains',[26] $p . (P''_t + L_{f,t})$, rather than merely the inflationary element of *ungeared* holding gains, $p . P''_t$. From the proprietors' standpoint it is unnecessary to index geared capital, because it requires maintenance only in money terms, the excess of the restated real terms amount over the money amount being the gain on borrowing, which is probably best deducted from interest payments.

It is therefore possible to disagree with Kennedy's detailed proposals for an eclectic income statement. The gearing adjustment may be unnecessary and it might be preferable to make the distinction between realised and unrealised holding gains (following Sweeney, 1936, or Edwards and Bell, 1961). It would also be desirable to show the gain on borrowing separately. However, it is difficult to disagree with the broad principle of reporting a variety of alternative income measures which can be used by different users for different purposes. Kennedy also deals effectively with a common criticism of this type of proposal:

> The suggestion that more than one measure of profit in the main statement of the accounts will confuse the users of the accounts has been greatly exaggerated. A user of accounts can simply pick on the line in the statement most appropriate for his purpose. In any case, even if he is confused, it is definitely preferable that he should remain so than that he should be misled by a single profit figure that he has not properly understood (Kennedy, 1978a, pp. 63–4).

8 Conclusion

The capital maintenance concept is a crucial component of income measurement. The measure of income, whether for pricing, taxation, dividend distributions, wage bargaining or share valuation, seems to have been a central concern of participants in the inflation accounting debate, and a variety of alternative concepts have been proposed. Fortunately, it is possible to devise an income statement which shows several alternative income numbers, based on different capital maintenance concepts. The three concepts which are most widely canvassed in the literature are the entity concept, the money proprietary concept and the real proprietary concept. The former raises the problem of defining the nature of the entity to be maintained, but if this issue can be resolved it seems likely that it will be useful to have a profit measure which excludes that portion of income which is pre-empted by the need to maintain the entity intact when the relative price of its assets is rising. The money proprietary concept has strong traditional and intuitive roots, and reflects the interests of the shareholder, but it needs to be modified for some purposes, in a period of inflation, by general price level adjustment, to yield real proprietary capital maintenance.

Each of these three basic concepts can be incorporated in a single income statement, so they need not be regarded as being mutually exclusive. The steps in the reconciliation are open to debate. Kennedy (1978a) proposes that these should include a gearing adjustment, but discussion of this adjustment failed to establish that it is anything other than an awkward compromise between the entity and the proprietary approaches. An alternative route would apply the general purchasing power adjustment across all sources of capital simultaneously, separating real holding gains (and losses) from fictitious gains due to inflation (or losses due to deflation, if that were to come about), and identifying the gain on borrowing and loss on holding monetary assets in a period of inflation. It might also be useful to separate realised holding gains from unrealised gains.

The exposition of this chapter has been mainly verbal and algebraic. In order to aid comprehension, Appendix A provides a set of simple numerical illustrations of alternative capital maintenance concepts. The argument has been conducted mainly in terms of *a priori* reasoning, but there is considerable scope for empirical work in order to establish the realism of the empirical assumptions of competing arguments, the materiality of the differences between capital maintenance concepts, and the utility of the resulting measures. Appendix B reviews the results of the empirical work which has been published to date. Finally, Chapter 7 attempts to provide an over-view of the previous discussion.

Chapter 6: Appendix A A numerical illustration of alternative capital maintenance concepts

1 Introduction

This appendix provides a numerical illustration of two important capital maintenance concepts not illustrated in the earlier chapters. These are the gearing adjustment (in its 'pure' Godley/Cripps/Kennedy/Gibbs form) and the general index 'real terms' adjustment, applied to a current valuation base. Finally, the Kennedy Appropriation Account is used to reconcile the profit figures resulting from using different concepts of capital maintenance.

The facts assumed are those of the 'Old Fred' example used in earlier chapters, the particular starting point for this illustration being Appendix B to Chapter 5, which gave current cost accounts, using replacement cost as the valuation base, and reporting both a money proprietary and an entity view of capital maintenance, in the spirit, if not the letter, of the Sandilands Report. Obviously, there is a bewildering variety of variations on the current value base (which were indicated in Chapter 5) and on the capital maintenance concept (which were indicated in Chapter 6). A valuable survey of capital maintenance concepts which have been proposed for practical application is provided by Tweedie (1979).

The object of the following examples is to illustrate the basic workings of some of the more popular techniques, rather than to deal exhaustively with all possible techniques and circumstances. The latter type of guidance will be found in the guidance notes and manuals published in association with accounting standards. For example, current UK practice, which incorporates a form of gearing adjustment (restricted to realised holding gains) and a monetary working capital adjustment, is defined in SSAP16 (ASC, 1980) and the *Guidance Notes* appended to it. Mallinson (1980) provides a thorough technical discussion of its implementation.

2 The gearing adjustment

Period 1: It will be recalled from Chapter 5, Appendix B, that Old Fred's opening balance sheet, on a current cost basis, was:

Balance Sheet at *t*

	£		£
Proprietor's Capital	150	*Fixed Asset*	
		Van (at cost)	100
Loan	50		
		Current Asset	
		Cash	100
	£200		£200

It will be observed that the gearing ratio is 1/4 (= 50/200), i.e. one quarter of the long-term capital is provided by loans. Applying this ratio to the current cost accounts for the period, as given in Chapter 5, Appendix B, a simple form of gearing adjustment will give us the following profit and loss account:

Profit and Loss Account for Period 1, *t* to *t* + 1

	£
Sales	120
Less Current Cost of goods sold	104
	16
Less Depreciation	10
Current Cost Operating Profit	6
Add Gearing Adjustment	7.50
Distributable Profit	£ 13.50

It will be observed that this profit and loss account is the same as that for the current cost accounts (Chapter 5, Appendix B) up to the calculation of Current Cost Operating Profit. Current Cost Operating Profit is based upon an entity concept of capital maintenance, holding gains being excluded from profit and treated as increases in the value of capital to be maintained. The gearing adjustment adds back that proportion of the holding gains which is financed by debt. In this particular case, the calculation is 1/4 (the gearing ratio) times £30 (the holding gain on stocks). The resulting profit figure (£13.50) is described here as 'distributable profit' because it is that profit which proponents of the gearing adjustment would regard as being distributable to the proprietor (or, in the case of a company, the

177

shareholders) without impairing the substance of the entity (i.e. the specific assets of the business, financed by a constant gearing ratio), on the assumption that further borrowing is possible in order to maintain the initial gearing ratio.

It should be noted that a number of variants of the gearing adjustment is possible. These include:

(1) Present UK practice is to apply the gearing ratio only to realised holding gains, but this practice is rejected by the original authors of the adjustment (Godley, Cripps, Gibbs and Kennedy), so we shall ignore it here.

(2) Gearing can be measured (as in the current SSAP16 in the United Kingdom) as the average for the year, rather than by reference to the beginning of year balance sheet.

(3) In the case of a company, preference shares may be regarded either as gearing (as in the earlier Hyde Guidelines for the UK) or as part of the proprietors' interest (as in the case of the current SSAP16).

(4) Long-term fixed interest loan stocks, or fixed dividend preference stocks, could be shown at market value, rather than nominal value, for the purpose of measuring gearing. Market value would be consistent with the *current* basis of current cost accounting, but nominal value is preferred in practice as being simpler to calculate and not subject to fluctuations as market interest rates change.

(5) The range of monetary liabilities and assets to be taken account of in determining gearing can be defined in various ways. Gearing is usually considered to be relevant to long-term financing, and short-term liabilities are often considered as an offset to current assets in determining net monetary working capital, for the purposes of a monetary working capital adjustment. In the simple example of Period 1, shown above, we assume no short-term liabilities, so that the latter problem does not arise. We also assume that the cash holding in the opening balance sheet was immediately converted into stocks, so that there was no monetary working capital during the period.

The closing balance sheet is the same as that for the current cost accounts (Chapter 5, Appendix B), except that the apportionment of the Proprietor's Capital is different, the ungeared holding gain (£22.50) being regarded as an undistributable capital maintenance reserve.

Balance Sheet at $t + 1$

	£		£	£
Proprietor's Capital		*Fixed Asset*		
Opening balance (at t)	150	Van (at cost)	100	
Add Capital reserve	22.50	*Less* Accumulated		
Distributable		depreciation	10	
profit	13.50		—	90
	186.00	*Current Assets*		
Less Drawings	30	Stock (at current cost)	26	
	—	Cash	90	
Closing balance			—	116
(at $t + 1$)	156			
Loan	50			
	£206			£206

Period 2: The gearing ratio in the opening balance sheet, calculated on the same basis as for Period 1, is 50/206. Applying this to the £50 holding gains shown in the current cost accounts (Chapter 5, Appendix B) gives the following final section of the profit and loss account.

Gearing adjustment to the Period 2, Current Cost Profit and Loss Account

	£
Current Cost Operating Loss	(37)
Add Gearing adjustment $\left(50 \times \dfrac{50}{206}\right)$	12.14
Distributable Loss	£(24.86)

The Proprietor's Capital in the Balance Sheet again must equal that in the current cost accounts (by definition, since it must equal $N_{t+1} + M_{t+1} - L_{t+1}$), but the division between distributable profits and undistributable reserves occurs under the gearing adjustment system:

	£
Proprietor's Capital	
Opening balance (at $t + 1$)	156.00
Add Appropriation to maintenance capital reserve	
(ungeared holding gains)	37.86
Distributable (loss)	(24.86)
	169.00
Less Drawings	106.00
Closing balance (at $t + 2$)	£ 63.00

In this example, we have implicitly assumed that a monetary working capital adjustment is inappropriate. However, the firm did receive net credit of £14 during Period 2, if we make the assumption (as for Chapter 4, Appendix B) that purchase transactions and settlement of initial debts took place at the beginning of the period, whereas sales took place at the end. This consists of £52 credit received from the supplier, less £38 held as a cash balance. The cash balance is assumed to be necessary for the running of the business, and therefore part of monetary working capital, i.e. in terms of the notation of Chapter 6, we define $M_{c,t+1}$ as £38 and $L_{c,t+1}$ as £52. We assume that the appropriate index by which to adjust the monetary working capital is the rise in the price of stocks during the period, 1.38 ($\approx 1.80/1.30$).

The monetary working capital adjustment is analogous to the cost of sales adjustment (i.e. the additional charge for the excess of replacement cost over historical cost) for stocks. When a net amount is invested in monetary working capital, the increase required to maintain this amount in real terms (according to the specific index chosen) is charged to the Profit and Loss Account in arriving at Current Cost Operating Profit. This charge is then abated by the gearing adjustment, because a proportion of the net monetary working capital is financed by long-term debt and, on the assumption of a constant gearing ratio, would not require maintenance by the properties of the entity. When, as in the present case, net monetary working capital is negative, i.e. borrowings exceed lendings and cash holdings, it is an addition (credit) to Profit and Loss, rather than a charge (debt), and so offsets the additional charge for replacement cost of stocks.

These adjustments would be implemented as opposite.

The effect of introducing the monetary working capital adjustment in this example is that the current cost operating loss is reduced by the full amount of the adjustment (£2.80) and the distributable loss is reduced by the ungeared proportion (£2.12). This results in a transfer of £2.12 from the capital maintenance reserve, to reduce the distributable loss, but the closing balance of proprietor's interest in the balance sheet is unchanged. This demonstrates that the monetary working capital adjustment is a capital maintenance concept, assisting the separation of capital from profit, but not affecting the evaluation of the proprietor's aggregate interest in the firm, which depends upon the valuation basis adopted for assets and liabilities (since $P_{t+2} \equiv N_{t+2} + M_{t+2} - L_{t+2}$).

Profit and Loss Account for Period 2, $t + 1$ to $t + 2$, with Monetary Working Capital and Gearing Adjustments

	£	£
Sales		135.00
Less Current Cost of Goods Sold	162.00	
Monetary Working Capital Adjustment		
($£14[180/150-1]$)	(2.80)	
		159.20
Trading (Loss)		(24.20)
Less Current Cost Depreciation		10.00
Current Cost Operating (Loss)		(34.20)
Add Gearing Adjustment $\left(\dfrac{50}{206}[£50-£2.80]\right)$		11.46
Distributable (Loss)		£(22.74)

Balance Sheet at $t + 2$, Proprietor's Capital section

	£
Opening balance (at $t + 1$)	156.00
Add Appropriation to Capital Maintenance Reserve	
($£37.86 - £2.12$)	35.74
Distributable (Loss)	(22.74)
	169.00
Less Drawings	106.00
Closing Balance (at $t + 2$)	£63.00

If net monetary working capital has been positive (assets exceeding liabilities), the effect of the monetary working capital adjustment would, of course, have been arithmetically opposite, increasing the capital maintenance reserve and reducing distributable profit.

It should be noted that the monetary working capital adjustment is subject to a wide variety of possible definitions. Of particular importance are the specification of the constituent assets and liabilities (e.g. whether cash should be included), the appropriate index or indices to be used (e.g. buying prices, selling prices or general purchasing power index), and the calculation technique (e.g. whether the adjustment should be based on the precise dating of transactions, as in the above example, or on some averaging method).

Period 3: The net borrowing during this period (as calculated in Chapter 4, Appendix B) was £215. Of this, £50 was a long-term loan. If we define the remaining items (creditors £180, less cash £15) as monetary working capital, the net borrowing during the period for the purposes of the adjustment is £165. Purchase prices rose during the period from £1.80 to £1.90, giving a specific index of approximately 1.06, which we assume to be appropriate

The Monetary Working Capital Adjustment is therefore

$$£165 \times \left(\frac{1.9}{1.8} - 1\right) = £9.17.$$

The Gearing Ratio, based upon the opening balance sheet is

$$\frac{50}{50 + 63} = 0.4425$$

The holding gains for the period (as in Chapter 5, Appendix B) are £51. The Monetary Working Capital Adjustment will, in this example (of net borrowing) be deducted from the holding gains in calculating the Gearing Adjustment:

Gearing Adjustment: (£51 − £9.17)0.4425 = £18.51

This is added to distributable profit, the remainder, £23.32 (= £51 − £9.17 − £18.51) being added to the capital maintenance reserve.

These adjustments appear in the accounts as follows:

Profit and Loss Account for Period 3

	£	£
Sales		180.00
Less Current Cost of Goods Sold	171.00	
Monetary Working Capital Adjustment	(9.17)	
Current Cost Depreciation	15.00	
		176.83
Current Cost Operating Profit		3.17
Add Gearing Adjustment		18.51
Distributable Profit		£ 21.68

The Proprietor's Capital section of the closing balance sheet, at *t* + 3, appears as follows:

	£
Proprietor's Capital	
Opening balance (at $t + 2$)	63.00
Add Appropriation to capital maintenance reserve	23.32
Distributable Profit	21.68
	108.00
Less Drawings	10.00
Closing balance (at $t + 3$)	£ 98.00

Period 4: The gearing and monetary working capital adjustments are not really appropriate to this period, as they are based upon the assumption of continuity of the business, whereas the business is being liquidated during the period. The only holding gain is a realised gain (on the van) for which no replacement is intended. It is not therefore necessary to amend the accounts given in Chapter 5, Appendix B, showing a trading profit of £6 and total gains of £21. In the context of the impending liquidation, all of the gains are distributable.

3 Real terms accounting

Here, we adjust the current cost accounts, given in Chapter 5, Appendix B, to show a 'real terms proprietary' concept of capital maintenance, i.e. the money value of the proprietor's capital, as calculated by deducting liabilities from the current value of assets (as defined for current cost accounting purposes), is increased by reference to a general price level index, for capital maintenance purposes. A similar exercise was carried out using historical cost accounts in Chapter 4, Appendix B. In this example, we assume that all sales took place either at the end of the period, or after all price changes of the period (both specific and general) had taken place, so that all figures in the accounts are expressed in end-of-period £s. Otherwise, if we wished to obtain a full set of 'real terms' accounts, measured in constant value £s, we should have to translate some of the profit and loss figures into year-end £s, as described in Chapter 4. It should also be noted that, for purposes of inter-period comparison, a full 'real terms' system would require that the accounts of previous periods be translated into current £s (or £s of any other common date, in which case the present period's accounts should be stated in the same unit), as described in Chapter 4. This is a purely mechanical piece of arithmetic which will not be demonstrated here.

Obviously, there are a great number of variations possible on the method of implementing real terms accounting. Very valuable sources of reference both for discussion and for numerical examples are the classic works of Edwards and Bell (1961) and of Sweeney (1936), particularly Chapter 3 of the latter.

Period 1: This starts with the same opening balance sheet (at t) as for the current cost accounting (Chapter 5, Appendix B) and for gearing adjustment (above). The 'real terms' capital maintenance concept is, however, to maintain the proprietor's capital P_t in real terms by multiplying by a general index p. The relevant values for period 1 are $P_t = £150$ and $p = 1.1$, so that closing capital to be maintained is £165, the increase of £15 being credited to a capital maintenance reserve. The Profit and Loss Account is as follows:

Real Terms Profit and Loss Account for Period 1, t to $t + 1$

	£
Sales	120
Less Current cost of Goods Sold	104
	16
Less Depreciation	10
Current Cost Operating Profit	6
Add Real Holding Gains	15
Real Profit	£ 21

The Real Holding Gains constitute the Holding Gains on Stocks of £30 (from Chapter 5, Appendix B), less the transfer to Capital Maintenance Reserve (£15) which is necessary to maintain opening capital in real terms. Alternatively, by looking at opening capital from the other side of the balance sheet, in terms of the components of net worth (i.e. as $N_t + M_t - L_t$ rather than P_t), we can attribute the real holding gains to particular classes of asset and liability held during the period, as follows:

	£
Real Holding Gains	
Gain on Stocks ($£30 - [£100 \times 0.1]$)	20
Gain on Borrowing ($£50 \times 0.1$)	5
Loss on Van ($£100 \times 0.1$)	(10)
	£15

The real gains and losses are calculated by deducting each item's indexed ('real') opening value from its actual closing value, i.e. in the case of an asset whose money value has not changed, by multiplying opening value by -0.1 ($=1-1.1$). The monetary gain on stocks (£30) was calculated in Chapter 5, Appendix B. The loss on the van arises because its replacement price did not keep pace with inflation. The loss was partly realised (in the form of the depreciation charge) and partly unrealised (in the form of the net value of the van, appearing in the closing balance sheet).

The closing balance sheet reflects the 'real terms' approach in the Proprietor's Capital section, the assets and liabilities being the same as in the current cost case.

Real terms Balance Sheet as at $t+1$

	£		£	£
Proprietor's Capital		*Fixed Asset*		
Opening balance (at t)	150	Van (at cost)	100	
Add capital maintenance		*Less* depreciation	10	
reserve	15			90
	165	*Current Assets*		
Add Real Profit	21	Stock (at current cost)	26	
	186	Cash	90	
Less Drawings	30			116
Closing balance (at $t+1$)	156			
Loan	50			
	£206			£206

Period 2: The opening balance sheet (at $t+1$) shows capital to be maintained of £156. Adjusting this by the rate of general price level change for the period, $p = 0.2$, gives an allocation to capital maintenance reserve of £31.20.

The profit and loss account will start with a calculation of current cost operating profit, as for current cost accounting (Chapter 5, Appendix B), but the final section will be:

	£
Current Cost Operating (Loss)	(37.00)
Add Real Holding Gains†	18.80
Real (Loss)	£ (18.20)

† £50 nominal holding gains (Chapter 5, Appendix B), *Less* £31.20 capital maintenance reserve.

Current value systems 2

The real holding gains can be decomposed as follows:

	£
Gain on stocks (£50 − [£130 × 0.2])	24
Gain on borrowing (£102 × 0.2)	20.40
Loss on holding money (£38 × 0.2)	(7.60)
Loss on van (£90 × 0.2)	(18.00)
Net Real Holding Gains	£18.80

As for the previous period, these gains and losses are calculated by deducting indexed opening value from actual closing value, in the case of assets and liabilities held during the period.

The closing balance sheet again (necessarily) shows the same proprietor's net worth as in the current cost case (£63), since the valuation basis is the same. The division between capital and profit is as follows:

	£
Proprietor's Capital	
Opening balance (at $t + 1$)	156.00
Add Allocation to capital maintenance reserve	31.20
	187.20
Add Real (Loss)	(18.20)
	169.00
Less Drawings	106.00
Closing balance (at $t + 2$)	£ 63.00

Period 3: The proprietor's capital at the start of the period (at $t + 2$) was £63. Indexing this by the inflation rate during the period (10 per cent, see Chapter 4, Appendix B) gives a transfer to capital maintenance reserve of £6.30. The adjustment to the profit and loss account is as follows:

	£
Current Cost Operating (Loss)	(6)
Add Real Holding Gains†	44.70
Real Profit	£38.70

† £51 (as in Chapter 5, Appendix B), *less* £6.30 capital maintenance.

The decomposition of the holding gains is as follows:

	£
Gain on Fixed Asset (£40 − [£80 × 0.1])	32
Gain on borrowing ([£180 + £50] × 0.1)	23
Loss on holding money (£15 × 0.1)	(1.50)
Loss on holding stocks (£11 − [£198 × 0.1])	(8.80)
	£44.70

It is notable that there was a real loss on holding stocks during this period, because the replacement cost of stocks failed to keep pace with the change in the general price level (p).

The proprietor's capital in the balance sheet appears as follows:

	£
Proprietor's Capital	
Opening balance (at $t + 2$)	63.00
Add Allocation to capital maintenance reserve	6.30
	69.30
Add Real Profit	38.70
	108.00
Less Drawings	10.00
Closing Balance (at $t + 3$)	£ 98.00

Period 4: The opening balance of proprietor's capital (at $t + 3$) is £98 and the general price level change (p) is 5 per cent, so the amount required for the capital maintenance reserve is £4.90 (= £98 × 0.05).

Profit and Loss Account for Period 4, $t + 3$ to $t + 4$

	£
Sales	44.00
Less Current cost of goods sold	38.00
Trading profit	6.00
Add Real holding gains	10.10
Real Profit	£16.10

The real holding gains are calculated as the realised gain of £15 (Chapter 5, Appendix B), less the real capital maintenance requirement (£4.90). Alternatively, the gains can be attributed to specific assets as follows:

	£
Gain on van (£15 − [£105 × 0.05])	9.75
Gain on borrowing (£50 × 0.05)	2.50
Loss on holding cash (£5 × 0.05)	(0.25)
Loss on holding stocks (£38 × 0.05)	(1.90)
	£10.10

The real loss on holding stocks arises because it is assumed that their replacement cost did not rise during the period before sale, so that their current cost value failed to keep pace with inflation.

Balance Sheet at $t + 4$

	£		£
Proprietor's Capital			
Opening balance (at $t + 3$)	98.00	Cash	169.00
Add Allocation to capital			
maintenance reserve	4.90		
	102.90		
Add Real Profit	16.10		
Closing Balance (at $t + 4$)	119.00		
Loan	50.00		
	£169.00		£169.00

4 The Kennedy income statement

In this section, we illustrate Kennedy's 'simplified income statement', which was described in section 7 of Chapter 6. This has the advantage of displaying a variety of information, including the 'geared' and 'real terms' profit figures illustrated above, and it provides a clear reconciliation of these figures. Alternative income statements of this broad type are illustrated and discussed in Edwards and Bell (1961).

Period 1

	£
Current Cost Operating Profit	6.00
Add Geared Holding Gains	7.50
Proprietary Profit	13.50
Add Ungeared Holding gains	22.50
Total Proprietary Gain	36.00
Less Inflationary element of ungeared holding gains	15.00
Inflation-corrected Proprietary Gain	£21.00

The format of this statement is identical with that illustrated in the text, except that lines which do not apply to this illustration (such as interest received) have been omitted. The numbers may be compared with those in the 'geared' and 'real terms' statements which were illustrated earlier in this appendix. 'Proprietary Profit' here is what was called 'distributable profit' in the gearing example, and 'Inflation-corrected Proprietary Gain' is the same as 'real profit' in the real terms example. 'Total Proprietary Gain' is the same as 'total gains' in Chapter 5, Appendix B (illustrating current value accounting) and the holding gains calculated there are the sum of the geared and ungeared holding gains reported here.

Period 2

		£
	Current cost operating profit (loss)	(37.00)
Add	Adjustment for maintenance of real value of monetary assets	2.80
	Entity Profit	(34.20)
Add	Geared holding gains	11.46
	Proprietary Profit (loss)	(22.74)
Add	Ungeared holding gains	35.74
	Total Proprietary Gain	13.00
Less	Inflationary element of ungeared holding gains	31.20
	Inflation-corrected Proprietary Gain (Loss)	£(18.20)

The only innovation in this period is the introduction of the monetary working capital adjustment (line 2), which was not relevant in the previous period. Because net monetary working capital was negative (net borrowing), this item is an addition to, rather than a deduction from, current cost operating profit.

Period 3

		£
	Current cost operating profit (loss)	(6.00)
Add	Adjustment for maintenance of real value of monetary assets	9.17
	Entity Profit	3.17
Add	Geared holding gains	18.51
	Proprietary Profit	21.68
Add	Ungeared holding gains	23.32
	Total Proprietary Gain	45.00
Less	Inflationary element of ungeared holding gains	6.30
	Inflation-corrected Proprietary Gain	£38.70

Period 4

Here, the gearing and monetary working capital adjustments were not considered relevant, so the statement will be simpler, the first three lines being taken from the current cost accounts (Chapter 5, Appendix B).

	£
Current cost operating profit	6.00
Add Holding gains	15.00
Total Proprietary Gain	21.00
Less Inflationary element of holding gains	4.90
Inflation-corrected Proprietary Gain	£16.10

Chapter 6: Appendix B Empirical evidence relating to alternative capital maintenance concepts

The capital maintenance concept is an essential ingredient in a profit calculation, so that the case studies described in Chapter 4 and Appendix A to Chapter 5, which compare the results of computing alternative profit measures, necessarily involve a choice of capital maintenance concepts and often involve a comparison of the use of alternative capital maintenance concepts. Thus, for example, the study by Hope (1974) involves a comparison of money proprietary, real proprietary and entity capital maintenance concepts, and the studies by Gibbs (listed in Gibbs, 1979), include estimates for individual companies of the effects of implementing gearing adjustments, and alternative capital maintenance concepts. Inevitably, shortage of data has meant that less of these studies have been concerned with entity concepts, which require current value data, the comparison of money proprietary (which is commonly the basis of published accounts) with real proprietary measures (which require only additional knowledge of movements in a general price index) being much more common.

Empirical research on capital maintenance concepts in isolation from income measurement is relatively rare, but some interesting lines of research have been started and the field might be a fruitful one for future research. One such line of research is the question of whether geared companies do, in fact, gain on borrowing in a period of inflation, as suggested by 'real terms' capital maintenance concepts. Briscoe and Hawke (1976) found that UK companies with high gearing did not appear to have particularly high gains in shareholder wealth, in the inflationary period 1965–74. They attributed this result to price competition, which caused gains on borrowing to be passed on in lower prices. Peasnell and Skerratt (1976b) have criticised this study on methodological grounds (in particular, the Briscoe and Hawke study did not allow for the effects of factors other than gearing, which might wrongly be attributed to gearing) and, more fundamentally, have argued that the basic hypothesis is not relevant to the case for general price level adjustment of capital. Even if heavily geared companies performed badly in times of inflation, this does not mean that they did not gain from borrowing, but merely implies that other aspects of their performance were bad. The latter criticism is particularly telling: the basic hypothesis certainly requires clearer specification before implications for accounting can be drawn. For example, the gain on borrowing is an offset to the interest rate, and companies will gain net from borrowing only if the interest rate fails to anticipate inflation fully. Furthermore, the issue of whether there has been a gain on debt should be separated, for financial reporting purposes, from the issue of whether this gain has benefited shareholders (through higher profits) or customers (through lower prices). It is clear that fuller specification of the theory and the empirical methodology is required before the tests of the debtor/creditor hypothesis can give insights into the choice of accounting method.[27]

Another relevant area of empirical research is the question of the adequacy of depreciation funds to finance new investment. This is relevant to the entity capital maintenance concept and its implication that a backlog depreciation problem might arise, although it was made clear in the earlier discussion (Chapter 6) that this is a problem of liquidity rather than income measurement. Several of the papers by economists referred to in Chapter 5, Appendix A (such as Meeks, 1974, and Merrett and Sykes, 1974 and 1980) have been concerned, *inter alia*, with this problem. A study by Nguyen and Whittaker (1976), based on data for 31 industrial groups in the United Kingdom, suggested that a rate of inflation in excess of sixteen per cent would lead to a serious shortfall of amortisation funds, calculated on the conventional historical cost basis, in relation to replacement requirements. There is clearly scope for much more work of this type, using better data, particularly at the level of the individual firm, and exploring the implications of such a shortfall, e.g. in terms of dividend policy or the appropriate rates of capital allowance for tax purposes.

Finally, the controversial question of the relevance to individual shareholders of general index adjustments has been explored by Peasnell and Skerratt (1978). They test the 'heterogeneity hypothesis', that changes in different individuals' purchasing power are not captured by changes in a general index, and find a 'remarkable degree of commonality' between groups, which leads them to reject the hypothesis and favour general index adjustment. Their study is based upon comparing the purchasing power of different income groups of individuals with changes in the general index, and this is an important limitation of the study. There is scope for further work, studying individuals, preferably selected from amongst the share-holders of a particular firm.

In conclusion, relatively little empirical work has been done which relates to the choice of capital maintenance concepts. It is to be hoped that theorists will, in future, pay more attention to the empirical assumptions and implications of work in this field, and that empirical researchers will make full use of the current cost accounting data which are now becoming available. In the United Kingdom, these data (published under SSAP16: ASC, 1980) include the controversial gearing adjustment, and an important area of research is to compare the effects of this adjustment with the pure gearing adjustment (of the Godley/Cripps/Kennedy/Gibbs variety, which is applied to unrealised, as well as realised holding gains) and with a thoroughgoing 'real terms' measure of proprietary profit.

7

Review

1 Introduction

The object of this chapter is to review the previous discussion, with three objectives in mind: firstly to summarise the current 'state of the art' of the theory of inflation accounting, secondly to identify the areas in which future research might make a particularly useful contribution, and thirdly to relate the theoretical discussion to the evolution of practice, a theme which will be developed in section 5. It should be clear from the earlier discussion that it is not appropriate, either here or later in the book, to offer uniquely 'correct' solutions. The approach is rather to discuss rational alternatives, each of which has its merits and its disadvantages, which might be more or less appropriate in different circumstances.

The next section of this chapter offers a brief outline of the more important issues discussed in the first five chapters: it is not intended as a comprehensive summary, still less as a substitute for reading these chapters. The following section draws on this discussion to identify the major contemporary issues of inflation accounting theory and practice. A section on the contribution of research, past and future, follows. Finally, a section on the historical evolution of inflation accounting adds an important dimension to the discussion and provides a link with the companion volume, *The Debate on Inflation Accounting*.

2 Review of the earlier discussion

The discussion has focussed on the problems raised by inflation for financial accounting, i.e. the periodic reporting of the economic performance of a whole business entity to shareholders and other users of financial information who are external to the entity, in the sense that they are not involved in day-to-day management. This restriction still leaves us with a wide variety of users and uses which financial accounting information has to satisfy. These were discussed in Chapters 1 and 2. In a realistic world of uncertainty and imperfect and incomplete markets, it is unlikely that it will be possible to identify unique measures of value, capital and income which will satisfy all of these needs. Thus, financial accounting faces serious problems, in defining the appropriate range of information which should be disclosed, even in the absence of inflation. The discussion of inflation is often complicated by the fact that it proceeds from an inadequately specified view of the rôle and content of accounts in the absence of inflation: thus, the problems of inflation become inter-twined with the fundamental problems of financial accounting, which are not necessarily aggravated by inflation.

The accountant's traditional basis for financial reporting is a profit and loss account and balance sheet based upon historical cost. This was discussed criticially in Chapter 3. Historical cost has the advantage of providing a record of actual transactions, which gives it an important use for control purposes. The transactions base also imparts a degree of objectivity to financial reports based upon historical cost, although the assessment of accruals (unexpired costs, recorded in the closing balance sheet) is an important exception to this, involving either a degree of subjectivity or the application of completely arbitrary allocation rules. Outside the unrealistic conditions of the 'stationary state' (in which all prices remain constant), historical cost valuation is seriously deficient in failing to record in the balance sheet the changes in value of assets[1] which take place between the date of acquisition (historical cost) and the date of the balance sheet (current values, the changes being unrealised holding gains and losses). The historical cost profit and loss account also fails to record the difference between historical cost and value at the time of use (current cost, the difference being realised holding gains and losses). Thus, historical cost accounts fail, in the presence of relative price changes but the absence of general inflation, to provide measures of value and income which are likely to be of use in assessing the economic performance of the accounting entity. These problems are exacerbated by the presence of general inflation (or deflation) which tends to widen the gap between current values and historical cost, due to the decline (or increase) in the value of the monetary unit, in addition to any distortion caused by relative price changes.

Inflation is commonly taken to imply an increase in the general price level, i.e. a declining value of money relative to goods. This can, in theory, occur when the prices of goods relative to one another remain constant. A method of eliminating the effects on accounts of general inflation is the Constant (or Current) Purchasing Power method (CPP) discussed in Chapter 4. This method is theoretically satisfactory, provided that inflation is of the pure 'no relative price change' variety. In practice, this is not the case, and we are faced with difficulties both in asset valuation and in defining the capital to be maintained for income measurement purposes. The asset valuation problem can be dealt with by adopting current values of the specific assets concerned. A current asset valuation base combined with CPP adjustment of items other than asset values yields 'real terms' accounting. The capital maintenance problem is dealt with in this system by applying a general purchasing power index, a 'proprietary' measure of capital, but some theorists have argued that an index specific to the assets of the firm should be adopted, implementing an 'entity' approach which aims to preserve the productive power of the entity intact. The divergence between the two capital maintenance concepts depends upon there being changes in the prices of the firm's assets relative to the general price index. It is also argued that the CPP adjustment method is ill-founded because the general index used does not reflect changes in the cost of living of individual shareholders: this argument also depends on there being relative price changes, although the relevant comparison is now between the cost of goods consumed by the individual shareholder and the general index.

It must, however, be stressed that given the limitations of accounting measurement discussed earlier, neither the isolation of the effects of general inflation nor the introduction of current values into accounts is likely to produce unambiguously 'true' figures for income or capital. The most that can be hoped for is that the accounts will yield a set of information relating to the economic progress of the entity, which will be relevant to a wide range of external users of financial information. In Chapter 5, various alternative valuation bases were examined from this standpoint. The two main competing bases are replacement cost and net realisable value. Both of these bases are based upon market prices and may therefore be regarded as being objective when such prices are available, although it is easy to conceive of situations in which they are unlikely to be available, e.g. in calculating the value of a partly used plant which has a highly specialised function. Each basis is clearly relevant to particular uses and circumstances. Replacement cost has obvious relevance for assessing the economic performance of a continuing business in which replacement will take place, but net realisable value is relevant to situations and purposes in which realisation is contemplated, e.g. in assessing the security for a loan. It is also clear that each basis requires a precise definition of the assumed uses and circumstances before it can be implemented in practice, e.g. replacement cost requires a definition as to whether it is to be based upon physical replacement ('reproduction cost'), replacement of the service ('maintenance of operating capacity') or some alternative criterion, and the choice of definition will be determined by the use to which the information is to be put, as well as the specific circumstances of the business. It is difficult to avoid the conclusion that both replacement cost and net realisable value would be of potential interest to a wide range of users of accounts and should therefore both be reported in a multiple-column format, although most writers on the subject have espoused a single valuation basis to the exclusion of all others.

A third valuation basis, which is potentially important for decision-making, is net present value, i.e. the discounted present value of assets in their current use. This suffers from the obvious problem of subjectivity, depending entirely upon estimates of future cash flows and discount rates. This makes it unsuitable for reporting purposes, although one possible practical approach is to select other market values as surrogates for net present value. This, however, amounts to using closeness to net present value as a means of selecting between the two more objective, market-validated bases (replacement cost and net realisable value), rather than being a direct application of the net present value basis. Furthermore, there are conceptual difficulties in relation to the level of aggregation appropriate for net present value calculations: if the object of the information is to provide a net present value of the whole firm (as might be the case if shareholders wished to value their investment) the whole firm should be valued, rather than summing estimates for individual assets. This is a formidable task (especially as different shareholders might wish to apply different discount rates) and it might be more realistically accomplished by providing information which might be the basis of estimates by individual users of accounts, rather than by attempting a direct estimate in the accounts. Moreover, even if net present values were reported, they should, for many purposes, be compared with valuations based on alternative assumptions about the disposition of assets (such as net realisable values), so that their use should not preclude the multiple-column approach.

An alternative to reporting either a single 'pure' valuation basis (such as replacement cost) or multiple column reporting of several bases, is to adopt an eclectic valuation basis which selects the valuation most appropriate to the circumstances of the particular asset being valued. An example of this is 'value to the owner' which selects either replacement cost, net realisable value or net present value, according to their relative values (it values at replacement cost or 'recoverable amount', whichever is the lower). Although this seems to be a sensible pragmatic principle if it is essential to report only one value, the theoretical foundations of value to the owner are not strong, and multiple-column reporting would provide more information, although it might raise the problem of 'information overload'.

Profit measurement is usually assumed to be an important purpose of accounts, and this requires a capital maintenance concept as well as a valuation basis. The main competing capital maintenance concepts were discussed in Chapter 6. The two central concepts of capital maintenance are the proprietary approach and the entity approach. The proprietary approach views the capital of the firm as a fund of wealth attributable to the proprietors (or equity shareholders). When the general price level is stable, the money amount of opening capital must be maintained before a profit is recognised. When the general price level changes, giving rise to inflation or deflation, it is the real purchasing power of opening capital which is to be maintained, real purchasing power being derived by the application of a general price index, to yield a capital measure which aims to maintain command over goods and services in general. The entity approach, on the other hand, aims to preserve the productive power of the business intact. When all prices are constant, this again leads to money capital maintenance, but when there are relative price changes, the entity approach requires the adjustment of opening money capital by changes in specific indices, so that the cost of maintaining the specific assets necessary to maintain productive capacity is deducted from revenue before a profit is recognised. Both of these approaches have their problems (e.g. of defining the appropriate indices to be applied when prices change) and both have their uses, but fortunately both can be reported in a single income statement, without resorting to multiple-column reporting, so that they need not be regarded as mutually exclusive alternatives.

One eclectic capital maintenance concept was discussed because it has received considerable attention in the theoretical literature and as a basis for practical reform of financial accounting. This treats the geared (loan-financed) portion of the firm's net assets on the money capital maintenance basis (i.e. the proprietary basis with no inflation adjustment). The ungeared portion (equity-financed) is treated on an entity basis, i.e. specific assets must be maintained before a profit is recognised. The gearing adjustment can be used as a step in the process of moving from an entity basis to a proprietary basis within a single appropriation statement, so that it need not be regarded as competing with the other bases. However, it is possible to question the value of the gearing adjustment relative to other intermediate steps which might, for example, divide holding gains on assets into real and fictitious (due to changes in the purchasing power of money) elements and recognise the gain on borrowing fixed money sums and the loss on holding fixed money sums during periods of inflation. However, the precise definition and measurement of holding gains is itself not without difficulty, especially in businesses in which holding assets is an integral part of operating activities.

3 The major issues in inflation accounting

It is clear from this review of the earlier discussion that the primary problem in inflation accounting is to establish what accounting system is appropriate in the presence of relative price changes but the absence of general inflation. Only when this prior problem is solved is it possible to define clearly what additional problems are introduced by general inflation and to suggest possible solutions. It is also clear that, although a wide range of possible models is available, it is unlikely, given the uncertainties and imperfections of the markets to which accounting information relates, that any single model will be appropriate to all users and uses. Thus, another important issue is the question of how much variety of information can be reported without imposing excessive costs on the reporting entity or creating confusion in the minds of potential users.

The following are important issues in deciding the appropriate form of reporting, even in the absence of general inflation:

(1) *The scope of the reports.* Balance sheets and profit and loss accounts are the fundamental *ex post* financial statements. The degree of detail offered is an important issue, but more fundamental is the question of providing additional statements, such as flow of funds accounts, value added statements, segmental reports, or cash flow statements. Perhaps of even greater importance is the question of providing *ex ante* data, which are of clear relevance to decision making but are highly subjective.

(2) *The valuation basis.* If it is not possible to produce a wide variety of valuations of each asset we must decide which are the most important valuation bases to be used in accounts and devise methods for choosing between them if they cannot all be reported.

(3) *The capital maintenance concept.* It seems likely that income measurement in some form will remain an important objective of financial reporting for some time to come. It is therefore essential to specify which capital maintenance concepts should be measured. Fortunately, it is possible to report a variety of capital maintenance measures, based upon alternative concepts, without undue complication, so that the choice of capital maintenance concept does not raise such acute problems as the choice of valuation base. Reporting a variety of measures may have a useful educational effect on those users who are 'functionally fixated' on a single profit measure, wrongly believing it to be a 'true' measure which is valid in all uses and circumstances.

Having established the appropriate form of financial reporting, we need to establish the problems raised by inflation, i.e. general price level changes. These problems may be subsumed under a single heading: *the choice of the unit of account.* The essential choice is between choosing a monetary until whose value will depend upon the date of the transaction or the valuation date and one whose value is constant in real terms. The difference between the two measuring units will be most apparent in the case of historical cost systems, in which a high proportion of asset values will be recorded in past purchasing power units of different dates. Current value systems largely eliminate this problem for asset values, since current values are, by definition, recorded consistently in current currency units, but the capital to be maintained will still need to be translated into current units if a 'real terms' proprietary measure is used. If an entity measure is used, the application of replacement costs or specific indices will ensure that the capital to be maintained is automatically expressed in current currency units. The remaining real terms adjustment to be made to conventional current value accounts will be to translate the transactions recorded in the profit and loss account into current (year-end) purchasing power units, where they are recorded in average-for-the-year prices. The time lag involved is relatively short, so this adjustment should not be very large, unless the rate of inflation during the year has been high. Finally, for comparative purposes, when current purchasing power is the standard unit (as opposed to constant purchasing power with a base in the past) data for past years should be translated into current purchasing power, and forecasts for future years should also be expressed in current units.

There are two important issues relating to the choice between a variable money unit ('actual £s') and a constant unit ('current £s'). First, there is the question of whether the concept of constant purchasing power has any operational meaning, and, secondly, it is important to recognise that, in many uses of accounting data, monetary measures are preferable to constant purchasing power measures. It has been argued, notably by the Sandilands Committee, that there is no such thing as a general price level, merely movements of individual prices, and it is not possible, therefore, to construct a unit of constant purchasing power using general indices. This view was discussed at some length in Chapter 4. In its more extreme form it might be taken to imply that inflation does not exist and there can be no problem of inflation accounting. On a more pragmatic level it leads to an argument about the construction of price indices and their utility to users of accounts. The second issue is less contentious: it is clear that not all accounting measures should be measured in 'real' units for all purposes for which they are used. For example, if we wish to evaluate an accounting income measure in terms of an interest rate observed in the market (e.g. by discounting the income measure to give an estimate of present value) no inflation-adjustment of the income measure is appropriate, since the market interest rate is applicable to money returns (in 'actual £s') not real returns ('current £s'). Equally, various forms of ratio analysis eliminate the scale effects of the changing value of the monetary unit, and this was suggested by the Sandilands Report as a method of avoiding the need for comparative historical data expressed in real terms. Thus, there is a case for expressing accounts in both 'money' and 'real' terms, and most reform proposals have adopted this approach, by making various inflation adjustments in supplementary statements rather than the main accounts.

This summarises the main theoretical issues which have to be considered in deciding upon the appropriate form of financial reporting in a period of inflation. There are, however, at least two types of practical constraint which have to be considered. First, there are the constraints on the volume of information which can be included in the accounts. On the supply side we have to consider the cost to the firm of providing a broad range of information, and on the demand side we have to consider the limitations of the user's capacity to absorb and interpret information. Secondly, there are the constraints imposed by the institutional environment in which accounting standards are framed. The practical reform of accounting practice is constrained by the current state of practice and the past experience and beliefs of accountants, managers, users of accounts and governments. This theme will be developed in the final section of this chapter and in the companion volume, *The Debate on Inflation Accounting*.

4 The contribution of research

Most of the ideas discussed earlier are the product of theoretical research, based upon *a priori* reasoning from assumptions, although the motivation to conduct the research was usually a practical problem. There has also been an encouraging feedback from theoretical research to accounting practice, e.g. Limperg's work was the inspiration of the Philips replacement cost accounting system (Goudeket, 1960), Schmidt's work in the 1920s influenced the West German accounting standard of 1975 (Coenenberg and Macharzina, 1976), and Sweeney's (1936) pioneering work was subsequently the basis for proposals for reform in both the USA and the UK.

Despite this progress, the work of the theorist is far from ended. Some important issues have been clarified, but what has emerged is not a single optimal system of accounting but a variety of methods of reporting the economic progress of a business, each of which might serve a useful purpose for a particular user in a particular situation. The next task of theory must surely be to address the specific problems of relating users and uses to information requirements. Although there is some literature of this kind, there is relatively little compared with the vast amount devoted to the advocacy of complete general-purpose accounting systems such as replacement cost or continuously contemporaneous accounting.[2] What is required is to derive the information requirements of such important uses as the dividend decision, the assessment of corporation tax, or the decision to lend to the firm, by considering the requirements of the decision rather than by starting from a general purpose information system and trying to relate the information to the decision.

This is not to deny that there is still scope for exploring and clarifying the properties of general systems. In fact, a number of important issues remain unresolved. One recent example of this type of work is the proposal by Scott (1976) that accountants should use the Hicks No. 3 consumption maintenance approach to income measurement, rather than the traditional Hicks No. 1 capital maintenance approach. Another example is Anderson's (1976) comparative analysis of competing 'general purpose' income measurement theories. Research should certainly continue in order to clarify the properties of such systems, but it should be complemented by research which seeks to derive the information requirements of specific uses of accounting data.

Theoretical research should also be complemented by empirical studies. Brief surveys of empirical research were given in Chapter 4 (section 7), and in the appendices to Chapters 5 and 6. In the past, the main contribution of empirical work has been in the form of case studies, such as Jones' (1949) study of the effects of CPP adjustment on US steel companies' accounts. These studies have been influential in emphasising the materiality of the adjustments involved, ruling out the possibility that the inflation accounting debate can be dismissed as dealing with matters which are of trivial importance. They have also demonstrated the practical feasibility of various alternative systems, thus forestalling the argument that traditional accounting is the only practical method. A more recent approach to assessing the materiality of alternative systems is the statistical approach, which uses statistical techniques, such as various forms of correlation analysis, to assess the degree of association between alternative accounting measures (Kratchman, Malcom and Twark, 1974). This type of work has, in the past, been inhibited by lack of data, but the recent requirements for disclosure of current value data in the USA and in the UK facilitate future work.

Some useful empirical studies have been carried out on the materiality of specific assumptions of alternative systems, notably the studies by Peasnell and Skerratt (1976a) and Bourn, Stoney and Wynn (1976) of the relationship between specific and general indices for plant valuation purposes. It is gratifying to note that the evidence from these studies was actually considered in the professional standard-setting debate (see Inflation Accounting Steering Group, 1976, pp. 57–8). Other areas in which a limited number of empirical studies have been carried out, and which require thorough investigation in the future are the gain on borrowing (Briscoe and Hawke, 1976) and the loss on holding monetary assets, including the problem of classifying assets as monetary or non-monetary (Wanless, 1976), the backlog depreciation problem (Nguyen and Whittaker, 1976), the differences between alternative methods of specific asset valuation (McDonald, 1968, Sterling and Radosevitch, 1969), and the relevance of general price indices to individual shareholders (Peasnell and Skerratt, 1978).

The utility of various alternative accounting measurement systems has also received some attention from empirical researchers, but this field is even less well developed than the assessment of materiality. Behavioural studies of sophisticated investors (Dyckman, 1969, Benston and Krasney, 1978) and of subjects untrained in financial matters (Tweedie, 1977), have made a promising start in establishing how different users interpret alternative types of accounting information, but a great deal remains to be done, and some important issues have not been touched upon, e.g. the crucial issue of whether multiple-column reports would convey a greater amount of useful information, or would merely serve to confuse the user, is replete with *a priori* arguments, but notably devoid of empirical evidence. Behavioural research on this topic is important not only to the choice of method of inflation accounting but also to the fundamental problems of financial reporting and accounting standard-setting. Another issue of fundamental importance, which could be explored by behavioural research, is the usefulness of general index adjustments: do individuals find it easier to interpret money units or constant purchasing power units derived by applying a general index?

Apart from behavioural studies a promising start has been made in testing the utility of alternative accounting systems by statistical methods. One approach is to use an objective criterion such as predictive value, which is assumed to have utility for the user of reports. The studies of self-prediction of alternative income measures (Frank, 1969, Buckmaster, Copeland and Dascher, 1977) and of the ability of general price level adjusted measures to predict corporate bankruptcy (Ketz, 1978b, Norton and Smith, 1979) are of this type. An alternative is to observe the effect of information on shareholders by estimating its impact on share prices. Examples of this type of work are Morris' (1975) study of the effects of CPP estimates for UK companies, Basu's (1977) study of the potential impact of CPP data on Canadian share prices, and Hillison's (1979) study for the USA. There will clearly be scope for extending this type of work in the future, as current value data become publicly available, recent examples being those discussed by Watts and Zimmerman (1980). These studies have, hitherto, typically used the Capital Asset Pricing Model as the analytical framework, but there are signs that this model may be refined or even superseded in the future, and it might be hoped that new models will give new insights.

The rôle of research in advancing the debate on inflation accounting should include a much greater emphasis on empirical studies than has been the case in the past. There is still scope for theoretical work, but it is to be hoped that theorists will pay careful attention to the empirical testing both of the assumptions and of the inferences of their theories. Equally, empirical research should have proper regard for theory in setting up its hypotheses. Theoretical and empirical research are complementary rather than competitive activities. The past has seen an undue emphasis on *a priori* theorising and this imbalance should be redressed, but this process should not be allowed to lead to an imbalance in the opposite direction. The apparent contempt of some writers (such as Nelson, 1973, and Watts and Zimmerman, 1979) for *a priori* theory suggests that there is a real danger that this may happen. However, a recent discussion document published by the United States Financial Accounting Standards Board (FASB, 1981), offers hope that, in the future, theoretical research, empirical research and the debate on inflation accounting standards will be more clearly related than in the past.

5 The historical evolution of inflation accounting

The earlier discussion has concentrated on explaining the alternative theoretical models which are available, with occasional references to the somewhat scanty empirical evidence. The variety of alternative models available, combined with the indecisiveness and piecemeal nature of the empirical results, would be quite sufficient to explain the lack of consensus in both academic and professional circles on the best system of inflation accounting. However, it would be misleading to suggest that this difficulty can be resolved merely by more research, refining and clarifying alternative theories and testing their assumptions and practicality. The reason for this is that the debate on inflation accounting is a historical and political process. The receptiveness of various groups and individuals to ideas relating to inflation accounting is coloured by their education and past experience and by the current state of accounting practice,[3] all of which are historical facts. Equally, different groups have different interests in relation to accounting data, and accounting standard-setting is therefore inevitably a political process, compromising between the interests of different groups. For example, it is not surprising that professional bodies have tended initially to favour historical cost based CPP systems as a method of inflation accounting: the index adjustments made in CPP rely on indices which are publicly available and accepted as being objective, so that their application involves the professional practitioner in much less risk of controversy than if he becomes involved in the more subjective valuations required by current value accounting. Equally, business managers, faced by rising production costs in a period of inflation, are likely to favour replacement cost or current cost accounting (probably excluding all holding gains from income) because it gives them an apparent justification for meeting the threat of rising costs by increasing prices, and possibly also by holding down wages (since the form of accounting which shows the lowest profit will presumably favour management's case in wage negotiations), and by paying less taxes and dividends.

This interpretation of the inflation accounting debate is not new. Sweeney, the great American pioneer of inflation accounting, explained developments during the inter-war period as follows:

> a period of inflation causes business management to arise in unanimous protest. For then expenses become

Review

> understated, profits and income taxes overstated, and
> union-and-stockholder desires insatiable. Business
> management is well informed, well financed, and well
> organized. It likes to bask in the spurious glory of overstated
> profits – but it likes to blast the accompanying excessive
> wages, income taxes and dividends (Sweeney, 1964, xxv).

In recent years, a number of writers have made similar observations. McRae and Dobbins (1974) surveyed the inflation accounting debate in Britain and concluded that technical arguments had been used 'to obscure the true issues which concern the personal interests of the various groups affected by inflation adjustment'. Aranya (1974) provides a historical survey of the evolution of British financial reporting, interpreted in terms of the conflicting interests of suppliers and users of reports. Beja and Aharoni (1977) demonstrate that many of the problems of inflation accounting are caused by the operation of legal and constitutional constraints, such as tax laws, dividend rules and debt levels. Mumford (1979) compares the pattern of the inflation accounting debate in the UK during the 1948–54 inflation with that in the 1973–78 period, finding certain parallels between the two periods. Watts and Zimmerman (1978) propose a 'positive theory of accounting', based upon the assumption that managers' attitudes to accounting standards are formed by the implications of the standards for their self-interest in such matters as taxes, public regulation and management compensation (salaries): from this they predict that large firms will favour changes which reduce reported earnings, and this is confirmed by an empirical analysis of corporate submissions in response to the FASB's Discussion Memorandum on General Price Level Adjustment. Finally, Watts and Zimmerman's 1979 paper concludes that 'the predominant function of accounting theories is now to supply excuses which satisfy the demand created by the political process; consequently accounting theories have become increasingly normative'.

Watts and Zimmerman's position is somewhat extreme and they admit that their evidence 'is somewhat "casual", and not as rigorous as we would like' (Watts and Zimmerman, 1979, p. 289). Their use of the pejorative word 'excuse' suggests that they have themselves made normative judgements about the process that they are describing: it is quite legitimate for a theorist to clarify the *case* for a particular system, and to describe this as an *excuse* introduces unwarranted imputations of bias. In this context, it should be noted that 'positive' theories are not free from value judgements, e.g. innumerable American empirical studies are based upon the maintained hypothesis that the stock market is efficient: fundamentally, the question being asked, which reflects the value of the person asking it, will always constrain the type of answer which can be obtained.

There is also a growing literature, particularly in the USA, on accounting as a political process, where 'political' includes national politics and social considerations amongst the interests which have to be reconciled. Solomons (1979) reviews some of this literature and presents the case against accepting that accounting is a political process. He draws an analogy between accounting and map-making, and seeks to establish the case for the accountant as a reporter of objective realities. By this he means that the accountant should not consciously distort his measurements in the hope of misleading users of them into behaving in a manner which supports national economic or social objectives: this judgement clearly is highly relevant to the question as to how accountants should treat inflation (if at all). Objectivity in this sense is a worthy aim (although this statement itself is a normative judgement), but it might be difficult to achieve in practice, given the variety of self-interested pressure groups operating to influence the choice of accounting standards (as described by Watts and Zimmerman). However, it seems more likely to be achieved if there is a full and free theoretical debate, which clarifies the issues involved, preferably supported by empirical research to ascertain any facts which are at issue.

Nevertheless, in tracing the course of the debate on inflation accounting and the possible directions which it might take in the future, we must take account of the historical and political constraints which have helped to shape it. This theme will be developed in the companion volume to this book, which will trace the worldwide evolution of ideas and practice in the area of inflation accounting.

6 Conclusion

This book has attempted to survey the various models which have been proposed to deal with the problems of accounting in a period of inflation, where 'inflation' is assumed to imply relative price changes in addition to changes in the general price level. The general drift of the argument should by now be clear: there is no universally 'correct' model which will serve all uses and users well in all circumstances. Financial reports should therefore provide a range of information, the precise contents being determined by a trade-off between utility to the user and cost to the preparer. For some purposes, such as taxation, it may be necessary to prepare an entirely different set of accounts, but even this decision is not independent of the decision about the contents of the main financial reports: if, for example, expensive information about current values is necessary for taxation purposes, the additional cost of providing this information in the financial reports will be much reduced.

Although it is not possible to discern a single correct model it is clear what type of information is most useful. Utility to users implies relevance to current or future decisions by them, and this in turn implies an emphasis on current values and information which has predictive value for the future. It is encouraging to see that this type of approach is increasingly favoured by standard-setting bodies, such as the influential United States Financial Accounting Board. It is perhaps even more encouraging to see that, in practice, professional accounting bodies have overcome their traditional loyalty to historical cost and have adopted systems of 'inflation accounting' which incorporate current values, such as SSAP16 (ASC, 1980) in the United Kingdom and FAS33 (FASB, 1979) in the USA. 'Inflation accounting' is used here in a broad sense, because 'accounting for price changes' would be a more accurate description, current valuation being a method of reporting specific price changes rather than changes in the general price level. The utility of general price level adjustments is one of the unresolved issues for the future: such adjustments are made in certain Latin American countries (such as Brazil) in which inflation is high, and they are incorporated in the current standard for the USA, but the British standard, in the tradition of the Sandilands Report, confines itself to specific price changes, combined with a gearing adjustment. The author's own view (Chapter 6) is that the gearing adjustment has an unsure theoretical foundation, and that a 'real terms' form of general price level adjustment is preferable.

Theoretical and empirical research have an important rôle to play in determining the evolution of accounting practice in relation to price changes. The fact that accounting reports have economic consequences which affect different groups differently and so bring accounting into the political sphere, should increase rather than diminish the importance of identifying the assumptions and implications of alternative models. However, it may be that the theoretical work summarised in this book has explored, if not exhausted, the most promising lines of theoretical research into comprehensive models, of the 'grand design' general purpose type. Perhaps future research should have more limited aims, concentrating on the specific information needs of particular decisions, and with much more emphasis on empirical research to establish both the materiality and the utility of particular types of information.

Nevertheless, the theoretical work of the past has given important insights into 'inflation accounting' (broadly defined), and the practical debate on accounting standards has not always reflected a satisfactory level of understanding of these insights: even such basic distinctions as those between valuation and the capital maintenance concept or between relative price changes and changes in the general price level, which were well-known to writers such as Sweeney half a century ago, are still ignored or misunderstood by some contributors to the debate on inflation accounting practice. One reason for this is that accounting is a new profession and that its practitioners are, in the main, unconvinced that the theory of the subject is worthy of serious study. One objective of this book has been to help to remedy this situation by demonstrating that the theory of accounting is not only important, offering insights into the solution of practical problems, but also has accumulated an interesting literature and has enough unsolved problems to offer a serious challenge to intelligent people.

Notes

Chapter 1 An introduction to inflation accounting

1 Much of the material in this chapter is based on the Deloitte, Haskins and Sells annual lecture, given at University College Cardiff on 6 March 1981.

2 Discussions of the treatment of inflation in management accounting will be found in Gee (1977), Carsberg and Hope (1976) and Scapens (1977), Chapters 8 and 9. It is, of course, possible that the method of financial accounting will have an influence on the methods used in management accounting: consideration of this was one of the tasks in the terms of reference of the Sandilands Committee (1975).

3 Admittedly only as *prima facie* evidence, more detailed costings and budgets typically being required to support a case. This qualification also applies to the use of financial reports in restrictive practices cases.

4 This is discussed in the Report of the Meade Committee (Meade, 1978), of which the present author was a signatory. An accessible discussion of the issue will be found in Kay and King (1980), Chapters 12 and 13.

5 Egginton (1980).

6 An analysis of recent world-wide inflation will be found in the United Nations, *World Economic Survey, 1979–1980*, Chapter III, from which Table 1.1 is extracted.

7 The latter qualification is necessary because otherwise, by accident, changes in the prices of other commodities in the index could offset changes in the price of the three commodities mentioned, so that changes in the index accurately reflected changes in the cost of living.

8 If we wanted to express the relative price change as a real gain in terms of the opening currency unit, the gain would be £2.50p ($= [£15/1.2] - £10$).

9 And in the companion volume, *The Debate on Inflation Accounting*, which will offer a broader historical perspective. These matters involve important political issues, such as whether oil companies should be taxed on their stock appreciation, so that the course of events cannot be

understood purely in terms of the rational evaluation of theoretical models.

10 *Statement of Standard Accounting Practice No. 16*, 1980.

11 For example, an article of theirs was very influential in persuading the Government to introduce Stock Relief in 1974, as an emergency measure to prevent the taxation of stock appreciation, the rise in monetary value of stocks held during a period. In Old Fred's case, the stock appreciation was £25, the difference between the current cost of goods sold (£125) and their historical cost (£100). Thus, exactly one half of Fred's historical cost profit (£50) could be attributed to stock appreciation, the remaining half being current cost operating profit.

12 Here we implicitly assume a discrete jump in the general price level between the purchase of the pineapples and their sale. Otherwise, we would have to adjust the sales figure upwards to current £s, offsetting this adjustment by a 'loss on holding money', which will be explained in Chapter 4.

13 Exposure Draft 8, *Accounting for Changes in the Purchasing Power of Money*, Accounting Standards Steering Committee, 1973.

14 This is because Fred does not end the period with any stocks or other assets on which unrealised holding gains could occur. If this were the case, it would be necessary to exclude unrealised real holding gains or losses from profit if the identity between the two profit figures were to be maintained. If Fred has started with a stock of such assets, further adjustments would have to be made with respect to unrealised real holding gains of previous periods, which would be incorporated in opening asset values in a real terms system, but not in a CPP system.

15 There is a corresponding loss on holding money in a period of inflation, which we avoid in this example. See note 12 above.

16 Here, we calculate gearing by reference to the opening balance sheet, although the current UK standard takes the average of the opening and closing positions. Our method is more consistent with maintaining opening capital.

17 The financial sector has an exceptionally high proportion of 'monetary' items (i.e. those whose value is fixed in nominal monetary units) in both its assets and liabilities. Oil companies have exceptionally large physical assets (stocks and reserves of oil) which have appreciated in value relative to the general price level in recent years.

18 Although in both cases, there is some controversy as to whether the gain should be reported separately from other profits, and, in particular, whether it should be regarded as distributable to shareholders.

19 In fact, Sweeney (1936) recommends that the CPP figures be first calculated in a common basic unit for all periods and then translated into current units.

211

Chapter 2 Fundamentals

1 It is notable that the first study of inflation accounting published by the Institute of Chartered Accountants in England and Wales was entitled *Accounting for Stewardship in a Period of Inflation* (Institute of Chartered Accountants in England and Wales, Research Committee, 1968).

2 The historical cost convention is usually modified by the conservative principle of 'cost or market value, whichever is the lower' in the case of stocks and work-in-progress.

3 Although this is written with the United Kingdom mainly in mind, the history of accounting in the United States is very similar, as is that in the rest of the English-speaking world.

4 The current rate of corporation tax is 52 per cent, but the effect of this is reduced by capital allowances, stock appreciation relief, and the imputation system. See Kay and King (1980) for an account of the system and quantitative estimates of the effects of the reliefs.

5 Secretary of State for Trade (1977).

6 See Kenneth S. Most (1977) for a good text-book account of developments in the USA. The Trueblood Committee Report (1973) was in many respects the USA counterpart to *The Corporate Report* and has served as a starting point for most subsequent developments in financial reporting in the USA, notably the Financial Accounting Standards Board's Conceptual Framework programme.

7 The most noted advocate of historical cost on this and related grounds is Ijiri (1971).

8 But not an identical figure, because the application of accrual conventions, such as the matching of costs to revenues, and the recognition of revenue itself usually involves a degree of subjective judgement.

9 See R. L. Mathews (1965) for a well-known statement of this view in the context of inflation accounting.

10 A leading critic of reporting a variety of valuation bases, on the grounds that this leads to unacceptable complexity for the user of accounts, is Chambers (1966) (particularly Chapters 7 and 8). A useful summary of the information economics approach to accounting, which treats accounting information as an economic commodity, will be found in the American Accounting Association Statement (1977), pp. 21–5.

11 See for example PSSAP7 (ASSC, 1974) and ED18 (ASC, 1976) and SSAP16 (ASC, 1980). The motive for supplementary disclosure is not purely a matter of reducing interpretation, e.g. audit considerations are also relevant, the auditor not being responsible for supplementary statements to the same extent as for the main statements.

12 Barton (1974) provides a critique of the economist's income concept as a model for accountants, under conditions of uncertainty.

13 See Bromwich (1977a) and Beaver and Demski (1979). Complete markets exist when there are markets for all commodities in all possible states of the world, so that all uncertainties can be insured against by dealing in futures markets.
14 Bromwich (1975a) examines some of the implications for current value accounting of imperfect markets.
15 Such as Bromwich (1977a) and Peasnell (1977).
16 See Whittington (1981) for a survey of literature on income measurement.
17 See Barton (1974 and 1976), Revsine (1970 and 1976) and Cook and Holzmann (1976).
18 See Revsine (1976).
19 G. Macdonald (1974) suggests that this articulation of accounts has had a restrictive influence on the development of accounting, by preventing the use of different valuation bases for different statements. There has historically been a shift in the focus of accounting and auditing, from the balance sheet, which was regarded as the primary financial statement during the first three decades of the twentieth century, to the profit and loss account, which receives primary emphasis today (Chatfield, 1974).
20 The notation used here was originated by R. J. Chambers, but Chambers would not approve of all the uses to which it will subsequently be put, because he is strongly committed to certain stringent measurement criteria which he claims to be met only by his 'CoCoA' (Continuously Contemporaneous Accounting) method, based on contemporary realisable market values (Chambers, 1978).
21 See, for example, *Statements of Source and Application of Funds*, Accounting Standard No. 10, issued by the Accounting Standards Committee in July 1975.
22 The profit and loss account will, of course, record gross flows, such as sales and purchases, whose net effect is reflected in the identity which follows. Profit is calculated as revenues (which are increases in assets or decreases in liabilities), less expenses (which are decreases in assets or increases in liabilities): the net profit is therefore an increase in net assets attributable to the proprietor. This relationship emerges clearly from the numerical illustrations given in the preceding chapter and in the appendix to this chapter.
23 This is not, of course, consistent with the economist's notion of 'pure profit', which is the residual after deducting a notional interest charge for 'normal profit'.
24 Useful analyses of the different approaches to income measurement of the accountant and the economist will be found in R. S. Edwards (1938), Alexander (1948), Solomons (1961) and Barton (1974). A survey of the literature and a bibliography will be found in Whittington (1981), a

collection of readings on the subject is Parker and Harcourt (1969), and a text book with clear numerical illustrations is Lee (1980).

25 The Hicks definitions are, of course, definitions for personal income. To translate them into appropriate definitions of the profits of a business, we must substitute 'distributed to the proprietors' for 'spent'.

26 The two sources of such gains, or losses, are changes in actual or prospective receipts from those originally expected, and changes in the discount rate which is applied in calculating the net present value of those receipts. Some writers define interest rate changes as being separate from windfalls.

27 This argument is stated more fully in Whittington (1974).

28 This is discussed in any good text book such as Bromwich (1976) or Bierman and Smidt (1980).

29 Calculate that discount rate r' which makes $V_0 = C_0$ where C_0 is the initial cost. The decision rule is then: invest when $r' \geq r$ (r being the market discount rate used in the net present value calculation).

30 Hirshleifer (1958) gives an elegant demonstration of this.

31 Note that it does not actually have to be maintained: it could be reinvested in the business, which should lead subsequently to increased returns.

32 This point is made cogently by Peasnell (1977) and by Bromwich (1977a).

33 The type of criticism, made by Nobes (1977) of the Sandilands 'deprival value' proposals for valuation, could also be made *a fortiori* in relation to some of Scott's proposals, particularly in relation to the treatment of monetary assets: the method of valuation to be used depends upon the intended use of the asset, which adds a further degree of subjectivity.

34 Vatter (1947) was a pioneer of cash flow accounting. Recent supporters in the United Kingdom have been Lawson (1971) and Lee (1972).

35 This point is made by Edey (1979).

36 A good critique of the use for share valuation of Sandilands operating profit, is provided by Kennedy (1976).

37 Kennedy (1976) points out that the valuation of shares based upon discounting Sandilands operating profit by an earnings yield obtained in the market would involve making the assumption that there would be no more inflation: surely an inappropriate assumption for an accounting system which purports to be 'inflation accounting'!

Chapter 3 Historical cost accounting

1 For example, Rayman (1980).

2 For an alternative discussion of this see Edwards and Bell (1961), Chapter 1.

3 We are assuming that pure goodwill (i.e. an excess of the economic value of the whole firm over the aggregate value of its individual assets) cannot exist, because long-run perfectly competitive equilibrium precludes the existence of pure profits.
4 These are discussed in any good microeconomic text book, such as Cohen and Cyert (1975).
5 This argument is expounded rigorously and at greater length by Beaver and Demski (1979).
6 Where there are intermediate repayments to the proprietor, the formulation is more complicated. This is illustrated in the appendix to this chapter.
7 This point is made by Wright (1978) in his comment on Kay's paper, and by Whittington (1979).
8 A similar interpretation can be made of current cost profit, as, for example, in Sale and Scapens (1978), which analyses the Sandilands concept of Distributable Operating Flow.
9 This would, for example, be necessary if we wished to value the firm by dividing standard stream income by a market discount rate, which included the market's anticipation of inflation.
10 For an analysis of the effects of pricing policy on profitability in periods of inflation, see R. N. Anthony (1976).
11 Mathews (1965) provides a strong statement of this view, in a critique of the HC basis of CPP accounting.
12 Thomas' criticism also extends to replacement cost systems, when depreciation is based upon allocations of the replacement cost of new assets rather than second-hand market values of used assets. The reporting of historical cash flows is one method of avoiding the accrual problem (Thomas, 1979).
13 This, and a number of other telling criticisms of Ijiri's argument, will be found in MacNeill (1971).
14 I am grateful to my colleague, Ian Davidson, for providing this.

Chapter 4 Inflation and the general price level
1 The paper mark equivalents of gold marks were as follows: July 1914, 1.00; July 1918, 1.786; July 1922, 159.603; July 1923, 264.034; 20 Nov. 1923, 1,000,494,971,000 (Sweeney, 1927).
2 Phase 3 of the counter-inflation policy. The retail price index in October 1973 was the base line and rises of 40p per week for those subject to threshold agreements were 'triggered' by each percentage point rise in the index from 7 per cent onwards. The 7 per cent 'trigger' was reached in May 1974 and ten further rises were triggered before the policy was abandoned in November 1974. I am grateful to Frank Wilkinson of the Department of Applied Economics, Cambridge, for this information.

215

3 *Sandilands Report* (1975), Chapters 18 and 20, particularly paragraphs 795–796. The latter chapter denies that inflation accounting is a form of indexation, because the form of reporting does not directly affect the money amount of contractual payments. This is a somewhat narrow interpretation of indexation.

4 Allen (1975) provides an accessible survey of the subject, and Afriat (1977) a more advanced treatise. Sen (1979) provides a lucid survey of the whole problem of making real income comparisons, at both the personal and the national levels. Deaton and Muellbauer (1980, Chapter 7) provide a concise account of the economic theory of index numbers, and Deaton (1980) provides an extended treatment of the subject, with special emphasis on the assumptions necessary for the practical use of index numbers in the measurement of welfare.

5 Although it should be noted that GNP only covers transactions which give rise to new value added and excludes transactions in second-hand assets, such as land and buildings.

6 This limitation of 'money-metric utility' measures is stressed by Sen (1979).

7 Deaton (1980) provides a good illustration of this approach.

8 Although it might be possible to justify some of the 'entity' capital maintenance concepts in this manner, such as the maintenance of operating capacity, as advocated by the Sandilands Report.

9 Here we ignore the choice between alternative current values, which will be discussed in the next chapter. The choice is not material in the case of quoted securities because buying price, selling price and net present value (at least as estimated by participants in the market) should not differ widely.

10 See, for example, *Accounting for Stewardship in a Period of Inflation*, Research Committee of the Institute of Chartered Accountants in England and Wales, 1968, pp. 6–8.

11 It should be noted that Sweeney preferred replacement cost to historical cost as a valuation basis, although his case studies, based on real-world examples, necessarily involved the CPP adjustment of traditional historical cost data.

12 The Accounting Principles Board (APB) preceded the Financial Accounting Standards Board as the voluntary, private sector standard-setting body in the USA.

13 Although the 1979 proposals contained in the first American standard on the subject (*FAS33*) also require some current cost disclosure and an element of 'real terms' reconciliation of current cost values with CPP restatement.

14 The author of *Accounting for Stewardship in a Period of inflation* was Mr (later Sir) W. E. Parker, who, at the time, was President of the ICAEW.

In conversation with the present writer, he acknowledged his debt to the American work, specifically mentioning Perry Mason's monograph and his personal association with George O. May, an active member of the Study Group on Business Income, which was at the centre of the debate on inflation accounting in the United States in the late 1940s.

15 Parker (1975) provides a lucid exposition of this. As W. E. Parker was instrumental in introducing CPP to the British profession (as author of *Accounting for Stewardship in a Period of Inflation*) this paper is a particularly interesting indication of the thinking which lay behind CPP.

16 A similar illustration will be found on pp. 12–13 of Accounting Research Study No. 6 (American Institute of Certified Public Accountants, 1963).

17 In practice, professional pronouncements such as the British PSSAP7 (Accounting Standards Steering Committee, 1974), have applied the conservative principle of 'restated historical cost or current value, whichever is the lower'.

18 A similar formulation will be found in Barton (1975).

19 This view is consistent with the arguments for an objective historical cost base in PSSAP7 (ASSC, 1973) and in *Accounting for Stewardship in a Period of Inflation* (Institute of Chartered Accountants in England and Wales, 1968).

20 This argument ignores income effects, which could negate these conclusions, especially when the commodity in question constitutes a high proportion of an individual's total expenditure.

21 This is preferred by Moonitz (1973) who uses a similar argument to that advanced here.

22 Strictly baskets. If we allow his consumption pattern to change as his income and relative prices change, even when his tastes are constant: this raises the traditional base-weighted versus current-weighted problem of index number construction.

23 These studies are surveyed by Ketz (1978a).

24 Dyckman (1975) criticises these later studies.

25 'Systematic' returns to holding a share are those which are correlated with returns on other shares ('the market portfolio'), and can be attributed to common factors such as changes in interest rates. 'Unsystematic' returns are the residual returns and are the result of factors unique to the individual company, such as the effect of new accounting information. This separation of systematic and unsystematic risk is obtained by using the Capital Asset Pricing Model (CAPM).

Chapter 5 Current value systems 1: valuation

1 It will be remembered from the previous chapter that the Sandilands Committee did not accept this.

2 Sandilands did not propose to recognise unrealised holding gains on stocks and work-in-progress, which are recognised in (5.6), as part of changes in N''. Sandilands proposed a specific form of current valuation, value to the owner, which is discussed later in the chapter.

3 The detailed proposals for implementation deviate from the model in some respects. For example, Sandilands did not propose the revaluation of 'non-monetary' long-term loans, although it was accepted that this would be desirable in principle. Also, Sandilands proposes certain approximate methods of calculation, such as the use of periodic averages and specific price indices.

4 Accounts in which the Profit and Loss Account and the Balance Sheet are part of the same double entry system, so that balance of the former matches changes in proprietors' interest in the latter.

5 *FAS33*, the most recent proposal, is eclectic in its attitude to 'inflation accounting', which is taken to include replacement cost accounting as one element in the required disclosures, some CPP information also being required, and a 'real terms' combination of the two elements is also allowed.

6 Earlier UK proposals by the Association of Certified and Corporate Accountants (1952) and the Institute of Cost and Works Accountants (1952) advocated replacement cost systems.

7 Limperg also was a pioneer of proposals of the 'value to the owner' type and Sweeney's advocacy of replacement cost is based upon similar reasoning. See Mey (1966).

8 Although Bell (1971) subsequently favours the service approach rather than reproduction.

9 Sweeney (1936) was an early advocate of reporting realised gains separately from real gains: he also advocated measuring gains in real terms, i.e. a gain would be measured as the amount by which the current replacement cost of an asset exceeded its indexed historical cost.

10 Factors leading to the decline in unit costs as the level of aggregation increases include bulk discounts (for materials), economies of scale and technical progress (replacement of a whole plant may enable a change of technique which is not possible in replacing one item which has to be compatible with the rest). Increases in unit costs as the level of aggregation increases could be due to inelastic supply, diseconomies of scale and loss of production due to the disturbance caused by a major reconstruction.

11 Drake and Dopuch (1965) and Prakash and Sunder (1979).

12 The unrealised holding gains represent the difference between the historical cost and the replacement cost of assets appearing in the closing balance sheet. The uncertainty surrounding realisation is an important reason for segregating unrealised from realised holding gains.

13 For longer accounts of Canning's work see Chambers (1979) and Whittington (1980a). A laudatory contemporary review is Fisher (1930).

14 Market replacement costs would also avoid this problem, but in practice replacement cost systems usually involve the allocation of depreciation of fixed assets (Thomas, 1974, Chapter 7).

15 Which postulates that the stock market is efficient in the sense that the market instantaneously impounds all new information into the share price.

16 Fama (1970) and Beaver (1973 and 1981) hold this view. This argument is, of course, based upon the view that investors are the primary users of accounting data, whereas, as was indicated in Chapters 1 and 2, the constituency of users is now much wider.

17 Goodwill being the excess of going concern value over the value of the aggregate net assets. The existence of goodwill can therefore be regarded as evidence of the aggregation problem, aggregate net assets being assessed on an individual basis.

18 Although, as stated earlier, where adequate second-hand markets are available, replacement cost depreciation could be assessed on second-hand values rather than on periodic allocations of the cost of new assets.

19 Including their covariance with returns to other investment, if we consider investment in a portfolio framework.

20 In particular, it was the starting point for the work of Wright (1964 and 1970).

21 This problem is analysed by Peasnell (1978) in the context of using present values as part of the deprival value base, which is discussed later in this chapter.

22 This point was made by Gellein (1971) in his response to Staubus' (1971) paper.

23 For this reason, the Edwards and Bell description of net realisable value as 'opportunity cost' is an over-statement. It is an element of the *external* opportunity cost of assets *already held* by the firm, and *may* be an element of the opportunity cost in other cases. In any case, opportunity cost will not be full net realisable value, but the *difference* between net realisable value and the value in the alternative use being considered.

24 The 'value to the owner' rule can be defined as: 'choose the lower of "netback" or RC'.

25 Stamp has since (1979) amended his rule to: 'The value to the firm of an asset is equal to its replacement cost except when it is clearly worth the owner's while to dispose of the asset immediately and not replace it. In the latter case, value to the firm is equal to net realisable value.'

26 It will be recalled that this argument arose in the discussion of Staubus' present value surrogates, earlier in this chapter.

27 It is surprising that neither Chambers nor Wright refers directly (in these

two papers) to Canning's contribution, as both have clearly been influenced by Canning's ideas.

28 Accounting Standards Committee (1980).

29 Institute of Chartered Accountants in Australia and Australian Society of Accountants (1975).

30 An estimate of PV was needed at an early stage of the algorithm, to decide whether the asset was worth replacing, but if RC did not emerge as the appropriate value (because it exceeded the 'netback', described as the 'recoverable amount'), NRV was the published value, as in Stamp's (1971) proposal.

31 It is notable that Barton (1975), whose paper is based upon a seminar given in Lancaster, also adopts the 'netback' approach to value to the owner, although he does not adopt the Gee and Peasnell extension.

32 The 'deprival' opportunity may, of course, be thought to be particularly relevant to the calculations of depreciation, but 'deprival value' is also advocated as the basis for calculating holding gains. Furthermore, depreciation is presumably planned and anticipated with reasonable accuracy, yet some writers (such as Solomons, 1966) have argued that consequential losses (losses occurring between deprival and replacement) should be added to RC in the calculation of value to the owner.

33 Although, of course, current cost data are supplementary under SSAP16, and historical cost remains the basis of the main accounts.

34 The work by Flemming, Price and Ingram (1976) has been followed up in a number of articles in the Bank of England Quarterly Bulletin.

Chapter 6 Current value systems 2: capital maintenance concepts and real terms accounting

1 Discounted net present value of future receipts is the measure of capital implicit in Hicks' No. 1 definition, so that this situation is one in which the Hicks No. 1 and No. 2 definitions of income lead to an identical measure, i.e. maintaining net present value in money terms maintains consumption in money terms. Alternatively if the No. 1 definition is taken to imply maintenance of net present value in real terms, it will be consistent with the No. 3 definition, real consumption maintenance, in this situation. The accountant's traditional approach to capital maintenance is not, of course, based upon maintenance of net present value.

2 It is therefore necessary to adjust figures for previous years into current pounds, for comparative purposes. It is also desirable to adjust the flows in the profit and loss account from average pounds for the year to closing pounds, to achieve consistency with the closing balance sheet (Edwards and Bell, 1961, p. 253, and Gynther, 1966, Chapter 12).

3 This is illustrated in Chapters V and VI of Edwards and Bell's book.

4 A general review of Baxter's work, with further comment on this point, is Whittington (1975).

5 He deducts the full replacement cost (rather than merely CPP-adjusted historical cost) of goods sold and depreciation, in calculating 'Current Operating Profit' (as in a CCA system) but then adds back 'real depreciation' (the excess of the replacement costs over CPP-adjusted historical cost) to obtain a 'Profit before Tax' which equals CPP-adjusted historical cost profit.

6 The converse is not true: certain advocates of replacement cost (notably Edwards and Bell) do not adopt an entity approach to capital maintenance. Samuelson (1980) argues that the entity view of capital is the only one which is consistent with replacement cost valuation. 'Current cost' and 'value to the owner' can be regarded as modified replacement cost, for present purposes.

7 Schmidt (1930) also includes a gearing adjustment. This is discussed in section 6 of this chapter.

8 An alternative and more detailed discussion of the case against the entity approach is in Baxter (1975, Chapter 8).

9 Gynther (1966, Chapter 15) points out that the Philips system treats real holding gains as capital (an entity approach) but real holding losses as losses (a proprietary approach).

10 A critical commentary on their argument is Whittington (1980b).

11 For simplicity, we are assuming no inflation in this argument. If inflation occurs, the proprietary approach must be interpreted in real terms (i.e. with a general index adjustment) and the holding gain should be defined as a real holding gain.

12 Samuelson (1980), in an interesting paper advocating the entity approach, appears not to realise that, by rejecting the 'cost-saving' argument for holding gains as being based upon a hypothetical opportunity, he is also rejecting the argument for preferring replacement cost depreciation rather than historical cost depreciation.

13 We should, however, remember that, as noted in Chapter 5, the validity and utility of this distinction have been questioned (Drake and Dopuch, 1965, Prakash and Sunder, 1979). In many business operations, holding assets is an integral activity and it is essentially arbitrary to distinguish between 'holding' and 'operating' gains.

14 Their 'current cost profit' is not strictly an entity concept, because, as Kennedy (1978a) points out, it is calculated after deducting interest, which is the financial return to the geared portion of the entity capital. Concentration on returns to proprietors, as represented by equity interests, is characteristic of the 'proprietary' approach, whereas a pure entity approach would focus on the returns to the total long-term capital of the entity, irrespective of the method of finance.

221

15 This is often the case when tax allowances are based upon depreciation charges: the consequent reduction in the tax burden may provide a significant proportion of the funds for replacement investment (Domar, 1953).

16 Preference shares have a fixed claim and conceptually are part of the gearing, although SSAP16 does not treat them as such.

17 The essential idea of the gearing adjustment appears on pp. 237–8 of the 1930 paper.

18 Although the Report did not specifically come down in favour of operating profit rather than total gains as the tax base.

19 The two other notable contemporary advocates of the gearing adjustment were Gibbs (1975 and 1976) and Kennedy, who has provided an excellent summary of the debate (Kennedy, 1978a).

20 This is demonstrated rigorously in Forker (1980).

21 *ED24* and SSAP16 use *average* gearing, rather than opening gearing, but the reason for this is not explained.

22 The entity orientation of the 'specific index' approach to equity capital maintenance can be seen clearly in Schmidt (1930).

23 Kennedy (1978a), p. 63. The whole question of using profit measures to determine dividend distribution is explored thoroughly by Egginton (1980), who concludes that income measures should be supplemented by liquidity measures for this purpose.

24 Although his system suffers from a minor error of double counting, which is demonstrated by Forker (1980), and discussed below (p. 174).

25 This assumes that all monetary assets are classified as working capital, $M_{c,t}$, or are maintained only in nominal terms, and are not deducted from L_f in calculating gearing.

26 This slip has been corrected in the illustration given above (p. 172).

27 Some American studies of the debtor/creditor hypothesis are surveyed in Freeman (1978).

Chapter 7 Review

1 Liabilities should be included in this definition as, conceptually, 'negative assets'.

2 A fuller discussion of this, in the context of income measurement, will be found in Whittington (1981).

3 For example, if some form of current value accounting had been the traditional method, and therefore the basis of generally accepted accounting principles, there would probably be strong resistance within the accounting profession (by individuals who would, no doubt, be described as 'backwoodsmen') to the idea of introducing a historical cost basis.

Bibliography

Abdel-Khalik, A. R. and McKeown, J. C. (1978), 'Disclosure of Estimates of Holding Gains and the Assessment of Systematic Risk', *Journal of Accounting Research*, Vol. 16, Supplement, pp. 46–77.

Accounting Principles Board (1969), *Statement No. 3, Financial Statements Restated for General Price-Level Changes*, American Institute of Certified Public Accountants, June 1969.

Accounting Standards Committee (1975), *Statement of Standard Accounting Practice No. 10, Statements of Source and Application of Funds*, ASC, London, July 1975.

(1976), *ED18, Current Cost Accounting*, ASC, London, 30 November 1976.

(1977), *Inflation Accounting – an Interim Recommendation by the Accounting Standards Committee* ('The Hyde Guidelines'), ASC, London, 4 November 1977.

(1980), *Statement of Standard Accounting Practice No. 16, Current Cost Accounting* ('SSAP16'), ASC, London, March 1980.

Accounting Standards Steering Committee (1971), *Inflation and Accounts, Discussion Paper and Fact Sheet*, Accountancy.

(1973), *ED8: Accounting for Changes in the Purchasing Power of Money*, ASSC, London, 17 January 1973.

(1974), *Provisional Statement of Standard Accounting Practice No. 7, Accounting for Changes in the Purchasing Power of Money* ('PSSAP7'), ASSC, London, May 1974.

(1975), *The Corporate Report*, ASSC, London, July 1975.

Adkerson, R. C. (1978), 'Discussion of DAAM: The Demand for Alternative Accounting Measurements', *Journal of Accounting Research*, Vol. 16, Supplement, pp. 31–6.

Afriat, S. N. (1977), *The Price Index*, Cambridge University Press.

Alexander, S. S. (1948), 'Income Measurement in a Dynamic Economy'. Originally pp. 1-97 of Study Group on Business Income (1948). Revised by David Solomons and reprinted in Baxter and Davidson (1977), pp. 35–85.

Bibliography

Allen, R. G. D. (1975), *Index Numbers in Theory and Practice*, Macmillan, London.

American Accounting Association, Committee on Concepts and Standards for External Financial Reports (1977), *Statement on Accounting Theory and Theory Acceptance*, American Accounting Association.

American Institute of Certified Public Accountants, Accounting Research Division (1963), *Reporting the Financial Effects of Price-Level Changes*, Accounting Research Study No. 6 ('ARS6'), American Institute of Certified Public Accountants, New York.

Anderson, J. A. (1976), *A Comparative Analysis of Selected Income Measurement Theories in Financial Accounting*, Studies in Accounting, 12, American Accounting Association.

Anthony, R. N. (1976), 'The Case for Historical Costs', *Harvard Business Review*, Vol. 54, No. 6, Nov/Dec. 1976.

APB: See Accounting Principles Board.

Aranya, N. (1974), 'The Influence of Pressure Groups on Financial Statements in Britain', *Abacus*, Vol. 10, No. 1, June 1974, pp. 3–12.

Arnold, J. and M. El-Azma (1978), *A Study of the Relative Usefulness of six Accounting Measures of Income*, The Institute of Chartered Accountants in England and Wales.

ASC: See Accounting Standards Committee.

ASSC: See Accounting Standards Steering Committee.

Association of Certified and Corporate Accountants, Taxation & Research Committee (1952), *Accounting for Inflation, a Study of Techniques under Conditions of Changing Price Levels*, Gee & Co.

Barton, A. D. (1974), 'Expectations and Achievements in Income Theory', *The Accounting Review*, Vol. 49, No. 4, October 1974, pp. 664–81.

(1975), *An Analysis of Business Income Concepts*, ICRA Occasional Paper No. 7, International Centre for Research in Accounting, University of Lancaster.

(1976). 'Surrogates in Income Theory: A Reply', *The Accounting Review*, Vol. 51, No. 1, January 1976, pp. 160–2.

Basu, S. (1977), *Inflation Accounting, Capital Market Efficiency and Security Prices*, The Society of Management Accountants of Canada, Hamilton, Ontario, September 1977.

Baxter, W. T. (1959), 'Inflation and the Accounts of Steel Companies', *Accountancy*, May 1959, pp. 250–7 and June 1959, pp. 308–14.

(1967), 'Accounting Values: Sale Price Versus Replacement Cost', *Journal of Accounting Research*, Vol. 5, No. 2, Autumn 1967, pp. 208–14.

(1971), *Depreciation*, Sweet and Maxwell.

(1975), *Accounting Values and Inflation*, McGraw-Hill, 1975.

(1976), 'Monetary Correction: Adjustments to inflation in three South American countries', *Bank of London and South America Review*, Vol. 10, No. 4/76, April 1976, pp. 184–94.

Baxter, W. T. and Davidson, S. (eds.) (1977), *Studies in Accounting*, 3rd edition. Institute of Chartered Accountants in England and Wales.

Beaver, W. (1973), 'What Should be the FASB's Objectives?', *Journal of Accountancy*, Vol. 136, No. 2, August 1973, pp. 49–56.

(1981), 'Market Efficiency', *The Accounting Review*, Vol. 56, No. 1, January 1981, pp. 23–37.

Beaver, W. and J. Demski (1979), 'The Nature of Income Measurement', *The Accounting Review*, Vol. 54, pp. 38–46.

Beja, A. and Y. Aharoni (1977), 'Some Aspects of Conventional Accounting Profits in an Inflationary Environment', *Journal of Accounting Research*, Vol. 15, No. 2, Autumn 1977, pp. 169–78.

Bell, P. W. (1971), 'On Current Replacement Costs and Business Income', Chapter 2, pp. 19–32 of Sterling (1971).

Benston, G. J. and M. A. Krasney (1978), 'DAAM: The Demand for Alternative Accounting Measurements', *Journal of Accounting Research*, Vol. 16, Supplement, pp. 1–30.

Bierman, H. and S. Smidt (1980), *The Capital Budgeting Decision*, Fifth edition, Macmillan, New York.

Bonbright, J. C. (1937), *Valuation of Property* (2 volumes), McGraw-Hill, New York.

Bourn, M., P. J. M. Stoney and R. F. Wynn (1976), 'Price Indices for Current Cost Accounting', *Journal of Business Finance and Accounting*, Vol. 3, No. 3, Autumn 1976, pp. 149–72.

(1977), 'Price Indices for Current Cost Accounting: A Rejoinder', *Journal of Business Finance and Accounting*, Vol. 4, No. 1, Spring 1977, pp. 145–7.

Briscoe, G. and G. Hawke (1976), 'Long-Term Debt and Realisable Gains in Shareholder Wealth: An Empirical Study', *Journal of Business Finance and Accounting*, Vol. 3, No. 1, Spring 1976, pp. 125–35.

Bromwich, M. (1975a), 'Asset Valuation with Imperfect Markets', *Accounting and Business Research*, Vol. 5, No. 20, Autumn 1975, pp. 242–53.

(1975b), 'Individual Purchasing Power Indices and Accounting Reports', *Accounting and Business Research*, Vol. 5, No. 18, Spring 1975, pp. 118–22.

(1976), *The Economics of Capital Budgeting*, Penguin.

(1977a), 'The Use of Present Value Valuation Models in Published Accounting Reports', *The Accounting Review*, Vol. 52, No. 3, July 1977, pp. 587–96.

(1977b), 'The General Validity of Certain "Current" Value Asset Valuation Bases', *Accounting and Business Research*, Vol. 7, No. 28, Autumn, 1977, pp. 242–9.

Buckmaster, D. A., R. M. Copeland and P. E. Dascher (1977), 'The Relative Predictive Ability of Three Accounting Income Models', *Accounting and Business Research*, Vol. 7, No. 27, Summer 1977, pp. 177–86.

Bibliography

Buzby, S. L. and H. Falk (1978), 'Discussion of DAAM: The Demand for Alternative Accounting Measurements', *Journal of Accounting Research*, Vol. 16, Supplement, pp. 37–45.

Canning, J. B. (1929), *The Economics of Accountancy: A Critical Analysis of Accounting Theory*, Ronald Press, New York.

Carsberg, B. V. and A. Hope (1976), *Business Investment Decisions under Inflation*, The Institute of Chartered Accountants in England and Wales.

Carsberg, B., E. V. Morgan and M. Parkin (eds.) (1974), *Indexation and Inflation*, Financial Times Publications.

CCAB (1975), *Initial Reactions to the Report of the Inflation Accounting Committee*, Accounting Standards Committee, London, October 1975.

Chambers, R. J. (1966), *Accounting, Evaluation and Economic Behaviour*, Prentice-Hall.

— (1970), 'Second Thoughts on Continuously Contemporaneous Accounting', *Abacus*, Vol. 6, No. 1, September 1970, pp. 39–55.

— (1971a), 'Evidence for a Market-Selling Price-Accounting System', Chapter 4, pp. 74–96 of Sterling (1971).

— (1971b), 'Value to the Owner', *Abacus*, Vol. 7, No. 1, June 1971, pp. 62–72.

— (1972), 'Multiple Column Accounting – Cui Bono?' and 'Quo Vado?', *Chartered Accountant in Australia*, Vols. 42 and 43, March 1972 (pp. 4–8) and August 1972 (pp. 13–15).

— (1976), *Current Cost Accounting – A Critique of the Sandilands Report*, ICRA Occasional Paper No. 11, University of Lancaster.

— (1977), *An Autobibliography*, ICRA Occasional Paper No. 15, International Centre for Research in Accounting, University of Lancaster.

— (1978), 'The Use and Abuse of a Notation: A History of an Idea', *Abacus*, Vol. 14, No. 2, December 1978, pp. 122–44.

— (1979), 'Canning's *The Economics of Accountancy* – After 50 Years', *The Accounting Review*, Vol. 54, No. 4, October 1979, pp. 764–75.

Chatfield, M. (1974), *A History of Accounting Thought*, The Dryden Press, Hinsdale, Illinois.

Coenenberg, A. and Macharzina, K. (1976), 'Accounting for Price Changes: an Analysis of Current Developments in Germany', *Journal of Business Finance and Accounting*, Vol. 3, No. 1, Spring 1976, pp. 53–68.

Cohen, K. J. and R. M. Cyert (1975), *Theory of the Firm: Resource Allocation in a Market Economy*, Second edition, Prentice-Hall, 1975.

Committee of Inquiry into Inflation and Taxation (1975), *Report: Inflation and Taxation*, 'The Mathews Report', Australian Government Publishing Service.

226

Cook, J. S. and O. J. Holzmann (1976), 'Current Cost and Present Value in Income Theory', *The Accounting Review*, Vol. 51, No. 4, October 1976, pp. 778–87.

Craswell, A. (1976), *A Manual on Continuously Contemporaneous Accounting*, Inflation Accounting Research Project, Department of Management Studies, Univesity of Waikato, Hamilton, New Zealand.

Cutler, R. S. and C. A. Westwick (1973), 'The Impact of Inflation Accounting on the Stock Exchange', *Accountancy*, Vol. 84, No. 955, March 1973, pp. 15–24.

Daines, H. C. (1929), 'The Changing Objectives of Accounting', *The Accounting Review*, Vol. 4, pp. 94–110. Reprinted in Zeff (1976).

Davidson, S., C. P. Stickney and R. L. Weil (1976), *Inflation Accounting. A Guide for the Accountant and the Financial Analyst*, McGraw-Hill.

Davidson, S. and R. L. Weil (1975), 'Inflation Accounting: What Will General Price Level Adjusted Income Statements Show?', *Financial Analysts Journal*, January–February, 1975, pp. 27–31 and 71–84.

Day, A. C. L. (1974), Article in *The Observer*, 3 November 1974.

Dean, J. (1951), 'Measurement of Profits for Executive Decisions', *Accounting Review*, Vol. 26, No. 2, April 1951, pp. 185–96.

(1954), 'Measurement of Real Economic Earnings of a Machinery Manufacturer', *The Accounting Review*, Vol. 29, No. 2, April 1954, pp. 255–66.

Deane, Phyllis M. (1979), 'Inflation in history', pp. 1–36 of David Heathfield (ed.), *Perspectives on inflation, models and policies*, Longman.

Deaton, A. S. (1980), 'Measurement of Welfare: Theory and Practical Guidelines', LSMS Working Paper No. 7, The World Bank Development Research Center, Washington D.C., October 1980.

Deaton, A. S. and J. Muellbauer (1980), *Economics and consumer behavior*, Cambridge University Press, 1980.

Devon, P. C. and R. Kolodny (1978), 'Price-Level Reporting and its Value to Investors', *Accounting and Business Research*, Vol. 9, No. 33, Winter 1978, pp. 19–24.

Domar, E. D. (1953), 'Depreciation, Replacement and Growth', *The Economic Journal*, Vol. 63, March 1953, pp. 1–32.

Dopuch, N. and L. Revsine (eds.) (1973), *Accounting Research 1960–1970: A Critical Evaluation*, Center for International Education and Research in Accounting, University of Illinois.

Drake, D. F. and Dopuch, N. (1965), 'On the Case for Dichotomizing Income', *Journal of Accounting Research*, Vol. 3, pp. 192–205.

Dyckman, T. R. (1969), *Investment Analysis and General Price-Level Adjustments*, Studies in Accounting Research, No. 1, American Accounting Association.

Bibliography

(1975), 'The Effects of Restating Financial Statements for Price-Level Changes: A Comment', *The Accounting Review*, Vol. 50, No. 4, October 1975, pp. 796–808.

Edey, H. C. (1974), 'Deprival Value and Financial Accounting', pp. 75–83 of H. C. Edey and B. S. Yamey (eds.), *Debits, Credits, Finance, and Profits*, Sweet and Maxwell.

(1979), 'Sandilands and the Logic of Current Cost', *Accounting and Business Research*, Vol. 9, No. 35, Summer 1979, pp. 191–200.

Edwards, E. O. (1975), 'The State of Current Value Accounting', *The Accounting Review*, Vol. 50, No. 2, April 1975, pp. 235–45.

Edwards, E. O. and Bell, P. W. (1961), *The Theory and Measurement of Business Income*, University of California Press.

Edwards, R. S. (1938), 'The Nature and Measurement of Income', *The Accountant*, July–October 1938. Revised and Reprinted in Baxter and Davidson (1977), pp. 96–140.

Egginton, D. A. (1980), 'Distributable Profit and the Pursuit of Prudence', *Accounting and Business Research*, No. 41, Winter 1980, pp. 1–14.

Emanuel, D. (1976), *A Manual on Current Purchasing Power Accounting*, Inflation Accounting Research Project, Department of Management Studies, University of Waikato, Hamilton, New Zealand.

Fama, E. (1970), 'Efficient Capital Markets: A Review of Theory and Empirical Work', *Journal of Finance*, Vol. 25, No. 2, May 1970, pp. 383–417.

Fane, G. (1975), 'The Case for Indexation', pp. 1–13 in Liesner and King (1975).

FASB (1974), *Exposure Draft. Financial Reporting in Units of General Purchasing Power*, FASB, Stamford, Conn., 31 December 1974.

(1977), *Field Tests of Financial Reporting in Units of General Purchasing Power*, FASB, Stamford, Conn., May 1977.

(1978), *Proposed Statement of Financial Accounting Standards. Financial Reporting and Changing Prices*, FASB, Stamford, Conn., 28 December 1978.

(1979a), *Exposure Draft. Constant Dollar Accounting*, FASB, Stamford, Conn., 2 March 1979.

(1979b), *Statement of Financial Accounting Standards No. 33 (FAS33): Financial Reporting and Changing Prices*, FASB, Stamford, Conn., September 1979.

(1981), *Invitation to Comment on the Need for Research in Financial Reporting and Changing Prices*, FASB, Stamford, Conn., 15 June 1981.

Fells, J. M. (1919), 'Some Principles governing the Ascertainment of Cost', *Incorporated Accountants' Journal*, November 1919, p. 34.

Financial Accounting Standards Board: See FASB.

Fisher, I. (1911), *The Purchasing Power of Money*, Macmillan, New York.
  (1920), *Stabilizing the dollar: a plan to stabilize the general price level without fixed individual prices*, Macmillan, New York.
  (1930), 'The Economics of Accountancy', *American Economic Review*, Vol. 20, No. 4, December 1930, pp. 603–18.
Flemming, J. S. (1976), *Inflation*, Oxford University Press.
Flemming, J. S., L. D. D. Price and D. H. A. Ingram (1976), 'Trends in company profitability', *Bank of England Quarterly Bulletin*, Vol. 16, No. 1, March 1976, pp. 36–52.
Forker, J. J. (1980), 'Capital Maintenance Concepts, Gains from Borrowing and the Measurement of Income', *Accounting and Business Research*, Vol. 10, No. 40, Autumn 1980, pp. 393–402.
Frank, W. (1969), 'A Study of the Predictive Significance of Two Income Measures', *Journal of Accounting Research*, Vol. 7, No. 1, Spring 1969, pp. 123–36.
Freeman, R. N. (1978), 'On the Association Between Net Monetary Position and Equity Security Prices', *Journal of Accounting Research*, Vol. 16, Supplement, pp. 111–45.
Friedman, M. (1974), *Monetary Correction*, IEA Occasional Paper 41, Institute of Economic Affairs, London.
Frisch, R. (1936), 'The Problem of Index Numbers', *Econometrica*, Vol. 4, pp. 1–38.
Gee, K. P. (1977), *Management Planning and Control in Inflation*, The Macmillan Press.
Gee, K. and Peasnell, K. V. (1976), 'A Pragmatic Defence of Replacement Cost', *Accounting and Business Research*, Vol. 6, No. 24, Autumn 1976, pp. 242–9.
Gellein, O. S. (1971), 'Response' (to Staubus, 1971), pp. 70–3 of Sterling (1971).
Gibbs, M. (1975), 'Why Sandilands is not the full answer', *The Times*, 18 September 1975.
  (1976), 'A better answer to the problem of inflation accounting', *The Times*, 23 February 1976.
  (1979), 'Inflation accounting and company taxation', *Fiscal Studies*, Vol. 1, No. 1, November 1979, pp. 11–19.
Gibbs, M. and Seward, W. (1979), *ED24 – Morpeth's New Proposals*, Phillips and Drew, 30 April 1979.
Godley, W. and F. Cripps (1975), 'Profits, stock appreciation and the Sandilands Report', *The Times*, 1 October 1975.
Godley, W. and A. Wood (1974), 'Stock Appreciation and the Crisis of British Industry', Department of Applied Economics, Cambridge, mimeo, October 1974. Later published in *The Economic Policy Review*, 1975.

229

Bibliography

Goudeket, A. (1960), 'An Application of Replacement Value Theory', *Journal of Accountancy*, July 1960, pp. 37–47. Revised and reprinted, with a Postscript by E. B. MacDonald, in Baxter and Davidson (1977), pp. 234–49.

Gray, S. J. (1975), 'Price Changes and Company Profits in the Securities Market', *Abacus*, Vol. 11, No. 1, June 1975, pp. 71–85.

(1976), 'Accounting for Price Changes: a Case Study of a Multinational Company', *Journal of Business Finance and Accounting*, Vol. 3, No. 1, Spring 1976, pp. 1–14.

Gress, E. J. (1972), 'Application of Replacement Cost Accounting: a Case Study', *Abacus*, Vol. 8, No. 1, June 1972, pp. 3–13.

Gynther, R. S. (1966), *Accounting for Price-Level Changes: Theory and Procedures*, Pergamon.

(1974), 'Why use General Purchasing Power?', *Accounting and Business Research*, Vol. 4, No. 2, Spring 1974, pp. 141–57.

Harcourt, G. C. (1958), 'The Quantitative Effect of basing Company Taxation on Replacement Costs', *Accounting Research*, Vol. 9, No. 1, January 1958, pp. 1–16.

(1965), 'The Accountant in a Golden Age', *Oxford Economic Papers*, Vol. 17, pp. 66–80. Reprinted in Parker and Harcourt (1969).

Heath, L. C. (1972), 'Distinguishing Between Monetary and Nonmonetary Assets and Liabilities in General Price-Level Accounting', *The Accounting Review*, Vol. 47, No. 3, July 1972, pp. 458–68.

Heintz, J. A. (1975), 'The Effects of Restating Financial Statements for Price-Level Changes: A Reply', *The Accounting Review*, Vol. 50, No. 4, October 1975, pp. 809–14.

Hicks, J. R. (1946), *Value and Capital*, Oxford: Clarendon Press. Pp. 171–181 of the second edition (1946) are reprinted in Parker and Harcourt (1969), pp. 74–82.

Hillison, W. A. (1979), 'Empirical Investigation of General Purchasing Power Adjustments on Earnings per Share and the Movement of Security Prices', *Journal of Accounting Research*, Vol. 17, No. 1, Spring 1979, pp. 60–73.

Hirshleifer, J. (1958), 'On the Theory of the Optimal Investment Decision', *The Journal of Political Economy*, Vol. 66, No. 4, August 1958, pp. 329–52.

Hope, A. (1974), *Accounting for Price Changes – a Practical Survey of 6 Methods*, Research Committee Occasional Paper No. 4, Institute of Chartered Accountants in England and Wales.

Hume, A. (1976), *A Manual on Current Cost Accounting*, Inflation Accounting Research Project, Department of Management Studies, University of Waikato, Hamilton, New Zealand.

Ijiri, Y. (1971), 'A Defence for Historical Cost Accounting', Chapter 1, pp. 1–14 of Sterling (1971).

(1976), 'The Price-Level Restatement and Its Dual Interpretation', *The Accounting Review*, Vol. 51, No. 2, April 1976, pp. 227–43.

Inflation Accounting Steering Group (1976), *Background Papers to the Exposure Draft on Current Cost Accounting*, Tolley Publishing Co. and The Institute of Chartered Accountants in England and Wales.

Institute of Chartered Accountants in Australia and Australian Society of Accountants (1975), *A Method of 'Current Value Accounting'*. Preliminary Exposure Draft, June 1975.

Institute of Chartered Accountants in England and Wales (1952), 'Accounting in relation to changes in the purchasing power of money', *Recommendations on Accounting Principles*, N15, 30 May 1952.

Institute of Chartered Accountants in England and Wales, General Educational Trust (1973), *Accounting for Inflation, a working guide to the accounting procedures, Part 1: Text* and *Part 2: Tables*.

Institute of Chartered Accountants in England and Wales, Research Committee (1968), *Accounting for Stewardship in a Period of Inflation*, The Research Foundation of The Institute of Chartered Accountants in England and Wales.

Institute of Cost and Works Accountants, Research and Technical Committee (1952), *The Accountancy of Changing Price Levels*, The Institute of Cost and Works Accountants.

Jackman, R. and K. Klappholz (1975), *Taming the Tiger*, Hobart Paper 63, Institute of Economic Affairs.

Jones, R. C. (1949), 'Effect of inflation on capital and profits: the record of nine steel companies', *The Journal of Accountancy*, January 1949, pp. 9–27.

(1955), *Price Level Changes and Financial Statements – Case Studies of Four Companies*, American Accounting Association.

(1956), *Effects of Price Level Changes on Business Income, Capital, and Taxes*, American Accounting Association.

Kaldor, N. (1955), 'The Concept of Income in Economic Theory', *An Expenditure Tax*, Allen and Unwin, pp. 54–78. Reprinted in Parker and Harcourt (1969).

Kay, J. A. (1976), 'Accountants, too, could be happy in a Golden Age: The Accountant's Rate of Profit and the Internal Rate of Return', *Oxford Economic Papers*, Vol. 28, No. 3, November 1976, pp. 447–60.

(1977), 'Inflation Accounting – A Review Article', *The Economic Journal*, Vol. 87, No. 346, June 1977, pp. 300–11.

(1978), 'Accounting Rate of Profit and Internal Rate of Return: A Reply', *Oxford Economic Papers*, Vol. 30, No. 3, November 1978, pp. 469–70.

Kay, J. A. and M. A. King (1980), *The British System of Taxation*, Oxford University Press, second edition, 1980.

Kennedy, C. (1976), 'Inflation Accounting, Profits, Profitability and Share Valuation', *Journal of Business Finance and Accounting*, Vol. 3, No. 1, Spring 1976, pp. 137–46.

Bibliography

(1978a), 'Inflation Accounting: Retrospect and Prospect', *Cambridge Economic Policy Review*, No. 4, Chapter 7, pp. 58–64.

(1978b). 'Fixed Assets and the Hyde Gearing Adjustment', *Journal of Business Finance and Accounting*, Vol. 5, No. 4, Winter 1978, pp. 393–406.

Ketz, J. E. (1978a), 'The Validation of Some General Price Level Estimating Models', *The Accounting Review*, Vol. 53, No. 4, October 1978, pp. 952–60.

(1978b), 'The Effect of General Price-Level Adjustments on the Predictive Ability of Financial Ratios', *Journal of Accounting Research*, Vol. 16, Supplement, pp. 273–84.

King, M. A. (1975), 'The United Kingdom Profits Crisis: Myth or Reality?', *The Economic Journal*, Vol. 85, March 1975, pp. 33–54.

Kratchman, S. H., R. E. Malcom and R. D. Twark (1974), 'An Intra-Industry Comparison of Alternative Income Concepts and Relative Performance Evaluations', *The Accounting Review*, Vol. 49, No. 4, October 1974, pp. 682–9.

(1975), 'The Comparison of Alternative Income Concepts: A Reply', *The Accounting Review*, Vol. 50, No. 4, October 1975, pp. 865–8.

(1976), 'Alternative Income Concepts and Relative Performance Evaluations: A Reply', *The Accounting Review*, Vol. 51, No. 2, April 1976, pp. 421–6.

Largay, J. A. and J. L. Livingstone (1976), *Accounting for Changing Prices*, Wiley.

Lawson, G. H. (1971), 'Cash Flow Accounting', *The Accountant*, 28 October and 4 November 1971, pp. 998–1002 and 1083–8.

Lee, T. A. (1972), 'A Case for Cash Flow Reporting', *Journal of Business Finance*, Vol. 4, No. 2, Summer 1972, pp. 27–36.

(1979), 'The Simplicity and Complexity of Accounting', Chapter 2, pp. 35–55 of Sterling and Thomas (1979).

(1980), *Income and Value Measurement: Theory and Practice*, second edition, Nelson.

Liao, S. S. (1975), 'The Comparison of Alternative Income Concepts: A Comment', *The Accounting Review*, Vol. 50, No. 4, October 1975, pp. 860–4.

Liesner, T. and M. A. King (eds.) (1975), *Indexing for Inflation*, IFS/Heinemann.

London Society of Chartered Accountants (1977), *Submission on ED18*, May 1977.

Ma, R. (1976), 'Value to the Owner Revisited', *Abacus*, Vol. 12, No. 2, December 1976, pp. 159–65.

MacDonald, G. (1974), 'Deprival Value: Its Use and Abuse', *Accounting and Business Research*, Vol. 4, No. 16, Autumn 1974, pp. 263–9.

(1975), *Profit Measurement: Alternatives to Historical Cost*, Haymarket.

McDonald, D. L. (1968), 'A Test Application of the Feasibility of Market Based Measures in Accounting', *Journal of Accounting Research*, Vol. 6, No. 1, Spring 1968, pp. 38–49.

McIntyre, E. V. (1975), 'The Effects of Restating Financial Statements for Price-Level Changes: A Reply', *The Accounting Review*, Vol. 50, No. 4, October 1975, pp. 815–17.

McKeown, J. C. (1971), 'An Empirical Test of a Model Proposed by Chambers', *The Accounting Review*, Vol. 46, No. 1, January 1971, pp. 12–29.

MacNeal, K. (1939), *Truth in Accounting*, University of Pennsylvania Press.

MacNeill, J. H. (1971), 'Response' (to Ijiri, 1971), pp. 15–18 of Sterling (1971).

McRae, W. T. and R. Dobbins (1974), 'Behavioural Aspects of the Inflation Accounting Controversy', *Accounting and Business Research*, Vol. 4, No. 14, Spring 1974, pp. 135–40.

Mallinson, D. (1980), *Understanding Current Cost Accounting*, Butterworths.

Mason, P. (1956), *Price-Level Changes and Financial Statements, Basic Concepts and Methods*, American Accounting Association.

Mathews, R. L. (1965), 'Price-Level Changes and Useless Information', *Journal of Accounting Research*, Vol. 3, pp. 133–58.

(1968), 'Income, Price Changes and the Valuation Controversy in Accounting', *The Accounting Review*, Vol. 43, July, 1968, pp. 509–16.

Mathews, R. L. and J.McB. Grant (1958), *Inflation and Company Finance*, The Law Book Co., Sydney.

Mathews Report (1975): See Committee of Inquiry into Inflation and Taxation.

Meade, J. E. (1978), *The Structure and Reform of Direct Taxation* ('The Meade Committee Report'), George Allen and Unwin.

Meeks, G. (1974), 'Profit Illusion', *Bulletin of the Oxford Institute of Economics and Statistics*, Vol. 36, No. 4, November 1974, pp. 267–85.

Merrett, A. J. and A. Sykes (1974), Article in *The Financial Times*, 30 September 1974.

(1980), 'Inflation accounting: how badly flawed is ED24?', *The Times*, 11 February 1980.

Mey, A. (1966), 'Theodore Limperg and his Theory of Values and Costs', *Abacus*, Vol. 2, No. 1, September 1966, pp. 1–23.

Middleditch, L. (1918), 'Should Accounts Reflect the Changing Value of the Dollar?', *The Journal of Accountancy*, Vol. 25, No. 2, February 1918, pp. 114–20, reprinted in Zeff (1976).

Moonitz, M. (1973), *Changing Prices and Financial Reporting*, International Centre for Research in Accounting, University of Lancaster.

Moore, B. (1980), 'Equity Values and Inflation: The Importance of Dividends', *Lloyds Bank Review*, No. 137, July 1980, pp. 1–15.

233

Bibliography

Morris, R. C. (1975), 'Evidence of the Impact of Inflation Accounting on Share Prices', *Accounting and Business Research*, Vol. 5, No. 18, Spring 1975, pp. 82–90.

Most, K. S. (1977), *Accounting Theory*, Grid Inc., Columbus, Ohio.

Mumford, M. (1979). 'The End of a Familiar Inflation Accounting Cycle', *Accounting and Business Research*, Vol. 9, No. 34, Spring 1979, pp. 98–104.

Nelson, C. L. (1973), 'A Priori Research in Accounting', in Dopuch and Revsine (1973).

Nguyen, D. T. and R. A. Whittaker (1976), 'Inflation, Replacement and Amortisation Funds: A Case Study of UK Industries', *Journal of Business Finance and Accounting*, Vol. 3, No. 1, Spring 1976, pp. 43–52.

Nobes, C. W. (1977), 'Current Cost Accounting – Valuation by Intent?', *Accounting and Business Research*, Vol. 7, No. 26, Spring 1977, pp. 95–9.

Norton, C. L. and Smith, R. E. (1979), 'A Comparison of General Price Level and Historical Cost Financial Statements in the Prediction of Bankruptcy', *The Accounting Review*, Vol. 54, No. 1, January 1979, pp. 72–87.

Parker, J. E. (1977), 'Impact of Price-Level Accounting', *The Accounting Review*, Vol. 52, pp. 69–96.

Parker, R. H. and G. C. Harcourt (1969), *Readings in the Concept and Measurement of Income*, Cambridge University Press.

Parker, Sir W. E. (1975), 'CPP Accounting. What is the Argument Really About?', *The Accountant*, Vol. 172, No. 5231, 3 April 1975, pp. 426–8.

Patell, J. M. (1978), 'Discussion of The Impact of Price-Level Adjustment in the Context of Risk Assessment and The Effect of General Price-Level Adjustments on the Predictive Ability of Financial Ratios', *Journal of Accounting Research*, Vol. 16, Supplement, pp. 293–300.

Peasnell, K. V. (1977), 'A Note on the Discounted Present Value Concept', *The Accounting Review*, Vol. 52, No. 1, January 1977, pp. 186–9.

(1978), 'Interaction Effects in CCA Valuation', *Accounting and Business Research*, Vol. 8, No. 30, Spring 1978, pp. 82–91.

Peasnell, K. V. and L. C. L. Skerratt (1976a), *Current Cost Accounting: The Index Number Problem*, International Centre for Research in Accounting, University of Lancaster.

(1976b), 'Long-Term Debt and Shareholder Wealth: A Comment', *Journal of Business Finance and Accounting*, Vol. 3, No. 3, Autumn 1976, pp. 137–41.

(1977a), 'How Well Does a Single Index Represent the Nineteen Sandilands Plant and Machinery Indices?', *Journal of Accounting Research*, Vol. 15, No. 1, Spring 1977, pp. 108–19.

(1977b). 'Price Indices for Current Cost Accounting – A Reply and Some Further Evidence', *Journal of Business Finance and Accounting*, Vol. 4, No. 1, Spring 1977, pp. 139–44.

(1978), 'Income-Group Inflation Rates and General Purchasing Power Adjustments: an Empirical Test of the Heterogeneity Hypothesis', *Accounting and Business Research*, Vol. 9, No. 33, Winter 1978, pp. 45–59.

Petersen, R. J. (1973), 'Interindustry Estimation of General Price-Level Impact on Financial Information', *The Accounting Review*, Vol. 48, No. 1, January 1973, pp. 34–43.

(1975), 'A Portfolio Analysis of General Price Level Restatement', *The Accounting Review*, Vol. 50, No. 3, July 1975, pp. 525–32.

(1978), 'Interindustry Estimation of a General Price-Level Impact on Financial Information: More Data and a Reply', *The Accounting Review*, Vol. 53, No. 1, January 1978, pp. 198–203.

Petri, E. and J. Gelfand (1979), 'The Production Function: A New Perspective in Capital Maintenance', *The Accounting Review*, Vol. 54, No. 2, April 1979, pp. 330–45.

Picur, R. D. and J. C. McKeown (1976), 'Alternative Income Concepts and Relative Performance Evaluations: A Comment and Extension', *The Accounting Review*, Vol. 51, No. 2, April 1976, pp. 415–20.

Prakash, P. and S. Sunder (1979), 'The Case Against Separation of Current Operating Profit and Holding Gains', *The Accounting Review*, Vol. 54, No. 1, January 1979, pp. 1–22.

Rayman, R. A. (1980). 'Is inflation accounting an academic confidence trick?', *The Financial Times*, 16 January 1980, p. 13.

Revsine, L. (1970), 'On the Correspondence Between Replacement Cost Income and Economic Income', *The Accounting Review*, Vol. 54, July 1970, pp. 513–23.

(1973), *Replacement Cost Accounting*, Prentice-Hall, 1973.

(1976), 'Surrogates in Accounting Theory: A Comment', *The Accounting Review*, Vol. 51, No. 1, January 1976, pp. 156–9.

Richardson Committee Report (1976), *The Report of the Committee of Inquiry into Inflation Accounting*, New Zealand Government Printer, Wellington.

Ross, H. (1969), *Financial Statements. A Crusade for Current Values*, Pitman (Canada).

Sale, T. and Scapens, R. (1978), 'Current Cost Accounting as a Surrogate for Dividend Paying Ability', *Accounting and Business Research*, Vol. 8, No. 31, Summer, 1978, pp. 208–16.

Samuelson, R. A. (1980), 'Should Replacement-Cost Changes be Included in Income?', *The Accounting Review*, Vol. 55, No. 2, April 1980, pp. 254–68.

Bibliography

Sandilands Committee (1975), *Inflation Accounting: Report of the Inflation Accounting Committee* under the chairmanship of F. E. P. Sandilands, Cmnd 6225, HMSO, September 1975.

Scapens, R. W. (1977), *Accounting in an Inflationary Environment*, The Macmillan Press.

Schmalenbach, E. (1959), *Dynamic Accounting*. Translated by G. W. Murphy and K. S. Most, Gee.

Schmidt, F. (1921), *Die Organische Bilanz im Rahmen der Wirtschaft*, Gloeckner, Leipzig.

(1931), 'Is Appreciation Profit', *The Accounting Review*, Vol. 6, pp. 289–93. Reprinted in Zeff (1976).

(1931), 'Is Appreciation Profit', *The Accounting Review*, Vol. 6, pp. 289–93. Reprinted in Zeff (1976).

Scott, M. FG. (1976), *Some Economic Principles of Accounting: A Constructive Critique of the Sandilands Report*, IFS Lecture Series, No. 7, The Institute for Fiscal Studies.

Secretary of State for Trade (1977), *The Future of Company Reports, A Consultative Document*, HMSO, Cmnd 6888, July 1977.

Securities and Exchange Commission (1975), *Notice of Proposed Amendments to Regulation S-X to Require Disclosure of Certain Replacement Cost Data in Notes to Financial Statements*, SEC, Washington, 21 August, 1975.

Sen, A. K. (1979), 'The Welfare Basis of Real Income Comparisons: A Survey', *Journal of Economic Literature*, Vol. 17, March 1979, pp. 1–45.

Short, D. G. (1978), 'The Impact of Price-Level Adjustment in the Context of Risk Assessment', *Journal of Accounting Research*, Vol. 16, Supplement, pp. 259–72.

Solomon, E. (1966), 'Return on Investment: the Relation of Book Yields to True Value', in *Research in Accounting Measurement*, ed. R. K. Jaedicke, Y. Ijiri and O. Nielsen, American Accounting Association.

Solomons, D. (1961), 'Economic and Accounting Concepts of Income', *The Accounting Review*, Vol. 36, pp. 374–83. Reprinted in Parker and Harcourt (1969).

(1966), 'Economic and Accounting Concepts of Cost and Value', Chapter 6, pp. 117–40 of M. Backer (ed.), *Modern Accounting Theory*, Prentice-Hall.

(1979), 'The Politicization of Accounting', pp. 25–39 of Zeff, S. A., J. Demski and N. Dopuch (eds.), *Essays in Honor of William A. Paton*, University of Michigan.

Stamp, E. (1971), 'Income and Value Determination and Changing Price Levels: an Essay Towards a Theory', *The Accountant's Magazine*, June 1971, pp. 277–92.

(1972), 'R. J. Chambers: Quo Vadis et Cui Bono', *Chartered Accountants in Australia*, August 1972, pp. 10–12.

(1979), 'Financial Reports on an Entity: Ex Uno Plures', Chapter 8, pp. 163–80, of Sterling and Thomas (1979).

Staubus, G. J. (1971), 'The Relevance of Evidence of Cash Flows', Chapter 3, pp. 42–69 of Sterling (1971).

Sterling, R. R. (1970), *Theory of the Measurement of Enterprise Income*, University Press of Kansas.

Sterling, R. R. (ed.) (1971), *Asset Valuation and Income Determination, A Consideration of the Alternatives*, Scholars Book Co., Houston, Texas.

Sterling, R. R. and R. Radosevitch (1969), 'A Valuation Experiment', *Journal of Accounting Research*, Vol. 7, No. 1, Spring 1969, pp. 90–5.

Sterling, R. R. and A. L. Thomas (eds.) (1979), *Accounting for a Simplified Firm Owning Depreciable Assets*, Scholars Book Co., Houston, Texas.

Stone, J. R. N. and G. Stone (1977), *National Income and Expenditure*, tenth edition, Bowes and Bowes.

Study Group on the Objectives of Financial Statements (1973), *Objectives of Financial Statements* ('The Trueblood Report'), American Institute of Certified Public Accountants, New York, October 1973.

Sweeney, H. W. (1927), 'Effects of Inflation on German Accounting', *The Journal of Accountancy*, Vol. 30, No. 1, July 1920. Reprinted in Zeff (1976).

(1928). 'German Inflation Accounting', *The Journal of Accountancy*, Vol. 45, No. 2, February 1928. Reprinted in Zeff (1976).

(1933), 'Capital', *The Accounting Review*, Vol. 8, pp. 185–99. Reprinted in Zeff (1976).

(1935), 'The Technique of Stabilized Accounting', *The Accounting Review*, Vol. 10, pp. 185–205. Reprinted in Zeff (1976).

(1936), *Stabilized Accounting*, Harper, New York. Reprinted 1964, by Holt, Rinehart and Winston, with a new Foreword by W. A. Paton and an essay 'Forty Years After: Or Stabilized Accounting Revisited', by H. W. Sweeney.

(1964), 'Forty Years After: Or Stabilized Accounting Revisited', pp. 17–39 of the 1964 reissue of *Stabilized Accounting*, Holt Rinehart and Winston, New York.

Thomas, A. L. (1969), *The Allocation Problem in Financial Accounting Theory*, Studies in Accounting Research, 3, American Accounting Association.

(1974), *The Allocation Problem: Part Two*, Studies in Accounting Research, 9, American Accounting Association.

(1979), 'Matching: Up From Our Black Hole', Chapter 1, pp. 11–33 of Sterling and Thomas (1979).

Bibliography

Tippett, M. (1979), 'ED24 – An Inefficient Means of Information Retrieval?', *The Accountant's Magazine*, Vol. 83, No. 881, November 1979, pp. 465–8.

Trevithick, J. A. (1977), *Inflation: a guide to the crisis in economics*, Penguin.

Trueblood Committee Report: See Study Group on the Objectives of Financial Statements.

Tweedie, D. P. (1977), 'Cash Flows and Realisable Value: the Intuitive Accounting Concepts? An Empirical Test', *Accounting and Business Research*, Vol. 8, No. 29, Winter 1979, pp. 2–13.

  (1979), *Financial Reporting, Inflation and the Capital Maintenance Concept*, International Centre for Research in Accounting, University of Lancaster.

United Nations (1980), *World Economic Survey, 1979–80, Current Trends in the World Economy*, United Nations, New York.

Vatter, W. J. (1947), *The Fund Theory of Accounting*, University of Chicago Press.

  (1966), 'Income Models, Book Yield and Rate of Return', *The Accounting Review*, Vol. 41, No. 4, October 1966, pp. 681–98.

Wanless, P. T. (1974), 'Reflections on Asset Valuation and Value to the Firm', *Abacus*, Vol. 10, No. 2, December 1974, pp. 160–4.

  (1976), 'Current Purchasing Power Accounting: A Study of a Cooperative Venture', *Abacus*, Vol. 12, No. 1, June 1976, pp. 61–72.

Wasserman, M. J. (1931), 'Accounting Practice in France During the Period of Monetary Inflation (1919–1927)', *The Accounting Review*, March 1931. Reprinted in Zeff (1976).

Watts, R. L. and J. L. Zimmerman (1978), 'Towards a Positive Theory of the Determination of Accounting Standards', *The Accounting Review*, Vol. 53, No. 1, January 1978, pp. 112–34.

  (1979), 'The Demand for and Supply of Accounting Theories: The Market for Excuses', *The Accounting Review*, Vol. 54, No. 2, April 1979, pp. 273–305.

  (1980), 'On the irrelevance of replacement cost disclosures for security prices', *Journal of Accounting and Economics*, Vol. 2, No. 2, August 1980, pp. 95–106.

Weston, F. T. (1971), 'Response' (to Chambers, 1971a), pp. 97–106 of Sterling (1971).

Westwick, C. A. (1980), 'The Lessons to be Learned from the Development of Inflation Accounting in the UK', *Accounting and Business Research*, No. 40, Autumn 1980, pp. 353–73.

Whittington, G. (1974), 'Asset Valuation, Income Measurement and Accounting Income', *Accounting and Business Research*, Vol. 4, No. 14, Spring 1974, pp. 96–101.

(1975), 'Baxter on Inflation Accounting', *Accounting and Business Research*, Vol. 5, No. 20, Autumn 1975, pp. 314–17.

(1976), 'Indexation: A Review Article', *Accounting and Business Research*, Vol. 6, No. 23, Summer 1976, pp. 171–6.

(1979), 'On the use of the Accounting Rate of Return in Empirical Research', *Accounting and Business Research*, Vol. 9, No. 35, Summer 1979, pp. 200–8.

(1980a), 'Pioneers of Income Measurement and Price-Level Accounting: A Review Article', *Accounting and Business Research*, Vol. 10, No. 38, Spring 1980, pp. 232–40.

(1980b), 'Inflation Accounting – Why the Debate Has Gone Off Course', *The Times*, 10 March 1980.

(1981), 'The British Contribution to Income Theory', Chapter 1, pp. 1–29, of *Essays in British Accounting Research*, edited by Michael Bromwich and Anthony Hopwood, Pitman.

Wiles, P. (1981), 'Equity Values and Inflation: The Importance of Dividends', *Lloyds Bank Review*, No. 139, January 1981, pp. 58–9.

Wright, F. K. (1964), 'Towards a General Theory of Depreciation', *Journal of Accounting Research*, Vol. 2, pp. 80–90. Reprinted in Parker and Harcourt (1969).

(1965), 'A Theory of Inventory Measurement', *Abacus*, Vol. 1, No. 2, December 1965, pp. 150–5.

(1968), 'Measuring Asset Services: A Linear Programming Approach', *Journal of Accounting Research*, Vol. 6, pp. 222–36.

(1970), 'A Theory of Financial Accounting', *Journal of Business Finance*, Vol. 2, No. 3, Autumn 1970, pp. 57–69.

(1971), 'Value to the Owner: a Clarification', *Abacus*, Vol. 7, No. 1, June 1971, pp. 58–61.

(1978), 'Accounting Rate of Profit and Internal Rate of Return', *Oxford Economic Papers*, Vol. 30, No. 3, November 1978, pp. 464–8.

Yoshida, H. (1973), 'Value to the Firm and the Asset Measurement Problem', *Abacus*, Vol. 9, pp. 16–21.

Zeff, S. A. (1976), *Asset Appreciation, Business Income and Price-Level Accounting, 1918–1935*, Arno Press, New York.

(1981), 'The Ordeal of Kenneth MacNeal', *Working Paper No. 8*, Jesse H. Jones Graduate School of Administration, Rice University, Houston, Texas.

Index

Index

Index

Index

Sen, A. K., 69, 216n.4
shareholders, 2, 14, 23–4, 69–70, 72, 73, 86–7, 90, 92, 93–4, 119, 156, 159, 168, 169, 197, 204; *see also* dividends, financial accounts, stewardship
Skerratt, L. C. L., 65, 88, 140, 191, 192, 203
Solomons, D., 132, 207, 220n.32
specific price changes, 5–6, 9, 13, 15–17, 30, 43, 47, 48, 62, 64–73, 85–6, Chapter 5 (110–51), 153, 155, 158–64, 166–7, 195, 198, 208; *see also* holding gains
SSAP16, 13, 20, 60, 136, 143, 153, 166, 168, 169, 170, 173, 176, 178, 208, 211n.10, 222n.16
stabilised accounts, *see* constant purchasing power
Stamp, E., 132, 133, 134, 136, 138, 219n.25, 220n.30
standard stream, 14–15, 111–12, 160
stationary state, 39–41, 47, 49, 194
Staubus, G., 129–30, 219n.22
Sterling, R. R., 123, 124, 127, 140, 203
stewardship, 23–4, 48–9
stock appreciation, 18, 20, 62, 112, 139, 145–50, 161–4, 169, 218n.2; *see also* holding gains, stocks
stocks, 6, 11, 47, 55–7, 118, 131, 144–50, 162–3, 211n.11; *see also* FIFO, LIFO, stock appreciation, work-in-progress
surrogates, 45, 49, 121, 129–30, 135, 137, 196
Sweeney, H. W., 11, 66, 71, 73, 75, 80, 82, 83, 90, 94, 95, 116, 131, 157, 171, 174, 184, 201, 205–6, 209, 211n.19, 215n.1, 218n.9

taxation, 2, 3, 9, 24, 63, 139, 169, 171, 192, 202, 211n.11, 212n.4
Thomas, A. L., 16, 40, 49, 120, 124, 127, 128, 135, 215n.12, 219n.14
Tippett, M., 111
Trueblood Report, 2, 46
Tweedie, D. P., 122, 124, 141, 176, 203

uses of accounts, 1–3, 9, 14, 23–7, 34, 42, 84, 119, 121, 122, 124–5, 137, 171, 174, 195, 196, 202, 208, 219n.16; *see also* shareholders, stewardship, taxation

valuation, 14–17, 26–7, 28–36, 40–2, 44, 47, 54–9, 73–4, 84, Chapter 5 (110–51), 152, 194–7, 199; *see also* current value, net realisable value, present value, replacement cost, value to the owner
value to the firm or business, *see* value to the owner
value to the owner, 110, 115, 116, 117, 122, 129, 131–7, 163, 197, 218n.7
Vatter, W. J., 45, 214n.34

Wanless, P. T., 83, 90, 203
Wasserman, M. J., 75
Watts, R. L. and Zimmerman, J. L., 141, 204, 206–7
Westwick, C. A., 97
Whittington, G., 46, 63, 124, 219n.13, 221n.10, 222n.2
windfall gains, 31, 33, 214n.26
work-in-progress, 120; *see also* stocks
Wright, F. K., 131, 133, 219n.20

Zeff, S. A., 75, 123

243

DATE DUE

OCT - 7 1989			